DISCARD

D1282139

AMERICAN FUEHRER

AVPT
E
748
.R6745
S56
1999

FUEHRER

AMERICAN

GEORGE LINCOLN ROCKWELL
and the AMERICAN NAZI PARTY

FREDERICK J. SIMONELLI

UNIVERSITY OF ILLINOIS PRESS
URBANA AND CHICAGO

© 1999 by the Board of Trustees of the University of Illinois
Manufactured in the United States of America
C 5 4 3 2 1

∞ This book is printed on acid-free paper.

Frontispiece photograph of George Lincoln Rockwell, with his
trademark corncob pipe, courtesy of James Mason.

Library of Congress Cataloging-in-Publication Data
Simonelli, Frederick J. (Frederick James)
American fuehrer: George Lincoln Rockwell and the American
Nazi Party / Frederick J. Simonelli.
p.   cm.
Includes bibliographical references (p.   ) and index.
ISBN 0-252-02285-8 (acid-free paper)
1. Rockwell, George Lincoln, 1918–1967.
2. Right-wing extremists—United States—Biography.
3. American Nazi Party—Biography.
4. National Socialist White People's Party—Biography.
5. Antisemitism—United States—History—20th century.
I. Title.
E748.R6745S56   1999
324.273'038'092—ddc21   98-58011
[B]   CIP

FOR DOROTHY

CONTENTS

Illustrations follow page 80

ACKNOWLEDGMENTS

Any work of history is really a collaborative effort. Mentors, colleagues, and other distinguished scholars unselfishly shared their time and insight to guide my work and minimize its flaws. Professor Richard O. Davies of the University of Nevada, Reno—my friend, mentor, and teacher—guided this work from its inception to completion. His skill as a historian and as a superb craftsman of the narrative form helped shape this book.

The late Professor Frank Kofsky of California State University, Sacramento, brought me to this topic and, more important, refused to allow me to withdraw from its more unpleasant aspects. A man of many talents and touching generosity, Frank Kofsky's legacy to us all is his uncompromising integrity and his passion for following truth, wherever it leads.

Several outstanding scholars evaluated and helped me to improve this manuscript throughout its development. I am indebted to Professors Jerome Edwards, Francis X. Hartigan, and Leonard Weinberg of the University of Nevada, Reno; Shirley Ann Wilson Moore and Karl von den Steinen of California State University, Sacramento; Jeffrey Kaplan of Ilisagvik College; and Michael Barkun of Syracuse University.

My colleagues and students at Mount St. Mary's College maintain a culture of intellectual inquiry that challenges all in our community to better understand the forces that shape our world. I am particularly grateful for the support and inspiration of Sister Karen Kennelly, distinguished historian and president of the college; Dr. Jacqueline Powers Doud, academic vice president and dean of the faculty; and Professor James Delahanty, chair of the Department of History and Political Science.

Richard L. Wentworth, director and editor in chief of the University of Illinois Press, believed in this project and advocated its publication. His professionalism, patience, and unflagging support helped make a long and arduous process bearable. Theresa L. Sears, managing editor at the Press, played a pivotal role—with skill and deftness—in bringing the manuscript to its final form.

I am indebted to William R. Massa Jr. of the Sterling Memorial Library at Yale University; Nancy Bartlett of the Bentley Historical Library at the University of Michigan; Sherry Williams and Becky Schulte of the Kenneth Spencer Research Library at the University of Kansas; Dorothy G. Knaus of the Special Collections Department of the Knight Library at the University of Oregon; the reference staffs of the Robert Manning Strozier Library at Florida State University, the Greschel Memorial Library at the University of Nevada, Reno, and the Carpenter Memorial Library, Manchester, New Hampshire; and William F. Buckley Jr., who generously granted me access to his private correspondence with George Lincoln Rockwell.

Professor Lawrence N. Powell of Tulane University kindly allowed me access to his manuscript in progress on Rockwell's activities in New Orleans in the spring of 1961. Dr. Herbert Adelstein and Stanley Adelstein, Esq., read portions of this manuscript regarding Rockwell activities in Cleveland, Ohio, and provided useful commentary.

Since so much of the information on George Lincoln Rockwell and the American Nazi Party is not contained in existing research facilities, I am grateful to those people who agreed to share their recollections of Rockwell and his movement through correspondence and personal interviews. Among them are members of the Rockwell family, especially P. Claire Rockwell, Nancy Smyth Stefani, Peter Smyth, and Emile Walter; former Rockwell followers and associates whose political and social views I do not share but whose willingness to relate their experiences to me I appreciate, including Emory Burke, R. E. Cooper, Dr. Edward R. Fields, Colin Jordan, Hal Kaiser, Lee Larson, James Mason, William L. Pierce, H. Keith Thompson, and several others who requested anonymity; and individuals whose special expertise or personal experiences gave them valuable insight on Rockwell and his times, including Hon. David Bell, Eldon Cutler, Gordon Hall, Victory J. Hillery, Bob Lane, Al Lerner, Eben Lewis, Stuart McKeever, Herman J. Obermayer, Harvey M. Spear, Fred L. Surber, Hon. Stanley R. Tupper, Tony Ulasewicz, and Laird Wilcox.

Alan Schwartz, Gayle Gans, and Helen Schneider of the Anti-Defamation League of B'nai B'rith were most helpful in providing materials from the ADL archives. Kenneth S. Stern, Sima Horowitz, and Michelle Anish of the American Jewish Committee faciliated my work at the AJC's Blaustein Library. Helen Ritter, archivist of the AJC, graciously made available to me the files and correspondence of Rabbi Solomon Andhil Fineberg and provided valuable assistance in innumerable ways.

My daughter, Laura Simonelli Adams, served as my research assistant while she was an undergraduate at the University of California, Davis. Her dedication, efficiency, and keen intellect added immeasurably to this work; her enthusiasm and graciousness made our work together enjoyable.

Because no repository of Rockwell materials existed when I began work on this book in 1990, the research phase entailed extensive travel to locate and interview Rockwell's family, followers, and adversaries. Throughout this arduous process one person above all others believed in this project and sacrificed for it. Her willingness to absorb far more of the burdens of home and family than one person should freed me to conduct my research; her unfailing good humor and gentle encouragement sustained me. The three decades that I have been privileged to share my life with this remarkable woman—friend, lover, wife, extraordinary writer, gentle soul—have been a gift of incalculable value, and I dedicate this work to her.

■■■

Portions of this book originally appeared in slightly different form as "The American Nazi Party" in *The Historian* 57 (Spring 1995): 553–66; "Preaching Hate with the Voice of God: American Neo-Nazis and Christian Identity" in *Patterns of Prejudice* 30 (Spring 1996): 43–54; and "The World Union of National Socialists and Postwar Transatlantic Nazi Revival" in *Nation and Race: The Developing Euro-American Racist Subculture*, ed. Jeffrey Kaplan and Tore Bjorgo (Boston: Northeastern University Press, 1998), 34–57.

AMERICAN FUEHRER

INTRODUCTION

I knew I would not live to see the victory which I would make possible. But I would not die before I had made that victory certain.
— George Lincoln Rockwell, 1961

Shortly before noon on 25 August 1967, a typically hot, muggy, late summer day in northern Virginia, George Lincoln Rockwell left a load of linen and underwear in two machines at a coin laundry in a seedy Arlington strip mall. He needed to get the car back to party headquarters, across the boulevard and up a steep hill, so his deputy, Matt Koehl, could drop off a crew of stormtroopers to distribute literature in an adjoining suburb. Rockwell was excited about this particular literature drop because it would introduce a new format for party propaganda. Earlier that year, he had changed the name of his American Nazi party to the National Socialist White People's party. Over the objections of Koehl, a rabid Germanophile, he had also eliminated the swastika and replaced it with a stylized eagle to "Americanize" the party's image and broaden its appeal. These changes were an important part of Rockwell's strategic shift from a "Nazi" to a "White Power" emphasis by which he hoped to kick-start his stagnant movement by tapping into the racial discord festering in American cities in the mid-1960s.

Rockwell rolled down the window to get some fresh air into the stiflingly hot car. By habit, he clenched his trademark corncob pipe, unlit, between his teeth and turned to look over his right shoulder as he slowly backed out of the parking spot. The first of two shots nicked his shirt and embedded itself in the coils of the car's front seat. In the second or two between shots, Rockwell took his foot off the gas pedal and leaned forward, lifting his eyes to the strip mall's flat, tarred roof. The second shot found its mark. As the assassin's bullet ripped into Rockwell's chest, it drove him against the seat and snapped his head back. His pipe dropped to the seat beside him. The car rolled backward, coming to rest against the rear bumper of a car parked on the other side of the narrow lot. Rockwell crawled across the front seat and opened the passenger-side door.

With blood pumping from a fatal wound—the bullet had ruptured his aorta—
he stumbled out of the car and onto the hot asphalt of the parking lot. In the
minute or two it took him to die, Rockwell laboriously turned his body toward
the refuge he had dubbed "Hatemonger Hill." From the spot where he lay,
he could see the rambling two-story farmhouse that had been his home and
headquarters during the tumultuous years of his public career.

People from the shops in the strip mall, from the laundromat and the bar-
bershop, came out into the sunlight when they heard the shots and the sound
of Rockwell's car hitting the parked car behind it. Most stood rooted to the
narrow walkway, frozen by the scene in the parking lot. A few were drawn to
a noise coming from the roof—the footsteps of the fleeing assassin. Most stared
at the man lying in a rapidly spreading pool of his own blood. No one went to
him. At two minutes past noon, George Lincoln Rockwell, with his eyes fixed
on Hatemonger Hill, died alone.

■ ■ ■

During the span of his public career—from 1958 to 1967—George Lincoln
Rockwell was the most widely publicized anti-Semitic and racist political figure
in America. He was also, some contend, the most reviled man in the country.
Rockwell openly displayed the swastika while proclaiming his admiration for
Adolf Hitler. He charged that virtually all U.S. Jews were communist traitors
and that all communist traitors deserved execution. He ridiculed African
Americans as ignorant and docile pawns of the Jews and vowed to place those
he could not drive into exile within "secure reservations" when his party took
power. He scorned homosexuals as "perverts," ominously pledging to "purge
the queers" even before he turned his attention to the Jews and the blacks. In
the words of an FBI surveillance document written at the height of his notoriety, Rockwell strove for "the shocking, the repulsive, and the horrifying" to
achieve the publicity he believed to be the lifeblood of his movement.[1]

Most historians, political scientists, and sociologists agree that fascism or
nazism, as political and social movements, have come nowhere near capturing a dominant position in American political life during the twentieth century. What, then, is Rockwell's significance? And what danger did he really
represent? His significance is in the strategic legacy he bequeathed the racist
right: "White Power" as a unifying concept and an organizing tool; Holocaust
denial as a means of rewriting history and muting the moral lessons of anti-
Semitism; and the link to the Christian Identity movement that gave the racists and anti-Semites who came after him a contrivance to camouflage their
purpose with the cloak of religion. Rockwell's danger was the same as that of
the hatemongering demagogues who preceded him—William Pelley, Charles

E. Coughlin, Gerald L. K. Smith—and those who followed him—David Duke, Lyndon Larouche, Tom Metzger: that under the right political, economic, and social circumstances a frightened and angry people could abandon their fragile Republic to the seduction of the man with a quick fix.

Within the racist right, leaders and movements tend to crest when circumstances are propitious, then recede and lay dormant until the next opportunity bids them forth. To Rockwell's misfortune, the conditions he needed to convert hatemongering to real political power did not exist during his active career; or, as the more optimistic among us would contend, those conditions were thwarted by a resilient political system before they could mature and be exploited. In either case, the challenge is to understand a man like Rockwell and the appeal of his message so that society can recognize the occasions that would make his answers attractive to the Republic's citizens.[2]

Rockwell represents but one manifestation of a psychological and political impulse that has surfaced and resurfaced throughout modern history. It has gone by many names—fascism, nazism, totalitarianism—but its ideology always rests on "a way of thinking and feeling, a group of cultural habits, of obscure instincts and unfathomable drives" that offer the comfort and the appeal of elemental answers to frustrating and complex societal problems. Rockwell embodied what Umberto Eco has called "Ur-Fascism," the recurring authoritarian impulse within the body politic. Like his ideological brethren, Rockwell offered the security of a "cult of tradition" that held firmly to a delivered and unalterable truth; the protection of the company of individuals with like blood rooted in an ancestral land—what Hitler's Nazis termed *Blut und Boden* (blood and earth); the exhilaration of action for action's sake; and freedom from the burden of analytical criticism, since disagreement is treason.[3]

Like his predecessors (and his successors), Rockwell scorned human diversity, showed contempt for the weak, created a cult of heroism within an atmosphere of sexual machismo, and exaggerated the power and cunning of "the enemy" while hoping to exploit the frustrations of the middle class. He obsessively railed against a conspiracy of the Jews to justify his depiction of life as permanent warfare and unrelenting struggle, with himself as the people's "Leader," expressing not his own desires but the "Common Will" of a monolithic and single-minded *Volk*.[4] It is as the prototypical authoritarian leader, keeping the flame of "Ur-Fascism" alive and passing it on to his philosophical children, and as an innovator who altered the flicker of that flame to make it more appealing, that George Lincoln Rockwell claims significance in the history of the racist right wing of American politics.

As the first biography of George Lincoln Rockwell by an author not connected with Rockwell's movement or sympathetic to his views, this study attempts to understand Rockwell's motivations and objectives and to place him within the historical context of his time and political milieu. This book is not meant to be a psychohistorical analysis of Rockwell, although his complex and conflicted relationships with his father and with the women in his life invite speculation into the way his inner struggles shaped his view of himself and the world. Neither is it intended as a comparative study of European and American variants of nazism, nor as an opportunity to revisit the fundamentals of authoritarian personalities or the politics of paranoia, both of which are well studied and amply documented. Rather, it is meant to provide a historical connection between Rockwell, a seminal figure in the postwar American racist right, and the major themes of that movement's manifestation at the dawn of a new millennium.

Throughout the twentieth century, the fascist impulse in human affairs has taken many shapes, its face adopting the contours of the people it seeks to arouse. In late twentieth-century America, the fascist impulse is manifested in hate-driven neo-Nazi movements that rally around three primary themes: racial purity, specifically an inclusive "whiteness" that embraces virtually all non-African ethnicities as a defining national characteristic; the existence of powerful forces, either openly or indirectly identified as Jewish, in control of the major institutions of modern society and capable of manipulating those institutions for gain; and a race-and-blood brand of Christianity that offers sanctuary for besieged white people and sanction for the violence they must use to prevent political subjugation and racial mongrelization. As this study will show, the hand of George Lincoln Rockwell is evident in each of these three major themes.

Rockwell shaped the transition from postwar neo-nazism to the present by introducing innovative elements to the tired themes of racism and anti-Semitism that energized them for new generations of haters. With the skill of the adman or the spin doctor, Rockwell crafted new themes from old lies and offered them to his eager disciples. While the older veterans of today's racist right venerate Rockwell, most of the foot soldiers of the neo-Nazi movement worldwide, overwhelmingly young and often angry and alienated, remember Rockwell, if they remember him at all, as a curiosity from a distant and irrelevant past. In truth, he is present in their slogans and in their strategies. He formed their conception of whiteness. He popularized Holocaust denial within the racist right, now a basic "proof" of Jewish control of history in the anti-Semite's belief system. And he brokered the marriage between racism and anti-Semitism and theology that provided a spiritual haven within the Christian Identity movement for those seeking justification from God for the hate that drives them. This is Rockwell's significance and his legacy.

1 THE FAMILY

We are the sheep and God is the Father,
So let us be good and not a bother.
For if we've been good unto the end,
A wonderful gift to us he will send.
But if you have lived the other way,
You'll be very sorry for your evil some day.
　　—George Lincoln Rockwell, 1929

George Lincoln Rockwell was born on 9 March 1918 in Bloomington, Illinois, the first child of George Lovejoy "Doc" Rockwell and Claire Schade Rockwell.[1] Doc Rockwell, a rising vaudeville comic, was well on his way to star status. By the 1920s, he headlined at the Palace Theater and Radio City Music Hall in New York City and appeared in the Billy Rose Revue at the Ziegfeld Theater; by the early 1930s, he earned the princely sum of $3,500 a week, making him one of the best-paid vaudevillians in the country. Claire Schade was a talented and beautiful woman, delicate and graceful, a toe dancer since childhood in her family's act, "The Four Schades." Although she never reached Doc's prominence on the stage, she had her admirers (as a child performer, she was the Shirley Temple of her era). But when Claire married Doc in 1915, she knew that as soon as the children came she would give up the theater for the full-time role of wife and mother. Doc wanted it that way. As in all things with Doc, she complied.

The Rockwell family was deeply rooted in New England. The first Rockwells arrived there from England in the seventeenth century. Doc Rockwell was the oldest child and only son of George Scott Rockwell and his second wife, a young Canadian farm girl of Scottish descent, Mary MacPherson. Doc's two younger sisters, Marguerite, whom the family called "Margie," and Helen, were in awe of their older brother, indisputably the star of the Rockwell clan. Helen would marry Roscoe Smyth and have three children—Nancy, Peter, and Bill—but would remain close to her brother throughout her life, helping to raise Doc's sons after he and Claire divorced in 1924. Margie, who never married, lived with her brother off and on and carried her devotion to Doc over to the next generation of Rockwells, especially to Doc's oldest son, George Lincoln.

Growing up, Doc Rockwell was known to his parents and sisters as "Georgie." He didn't pick up the nickname "Doc" until his early years in vaudeville, when he introduced the shtick that would become his trademark: a rapid-patter monologue delivered while dressed in a white lab coat with a stethoscope draped around his neck and a five-foot banana stalk as his only prop. The act was so successful that "Georgie" was known thereafter as "Doc" and was always billed as *"Doc Rockwell—Quack, Quack, Quack!"* At first, the staid Rockwells—Doc's elderly father, his proper Victorian mother, and his adoring sisters—didn't quite know how to react to this star in the family. Moreover, they didn't quite know how they'd fit into the fast-paced life of vaudeville. But Doc swept them along, willing or not. His life, at least vicariously, became theirs because *his* life was the only one that really mattered.[2]

Although of small stature—barely 5'4" and slim; in the words of his nephew, Peter Smyth, "just a little, tiny fella"—Doc Rockwell dominated a room and the people in it. He walked fast, talked fast, and spoke loudly; he told jokes, danced, played the pennywhistle, and was an accomplished magician; and he drew outrageous caricatures with an offhanded ease while enthralling those around him with an improvised monologue (his mimicry was legendary). He was always "on," the prime purpose of all those around him being to serve as his attentive audience. Whether at home or before a sellout crowd in any of the countless theaters he played in big cities and little towns across America, Doc Rockwell demanded the center of the stage.

Doc drew his friends from the upper crust of the entertainment world: Fred Allen, Doc's closest, lifelong friend, and his unconventional wife, Portland; Fanny Brice; Benny Goodman; Groucho Marx; Walter Winchell; Jack Benny; George Burns; Rudy Vallee; Ray Bolger; Martha Graham. The Allens were frequent summer guests at Doc's oceanside retreat in Maine; along with Groucho Marx, Jack Benny, and George Burns, they attended the christening of Doc's firstborn son, George Lincoln.[3]

Doc Rockwell met Claire Schade at the theater her father managed in Bloomington, Illinois. Claire, a slight, soft-spoken young woman with finely chiseled features and captivating eyes, lived in the house, and under the rule, of her gruff, overbearing German-born father, Augustus Schade.

"Gus" Schade emigrated from his native Germany in the 1880s to seek his fortune in America. He worked hard, spent little, and by the early years of the new century had accumulated comfortable savings and minor investments in property in and around Bloomington. There, he met and married an enchanting younger woman, a willowy French brunette named Corrine Boudreau. Gus and Corrine had two daughters. The elder, like Gus, was hefty, big-boned, and overbearing. They named her Arline.[4] The younger, Claire, was a delicate creature, just like her mother, with the beauty and grace her sister lacked. As soft-willed as she was soft-spoken, Claire always subordinated her wishes to those of her father and, increasingly, to those of the domineering Arline.

Gus Schade was involved in show business as the manager of the Majestic Theatre, Bloomington's largest and busiest live performance house. By the turn of the century, the booming new vaudeville caught Gus's imagination. He'd seen enough good acts, and bad ones, to know that his talented six-year-old was a natural for the stage. Claire could sing and dance and had already mastered the difficult art of toe dancing. Gus built a family act around her, billed it "The Four Schades," and took it on the road when the Majestic Theatre was dark. Claire was a hit and Gus prospered. The novelty of the act faded as Claire entered adolescence. By 1915 she was earning a living in vaudeville— no small feat—but any aspirations to stardom were long since dashed on the rocks of reality.

Claire Schade met Doc Rockwell in 1915 when she was twenty-one. Once he decided that this captivating beauty was going to be his wife, there was little left to do but pick the date. There is no hint from those early years of just how Claire felt about her peculiar and persistent suitor. She left no record of whether she was madly in love with him or merely acquiesced to his will, moving compliantly from the orbit of one dominant man to that of another. Nor is there a record of how Gus Schade felt about the union, although it is likely that he approved heartily since having Doc Rockwell at the Majestic Theatre would have been very good for business.

Doc and Claire were married in Bloomington and settled down not far from Claire's parents and the Majestic Theatre. Early in their marriage, Claire accompanied Doc on the vaudeville circuit. When their first child, George Lincoln (or "Lincoln," as he was often called), was born in 1918, she "retired," though she still traveled with her husband, performing occasionally when illness or the effects of a drinking binge left a hole in the program. Claire retired for good when their second son, Robert, was born in 1919. By the time their last child, Priscilla, was born in 1921, Doc was an established star who commanded top billing and a healthy salary. Claire, housebound and broken-spirited under Doc's smothering personality, struggled unsuccessfully to salvage an increasingly shaky marriage. They divorced in 1924, making George Lincoln, age six, the man of the house.

The divorce devastated Claire and traumatized Lincoln, who idolized his father. Doc, never an attentive husband or doting father, structured the divorce to his convenience. Claire, as she did in all things throughout their marriage, agreed to Doc's demands. If Claire even briefly entertained any notions of opposing him on custody, alimony, or child support questions, she did not act on them. Her daughter, Priscilla, who cared for her mother until Claire's death in 1991 at age ninety-seven, believes that Claire was so insecure over her lack of formal schooling—she'd left school at the age of nine because of the demands of her vaudeville career—that she refused to contest Doc in court, considering herself incapable of disputing him credibly. A lifetime of submissive acquiescence conditioned her to accept whatever Doc decided was best for her—which included only sporadic alimony and child support payments, despite his large income and comfortable lifestyle. One of young Lincoln's bitterest memories was of a sheriff's auction at his home to satisfy his mother's creditors.[5]

Doc's career continued to soar, and he continued to prosper. In 1928 he launched *Doc Rockwell's Mustard Plaster* from his home in Boothbay Harbor, Maine. This successful magazine introduced an offbeat humor that was the forerunner of a later cult favorite, *Mad* magazine. Doc also wrote a regular humor column for *Downeast Magazine* that ran for twenty years. In 1937 he appeared in a musical comedy feature film, *The Singing Marine,* with Dick Powell.

While Claire Rockwell and the children struggled with unpaid bills and unsatisfied creditors, Doc settled down on the coast of Maine with his common-law wife, Madline, writing, fishing, dabbling in radio and the movies after the fade of vaudeville, and entertaining old friends. He seems to have paid little attention to his daughter and saw his sons only on his own terms, bringing them to Maine every summer.

For George Lincoln Rockwell, those summers in Maine were the best times of his life. Doc held the boy in his thrall and spun his magic over him, as he had over every person, and every audience, he encountered in his life. He took Link (the boy's family nickname) and Bobby deep-sea fishing and on moonlight sails, and his big house in Boothbay Harbor was always filled with magicians and show people, including, for Link, a particularly memorable pair of luncheon guests: an organ-grinder and his monkey.

According to Lincoln, Doc did more than entertain his sons; he taught them to be curious about the world around them, quizzing them, even at a young age, on "politics, history, magic, art." He taught them to question, to analyze, to argue. He encouraged them to be curious about all sorts of things, even performing elaborate—and wildly funny—"autopsies on fish to see what they had been eating." And then there were the stories, mad flights of wonder and imagination from a master of imagery and inflection, that held his wide-eyed boys in awe. As an adult, Link wrote: "Even now, I get goose flesh as I remember the smell of his pipe, the hushed voice and the magic of the Maine dusk as we listened to these superb flights of imagination."[6]

Those idyllic summer days in Maine, of which Lincoln spoke and wrote so fondly, were marred by another side of his father's personality. Lincoln did not often recognize those darker memories as part of his childhood, at least not consciously—and certainly not publicly. But no matter how diligently he pushed them back into the shadows, they helped to shape how he saw himself and how, through his eyes, he saw the world.

Doc Rockwell gave his son the attention a performer gives his audience. Lincoln's adulation fed Doc's voracious ego. But what the boy really needed (guidance) and really craved (love) were absent from the relationship. Lincoln always sought his father's approval but seldom got the hoped-for word of encouragement or look of confirmation. There was just no room for the son's needs in the father's world. "As far as Uncle George was concerned," Doc's nephew Peter Smyth recalled years after the death of both Doc and Link, "the sun went up and down on what *he* was doing. Period." Another Rockwell cousin could not recall one instance of affection expressed by Doc toward Link.

As Lincoln grew into young manhood, he quickly eclipsed his father in stature. At maturity he was almost 6'4" and towered over his diminutive father, raising yet another barrier between them. Doc was always sensitive about his lack of height, often compensating for his discomfort on the subject with humor. His oldest son's height and athleticism emphasized the very aspect of himself that Doc felt most insecure about. And he made sure Link suffered for it. Biting wit was his weapon, and his rapier-like sarcasm slashed the sensitive teenager's fragile self-image. Family members describe Doc as "compulsively competitive" with his teenage son, his anxiety about his own stature aggravated by Link's height. For his part, Link tried desperately to win his father's approval, emulating the way he talked, seeking to sound like him, to be like him. Ironically, of the three Rockwell children, George Lincoln was the most like Doc in many ways. Beyond adolescent attempts at copying his father, the Lincoln Rockwell his family remembers as a young man spoke loudly and in a rapid staccato—just like Doc; he was a talented cartoonist and mimic; he was always "on," always trying to impress and, if he could not impress, to intimidate. He became, at heart, one close relative believes, "an opportunist, a con-man, just like his father."

Doc's emotional distance and his coldness and detachment from his son's feelings and passions created, in Peter Smyth's words, "an emotional wasteland" for Link as he realized that in matters of importance to him, quite simply, "his father probably didn't care." Smyth remembers that at the time of Lincoln's death, Doc kept himself removed from the events that grieved the rest of the family. "That speaks to the essential Doc Rockwell," Smyth believes.

Doc just couldn't be bothered. "As for being a *father,* Good Lord! That's a contradiction in terms!" says Smyth.

Being away from Doc offered Link no relief. Every fall the Rockwell boys left Boothbay Harbor and returned to their mother's house. Claire moved from Bloomington to Atlantic City, New Jersey, to live with her spinster sister. Alone with her three children, insecure, scraping to put food on the table, Claire turned to Arline, who offered a seemingly secure refuge. Arline was everything Claire was not: strong, both physically and emotionally, confident, opinionated, and unafraid. A massive woman with the flat, broad, humorless features of the Schades, she filled Claire's deepest needs. Arline took over Claire's finances, managed her money, and fought with the courts over Doc's delinquent child support payments, and disciplined the children. Her brand of discipline was swift and harsh, and was most often directed at Link. Priscilla, docile and compliant like her mother, gave Arline little trouble; Bobby, a natural diplomat, eluded Arline's wrath; but Link confronted his aunt and defied her at every turn. To Arline, he was just like Doc, a man she detested. Doc may have been beyond her control, but Link was not.

Priscilla describes Arline as "vindictive" and remembers her relentless determination to break Link's willfulness, to make him less like his despised father. Whatever freedom of spirit Link brought back from Maine each fall was quickly beaten out of him by Aunt Arline. Link later likened returning to her home (for it was far more her home than Claire's) to a return to the "penitentiary." She beat him from the time he was six years old to when he was fifteen and beyond her physical powers. Her psychological abuse—the names, the taunts, the constant revilement of his beloved father—continued until he left her house for good to attend Brown University. Link later wrote of being forced, as a young boy of seven years, to listen to hours-long tirades by Arline on "the rottenness and vileness of my father." When he rebelled, as he often did, Aunt Arline—whom Link relished referring to later as "this human dirigible"—"suppress[ed] the mutiny." Arline's lectures often lasted far into the night, with young Link sitting for hours in a straight-back wooden chair as his aunt paced and ranted. When he fell asleep, she would bring her fleshy, red face within inches of his and scream his name until he awoke. Claire—"my poor, patient, weak mother"—would try her best to shield the boy, but she could no more stand up to Arline than she could to Doc. Claire tried to get Link to placate Arline by doing as she and Bobby did, to "give in and crawl out," but Link simply "could not do it."

Lincoln held his rage for Arline all his life. At forty, he was still trying to reconcile his mother's actions in abandoning him to Arline's wrath. In 1958, he wrote to his mother of his twenty-five-year anguished, emotional struggle trying to understand the complex family dynamics that left him exposed to his aunt's abuse. Lincoln loved his mother deeply and tried to find a way to understand and forgive her. In the end, he couldn't understand her weakness, but he could, and did, forgive her, even though the scars of her abandonment left an indelible mark on his psyche.[7]

In 1966, at the height of his public anti-Semitic and anti-black agitation, and in the grips of what many believed to be a paranoiac state, Rockwell found that Aunt Arline still rode heavily on his mind. Again writing to his mother, he reached back to his childhood with a bitter immediacy, likening the hardening he experienced at his aunt's hands to the protective shell he had to develop to withstand the onslaught of the "Jews and liberals and commies" that assaulted him in 1966. Rockwell's passionate letter alternated between graphic images of Arline Schade's "bullying" and the "gangs of Jews, Negroes and Commies" he saw as "bullying" his country. He attributed his ability to stand up to them to his youthful resolve not to submit to his aunt's tyranny. The "bullies" that haunted Rockwell in 1966 were a confused blend of those he perceived as political enemies there and then—Jews, blacks, Communists— and the "mobs of bullies" at school that he fought thirty years earlier because, according to his memory, Aunt Arline insisted that he wear knickers, and even short pants, to school, which made him the butt of ridicule.[8] The rage jumps off the pages of his plaintive letter to his mother, but the object of that rage is as confused for the reader as perhaps it was for Rockwell himself. His sister believes he was a "broody and unhappy" man because of his "terrible childhood" and says their mother carried the guilt of Link's childhood to the grave.

Those looking for the key to Rockwell's pathological anti-Semitism in his family or his upbringing will be largely unsatisfied. The three households where Rockwell spent his developmental years—his aunt's house, his father's Boothbay Harbor compound, and the Roscoe and Helen Rockwell Smyth house, where Link and his brother often sought refuge from Aunt Arline— reflected the pervasive anti-Semitism and racism that existed throughout middle-class America in the late 1920s and 1930s, but none did so to an extent that would clearly identify it as the undisputed source of what would become a lifelong obsession. Rockwell grew up in an atmosphere where Jews were regularly referred to as "kikes" and African Americans as "niggers"—but so did Bobby, Priscilla, and their cousins Nancy, Pete, and Bill, yet only Link made the prejudices of his milieu the core of his worldview.

The Smyth household, in which Link spent time with Uncle Roscoe, Aunt Helen, and his cousins, was perhaps the most openly anti-Semitic of the three. Peter Smyth describes it as a base-level anti-Semitism. There was, he says, an unchallenged "anti-Jewish feeling throughout the family." Smyth remembers that "[his] father came home and did nothing but rant about the Jews all the time," adding, "but that's because he was in the garment business." Smyth's sister, Nancy Smyth Stefani, describes her family as "Archie Bunker types," very anti-Semitic, anti-black, anti-Catholic, anti-Italian, but she firmly notes that these were feelings they "didn't talk about outside the family."

There is little extant material on Claire Rockwell's attitude toward Jews and blacks, but a letter Link wrote to his mother in 1952 while stationed in Iceland during his second tour of duty in the U.S. Navy, a period long before his emergence as a political activist and public anti-Semite, suggested a casual anti-Semitism shared by mother and son. In the letter Link describes the harsh weather on the air base, with winds in excess of 110 mph that blew several people out onto the rocks. Claire lived in Brooklyn, New York, at the time, in a neighborhood with a large Jewish population. Link concluded his letter with a joking reference to the desirability of such a wind striking Brooklyn and blowing the Jews out to sea.[9]

The most problematic of the three households in which Link found himself was his father's. Many of Doc's intimate friends from show business were Jews, including Portland Allen, and many of them came and went as Doc's houseguests during the summers Link spent with his father. Doc, more than any other member of the family, was embarrassed by Link's blatant anti-Semitism during his public career and on several occasions tried to get his son to tone down his anti-Semitic pronouncements. About two years into his Jew-baiting phase, Link wrote to his mother about what he regarded as his father's hypocrisy regarding Jews, suggesting that Doc's private and public comments about Jews were at great variance.[10] Later, he wrote mockingly to his closest boyhood friend, Eben Lewis, about Doc Rockwell's repeated failure to satisfactorily defend the "kikes and coons and queers" that Link believed were running the country.[11]

It is likely that Doc Rockwell, in the privacy of his home, used the epithets that were common in his family and among his class. But his reaction to Link's later overt and brutish anti-Semitism and the lifelong friendships he maintained with Jews suggest that his anti-Semitism was reactive and superficial. The anti-Semitic sentiments he'd heard and absorbed all his life surfaced when his guard was down. They seemed to be "natural" responses to Jewish people and situations involving Jews, and he never thought to challenge their underlying assumptions. In fairness, Doc was not really a reflective man. He gave little thought to the meaning of the words he spoke in anger or in jest, and he apparently had no awareness of their impact on his children.

In 1961, Harry Golden, a *New York Post* columnist and editor of *The Carolina Israelite,* wrote to George Lincoln Rockwell in outrage over some particularly vicious piece of American Nazi party literature. "If you love Hitler," Golden wrote, "you will have to liquidate your father somewhere along the way because your father was 'contaminated' many years ago. Old Doc Rockwell, a lovable old man, ate dinner at my home on the Lower East side of New York, on the Jewish Sabbath too, and my old pious mother . . . served him with affection and your father responded with grace and good will. . . . He was our friend." Doc's friendship with the Goldens was genuine and long-lived. He employed Harry's brother, Jacob, when the latter needed work; and Claire would send letters to Doc, when he was on tour, in care of the Taft Hotel in New York, which was run by the Golden family. Harry Golden could not see Doc in Link. "Get thee to the couch of a psychiatrist as quickly as you can!" he pleaded. "There is time yet. Fall upon your knees and beg forgiveness of Almighty God!"[12]

Rockwell was unmoved. His father's old friend was no friend of his. He would break no Sabbath bread with the likes of Harry Golden. However, he would respond to Golden's plea. In late October 1961, Rockwell wrote to Harry Golden, reminding him that the American Nazi party platform called for the gassing of "Jew-traitors" when the party took control, and he ominously warned Golden that when that day came, George Lincoln Rockwell would personally review Harry Golden's words and actions to judge Golden's loyalty to America.[13]

2

THE ARTIST AND THE WARRIOR

Destiny smiles most on those who fight the hardest.
—George Lincoln Rockwell, 1966

From 1931 to 1936, George Lincoln Rockwell attended four high schools, graduating from two of them.[1] These were years—from thirteen to eighteen—when Rockwell showed flashes of brilliance, outbursts of rage, and fits of rebellion amid a growing alienation from both his family and societal convention. He was an angry young man, and he channeled that anger into acts of rebellion against the structure and authority of high school. Among other things, he organized a student boycott over bad cafeteria food and held a one-man "strike" against a particularly authoritarian civics teacher—projecting what were essentially personal grievances onto a larger stage. Rockwell found both a forum for his ego and an outlet for his anger by provoking the authority figures in his life. If he couldn't challenge his aunt Arline or penetrate his father's disinterest, then his teachers and the school's administrators would have to do.

Rockwell spent his longest stretch of time at any educational institution at Atlantic City High School. His home—with his mother, Aunt Arline, Bobby, and Priscilla—was, to him, "a penitentiary." Each fall he reluctantly returned to Atlantic City from Boothbay Harbor and the company of his father. He hated Arline—her look, her voice, her vitrolic attacks on Doc Rockwell, and her endless, irrational midnight ravings that went on throughout his adolescent years. Most of all, however, he hated what living with her had done to his mother. Claire, always meek and submissive, had lost any sense of herself in Arline's shadow. She never talked back or challenged Arline's rules or even stood up for her children when Arline decided one of them—usually Link—required physical punishment or verbal "correction." Link didn't seem to mind his father's domination of Claire—that was her place in the world, and Doc could do no wrong—but he chafed under his aunt's usurpation of that role.

The anger and frustration he could not vent at home spilled over in school. During his senior year, Rockwell tangled with a strict old-school civics teacher named Schwab. He bristled under Schwab's tedious rules and "stupid ideas." He particularly hated Schwab's method of instruction by repetition, complaining that such effort was useless and a waste of time, "as if one could fill one's head as one filled a bucket." Rockwell refused to bend to Schwab's "tyrannical folly" just as he refused to break under "the lectures and arguments with Arline." Rockwell wrote that Schwab's demands were "an outrage against all reason and I rebelled as I . . . rebelled at my Aunt Arline's outrages against reason."[2]

Rockwell struck out at Schwab with a flamboyant public gesture meant to provoke and enrage his oppressor while holding him up to ridicule—a technique he would also utilize later in his career. He brought a "stack of pulp Western[s]" to Schwab's class, and with a studied casualness designed to draw attention to his protest, spread the magazines over his desk, picked up a particularly juicy one, sat down with his long legs draped across the desk, and refused to recognize the teacher's presence, much less participate in his rote drills. Rockwell describes the other students as "awed" by his brazenness and "impudence in the face of the 'almighty.'"[3] It was the last semester of his senior year, and he was given an ultimatum: end his "strike" and resume his classwork or face the consequences. Rockwell refused and was not allowed to graduate.

That summer, perhaps because he was becoming too much for even Arline to handle, Rockwell was sent to live with his paternal grandmother, Mary MacPherson Rockwell, and her spinster daughter, Margie, in Providence, Rhode Island. His stay in Providence was one of the happiest periods of his life. Undoubtedly, having distanced himself from the despised Arline helped. Aunt Margie, the opposite of Arline in virtually every way—a Rockwell, not a Schade—was one of the few people in his life he genuinely loved. More important, she was one of the few people who seemed to genuinely love him. She gave him time to talk of his anger and frustration and was the one sympathetic adult in what he viewed as an increasingly hostile world. She wasn't particularly learned or talented or beautiful, but she truly cared about her nephew and was not reluctant to express her affection for him.

Rockwell's grades at Providence's Central High School were significantly better than the mediocre grades he earned in Atlantic City. He was the editor of the school newspaper and developed his talent as a cartoonist. At Central, he had his first romance and, at eighteen, his first kiss. He graduated in 1936 and decided to go to college. His father, who had kept in much closer contact with Link since he moved to Providence, set his sights on Harvard. Link was unquestionably bright, but his grades were inconsistent, and the episode at

Atlantic City High School was not going to impress the Harvard entrance committee. So Doc decided Link should spend an extra semester at Hope High School, known in Providence and throughout New England for its outstanding English program. Link dutifully performed for Doc and graduated from Hope, receiving his second high school diploma in less than a year. Harvard rejected him nonetheless.

Father and son were so sure of a favorable decision from Harvard that Link neglected to apply to any other college. As the 1937 school year approached, Link would have been content to stay with his grandmother Rockwell and his aunt Margie and get a job, or else try his hand at freelance illustration, but Doc wanted his son to gain entry to an Ivy League school. He decided that an idle year was not compatible with that goal and enrolled Link at Hebron Academy, a boy's boarding school in rural central Maine, determined to knock at the gates of Harvard, or another elite college, the following fall. Link was reluctant to leave his aunt and he wasn't anxious to tackle yet another college preparatory course, but he never considered disputing his father's plans.

To his surprise, Link liked Hebron. He enjoyed the rough campus and the Maine woods. He made friends he would hold for life, friends who stood by him even when his career veered toward fringe politics, although they abhorred the crude anti-Semitism and racism he espoused and were mystified by the turn his life took. At Hebron, Rockwell read serious books for the first time, including works by Will Durant, Sinclair Lewis, and John Steinbeck. He also later claimed that it was at Hebron that he "lost [his] belief in Christianity," and he traced the origins of his adult agnosticism to examining things previously accepted on faith by the light of science and reason during that year. He rejected his Methodist upbringing—with its stifling strain of predestination—and began to form the belief in his own agency for greatness, for salvation by his own light, that would sustain him as he became increasingly isolated in later years.

Just as they had done at Atlantic City High School, Rockwell's demons found him in the Maine woods. This time the villain's name was Foster, not Schwab, but the grievances and the remedy were the same. Foster, a chemistry instructor, was, according to Rockwell, a "petty tyrant" who plotted against Rockwell for no other reason than to give him and his friends "huge numbers of demerits." Rockwell's tactics, which had become more sophisticated, included organizing his Hebron mates to burn Foster in effigy. He also led nighttime marches around the campus, moving on to Foster's residence, once a sufficiently raucous crowd had gathered, where the boys chanted slogans and shouted epithets. Rockwell later bragged about plaguing "the poor man" and driving him away. At the end of the school year, Foster resigned his position.

Rockwell learned other lessons at Hebron. He found that he could move people with words and that he could make others see the world as he saw it. He discovered that he could defy authority and prevail. He recognized that he could release the anger he felt and, by doing so, alleviate the pain. He also found pleasure in tormenting boys who were slow, naïve, or just different, boasting of his cleverness in "making life miserable for such characters."[4]

The door to Harvard remained closed to Rockwell, but he gained admission to another elite Ivy League school, Brown University. Rockwell's academic record did not meet Brown's standards, but his high score on the College Aptitude Test won him a prized place in the Class of 1942. During the summer between his year at Hebron and his freshman year at Brown, Rockwell worked as a waiter at a small Boothbay Harbor summer hotel, The Green Shutters, and met his future wife, Judith Aultman.

At Brown, Rockwell cultivated few close friends, although those who knew him then describe him as generally friendly and likable.[5] Rockwell joined two sophomores, Victor J. Hillery and Bob Grabb, to revive a campus humor magazine, *Sir Brown!* that had ceased publication years before. Rockwell continued to hone his skills as an illustrator and cartoonist, working as art editor of the magazine and periodically contributing cartoons to the college newspaper, the *Brown Daily Herald*. At this time Rockwell also developed an affinity for esoteric political tracts and conspiracy theories. He was drawn to such works as *The Law of Civilization and Decay* by Brooks Adams and *The Crowd* by Gustave Le Bon, all of which shaped the core of his beliefs on collective behavior, social psychology, and historical determinism.[6] Rockwell majored in philosophy and developed an increasingly pessimistic view of society and people. By his second year, he had turned on the institution itself, seeing it as a haven of "intellectual dishonesty." To Rockwell, no one—not his professors or his friends—would challenge the liberal orthodoxy that he saw stifling creativity and freedom. His increasingly strident attacks on professors and administrators once again brought him into conflict with authority. Only the intercession of his aunt Margie convinced him to mute his outspokenness enough to pass his sophomore courses with a C average. Rockwell later described a college community "infected" with communism: "the campus, dorms, fraternity houses and classrooms of Brown University were crawling with the filthy thing." Of course, in Rockwell's memory, no one saw it as clearly as he did, and those who did were part of the conspiracy to cover up and protect the subversion.[7]

At a fall dance during his sophomore year, Rockwell recognized a Pembroke College freshman whom he had met briefly during the summer before he entered Brown. Judith Aultman was a pert, bright, attractive brunette from a respected and financially comfortable Rhode Island family. Rockwell later remembered her as a "sassy little jaybird." He was captivated by her. Politics and conspiracies faded fast in Link's mind as he pursued her down a path of "glorious hope and miserable despair." Judith, one of the most popular Pembroke freshmen, "played the field" and enjoyed the experience of being courted by so many handsome and eligible young suitors. But she kept coming back to the aggressive, fast-talking, tall, angular, handsome young man from rural Maine with the flashing dark eyes. She alternately drew Link to her and turned him away, driving him to desire her all the more. "I had to have her," Link recalled many years later, "and I doubled and redoubled my efforts to that end."[8]

Bored with college, frustrated by Judith, his unpredictable passions drawn to the war in Europe, Rockwell left Brown and joined the U.S. Navy in March 1941. Like thousands of other young men that year, he saw the European war driving closer and closer to an isolated America. Although no fan of Franklin Roosevelt, Rockwell agreed with the president's assessment of the Axis menace and wanted to be on the front line fighting Hitler, Mussolini, and Tojo when his country recognized the inevitable and joined the fray. Seaman 2d Class Rockwell was accepted as an aviation cadet and received his flight training at the naval air station at Squantum, Massachusetts. He was commissioned an ensign naval aviator on 9 December 1941, two days after the Japanese attack on Pearl Harbor. Before being shipped off to his first assignment as a navy pilot aboard the cruiser USS *Omaha,* Link returned to Brown to see Judith. Perhaps it was the sight of the dashing young pilot in his uniform or the emotional fervor of the first months of America's war that inspired Judith to pledge her love to him alone. Link was ecstatic. He had everything he thought he wanted: the thrill of anticipated air combat, the prestige and glory of a commission in the navy, and the betrothal of the beautiful young woman he'd pursued for a year. Rockwell the warrior, the hero, the conqueror prepared to devour life's exhilarating experiences.

George Lincoln Rockwell conducted himself honorably as a navy pilot throughout the war. He saw service, primarily in support, photo reconnaissance, transport, and training functions, aboard a sequence of ships after the *Omaha:* the USS *Pastores,* the USS *Wasp,* and the USS *Mobile,* where he served as senior aviator. He was promoted to lieutenant in 1944 and performed in a support function at the battle for Guadalcanal and during the invasion of Guam. Although he never actually flew in combat, he claimed to have gotten in on "the tail end of the action" at Guadalcanal, flying a few "mop-up" operations after the battle was won. Based on his service in the Pacific, he was promoted to lieutenant commander in October 1945. He also received several commendations and was generally considered a competent pilot and efficient officer.

In April 1943 Rockwell married Judith Aultman at St. John's Church in Barrington, Rhode Island.[9] They had a small wedding and a short honeymoon. Judith returned to Pembroke to complete her degree and Link shipped out to sea. Doc Rockwell, who was inexplicably absent from his son's wedding, nonetheless managed to make himself the center of attention—arriving in Barrington two days *after* the ceremony.[10]

Link and Judith's marriage got off to a rocky start. Judith's father, Merwyn L. Aultman, disliked the Rockwells and was never comfortable with Link, but his reservations about his future son-in-law served only to make his willful daughter more determined than ever to go through with the nuptials. Rockwell soon discovered that the well-educated and spirited Judith was nothing like his mental image of a wife—based on the demure and submissive Claire. He quickly eroded whatever relationship he had with the Aultmans by blaming them for not "training" Judith for the "proper"—meaning docile and compliant—role of a wife and mother, which was, in his view, the only appropriate station for a woman. What little time the newlyweds shared during the war was marred by loud and violent arguments. On at least one occasion Link struck Judith. By the time he was discharged from the navy, their relationship was strained and the marriage in jeopardy.

After the war Rockwell maintained his commission as an officer in the naval reserve. He loved the navy and would probably have stayed in the service if postwar demobilization hadn't dried up most opportunities for navy fliers. The reserve enabled him to keep his contact with the navy. Besides, the small monthly stipend came in very handy. In late 1945, Rockwell faced an uncertain future. Like millions of recently discharged servicemen, he had a wife to support and little experience at earning a living. He had neither a college degree nor immediate prospects for a job, so he and Judith moved near his father's Boothbay Harbor home in Maine. Rockwell tried his hand as a sign painter while practicing at night on his art and drawing. He scrounged out a meager living during 1946 as the proprietor and sole operator of Maine Photo-Art Service, painting signs and doing freelance photography. His small shop was rent-free, on land owned by his father, which was really the only reason that the business was profitable enough to support Link and his then-pregnant wife.

In September 1946 Rockwell entered the Pratt Institute of Commercial Art in Brooklyn, New York, one of the country's most respected institutions for the study of commercial illustration. Rockwell saw Pratt as the key to a lucrative career as a commercial artist. He and Judith closed their little shop and moved to New York. Penniless, they moved in with Doc Rockwell's sister, Helen, and her husband, Roscoe Smyth. The Smyths had three children of their own who shared their small home in suburban Mount Vernon, so the house was cramped, especially after Judith gave birth to the Rockwell's first child, Bonnie, later that fall. After Rockwell's first year at Pratt, G.I. housing became available in Brooklyn and he moved his family out of the Smyth home.

Rockwell did well at Pratt. He had modest talent and learned quickly. He studied there from September to June, returning to Maine each summer to work in his small sign-painting and photography business. In 1948 he won a prestigious illustration competition sponsored by the New York Society of Illustrators for a newspaper poster he'd done for the American Cancer Society.[11] The award carried a handsome honorarium—$1,000—and national recognition, which should have opened doors for him. But Rockwell inexplicably left Pratt before completing his course of study. Instead of exploiting his success in New York, he packed his wife and daughter off to Maine, where he opened an advertising agency in Portland with two partners, Al Bonney and Norton Payson. Maine Advertising, Inc., was an initial success, but Rockwell soon fell out with his partners and they bought him out in 1949. He then struck out on his own, finished with partners and more resistant than ever to working for a large company where he'd be under someone else's thumb. Resolved to "launch a personal assault on the business world," he started the Rockwell Publishing Company—another one-man outfit—to produce *The Olde Maine Guide,* a tourist magazine, and *What's Next?* a radio listings guide. Both publications were modestly successful and reflected the positive side of Rockwell's talent. He was a good "idea man" and often came up with a concept or gimmick that preceded trends. *The Olde Maine Guide* was the first of many similar tourist magazines distributed free of charge through motels and restaurants and funded by local advertisers, and *What's Next?* was virtually identical in concept and format to the later *TV Guide.* Rockwell's flaw, however, was a chronic inability to see a project through and to stick with an idea, even a great one, long enough to reap the rewards of commercial success.

Once the excitement of creation passed, Rockwell quickly grew bored with both publications and simply let them drift out of his control. He craved new challenges, new excitement. His restlessness severely strained Judith's patience, and by the time the U.S. Navy recalled him to active duty at the outbreak of the Korean War in 1950, their marriage was in trouble. When Link left for his assignment as an instructor at the Naval Air Support School in California, Judith did not accompany him. She took their daughters—a second girl, Nancy, was born in 1949—to live with her grandmother in Connecticut.

Lieutenant Commander Rockwell quickly readapted to a military regimen. At the San Diego Naval Air Station, he took the controls of an F8 Bearcat and was again the warrior in charge of his own destiny, in a man's world where the enemy was right out in front, easy to see, easy to engage. Rockwell trained navy and marine pilots at the ground school in Coronado, outside San Diego, and supervised their flight training in El Centro, in the California desert. But he missed his daughters and convinced Judith to give their marriage another chance. She agreed and joined him in a small rented house on the outskirts of San Diego. Before long, however, the fighting began again. From time to time Rockwell left home and moved into the Bachelor Officers' Quarters on the base, but each time, after a cooling-off period, he convinced Judith to take him back, to try one more time. Rockwell stubbornly resisted the idea of divorce, probably remembering the anguish he suffered as a six-year-old when his parents split up and unwilling to submit his daughters to the same fate. Link and Judith's third daughter, Phoebe-Jean, was born at the base hospital in San Diego. The fighting resumed shortly after Judith got home from the hospital. Their life together was now little more than periodic violent outbursts in a sea of cold, loveless silence. In 1952 the navy transferred Rockwell to the Keflavik Naval Air Station in Iceland. With the transfer came a promotion to full commander. He drove his family—Judith and the three girls—to the Aultman home in Barrington, Rhode Island, kissed the girls good-bye, hugged them, and promised to see them soon—a promise he knew he couldn't keep. Link and Judith never spent another night together as husband and wife.

Something happened to Rockwell during that last year or so in San Diego; or, more accurately, something probably happened within his mind, within the complex labyrinth of human thought and human reasoning. At some time during one of the bitter arguments with Judith, or during a night alone in his room at the Bachelor Officers' Quarters, or perhaps while behind the controls of an F8 Bearcat out over the blue Pacific off the Coronado coast, George Lincoln Rockwell met Adolf Hitler. Rockwell's autobiography gives an account of an almost mystical awakening to the "truth" of what Hitler had been preaching concerning the insidious Jew-led world communist conspiracy, and he anguished over the part he played in Hitler's defeat. But that account was written in later years and for an audience of believers. We'll probably never know the precise moment that Rockwell went from an eccentric crank with oddball political notions, a hatred for authority figures of all stripes, a hair-trigger temper, a conviction that some great conspiracy was afoot to deny him glory and prosperity, and a visceral dislike for Jews and blacks to a committed revolutionary who advocated race war and genocide. What we do know is that when U.S. Navy Commander George Lincoln Rockwell landed at Keflavik, Iceland, he had left behind his family, his art and his struggle for commercial success, his concern for his navy career, his life and his identity. He would never go back to those things. He had become, and would remain, Adolf Hitler's warrior.

3   THE COMING OUT

*If [the Jews] think Hitler was rough on them, that was because
they have not yet experienced Rockwell.*
—George Lincoln Rockwell, 1963

Just before he shipped out for Iceland in late 1952,
Rockwell visited his cousin Peter Smyth in Norfolk, Virginia. During that visit,
over dinner, Rockwell became increasingly agitated as he described for his
cousin the magnitude of the Jewish conspiracy to control America. Casual anti-
Semitism was not uncommon in the Smyth and Rockwell households while
the boys were growing up, but Pete was struck by the intensity Link displayed
and the viciousness of his attacks on unnamed "Jewish traitors." As Rockwell
went on and on about the wickedness and the cleverness of the Jews, Smyth
sat in stunned silence. "It was such a departure from anything he had done
before" that Smyth was not sure how to respond. He describes Rockwell as
"very excited," as though he had made an important discovery. For the first
time, Rockwell talked about the need for a Nazi party—an *American* Nazi
party—to rectify the error the United States had committed by fighting on the
wrong side in the recent world war. Smyth wasn't sure, at that time, if Rockwell
was serious about such an outrageous notion or if the Rockwell he thought he
knew, the fast-talking con man, wasn't just cooking up some new scheme to
get rich quick. Rockwell and Smyth marked their last night together for a while
by getting drunk.[1]

Rockwell's erratic behavior during late 1951 and 1952, during the time of
his final breakup with Judith, was evident in more than his sudden fascination
with Hitler and nazism. In late 1951 he visited his cousin Nancy Smyth in Reno,
Nevada. Nancy was going through a painful divorce and welcomed the com-
forting visit from her handsome older cousin. While they were growing up,
Nancy had a crush on Link, a crush that took on sexual overtones when she
entered puberty. One of her earliest memories was of "snuggling" with him
when she was eleven and he was eighteen. Many years later, Nancy recalled

the incident as the first time she felt real affection, and the first time she experienced sexual arousal. In Reno, Link's visit took a turn Nancy neither expected nor welcomed. He clumsily tried to seduce her, becoming more and more insistent that "she go to bed with him." Nancy remembers that Link was "roaring drunk" but, in the end, respected her refusal. He mumbled an apology of sorts and left, but the close lifelong bond between them was breached. Although she still loved him deeply—and continues to believe that she was only one of two persons he ever truly loved (the other being his aunt Margie)—Nancy never saw Rockwell again during the remaining years of his life.[2]

Rockwell turned to alcohol during periods of great stress throughout his life. He seems to have understood, at least to some degree, the connection between alcohol and the increasingly frequent fits of anger and irrationality that were darkening his life. From Iceland, he wrote reassuringly to his mother that he was busying himself with work and "hobbies" to avoid the temptation, so common to servicemen in isolated posts, to drink merely to pass the time. From the tone of his letter, Claire seems to have been concerned in this regard, and he assured her that he kept himself busy "so that I am not driven to the bottle like the rest."[3]

Rockwell served two one-year tours of duty in Iceland. His marriage to Judith was over, although the divorce would not become final until 1953, during his second tour. He buried himself in reading and studying, especially Hitler's *Mein Kampf*, which he read "a dozen times" during his first long, dark winter in Iceland. He'd bought the book in San Diego and said that reading it "was like finding part of me." As he read and reread, he came to believe that "national Socialism, the iconoclastic world-view of Adolf Hitler, was the doctrine of scientific, racial idealism," a "new 'religion' for our times." He also devoured the anti-Semitic writings of Gerald L. K. Smith and Conde McGinley and read, for the first time, the notorious forgery *The Protocols of the Learned Elders of Zion*.[4]

About halfway through his first tour of duty, Rockwell, as a naval officer, was invited to a diplomatic reception in Reykjavik, the capital of Iceland. At the party, held in the home of the first secretary of the Norwegian Embassy, Rockwell was introduced to—and was "captivated . . . instantly and completely" by—a stunning Icelandic beauty, Thora Hallgrimsson. For one of the few times in his life he was speechless. Thora was twenty-three, tall, blonde, blue-eyed, with a model's figure and the aristocratic bearing of a woman born to wealth and privilege. She also spoke perfect English. As they danced, Rockwell learned that she was recently divorced, with one son, Fridthrik. Thora was the daughter of a well-to-do Icelandic businessman, one uncle was a high-level diplomat, another was the archbishop of Reykjavik. By the end of the evening, Rockwell was madly in love with her. "I knew in my soul," he wrote, "that I had found THE woman in my life." Thora did not return his ardor, at least not yet. She allowed him to escort her home from the reception, and when they parted she was friendly but "cool" and proper, handing Rockwell her personal engraved card. By early 1953 they were dating regularly and their courtship became intense. They were married in an Icelandic service in the National Cathedral of Reykjavik on 3 October 1953. Thora was two months pregnant.[5]

The Rockwells honeymooned in the Bavarian Alps in West Germany, where they visited Berchtesgaden, the site of Obersalzberg, Hitler's mountain retreat. Rockwell claims to have fully confided in Thora about his racial beliefs and his political ambitions and to have warned her of the hardships they would encounter when he entered politics back in the United States. Thora, according to Rockwell's account, pledged to "follow him" regardless of the consequences.[6] In May 1954, Lincoln Hallgrimmur, their first child together and Rockwell's first son, was born at the base hospital in Keflavik. At the end of 1954, Rockwell's second tour in Iceland ended. He was returned to the United States with his new family—Thora; his stepson, Fridthrik, whom they called "Rickey"; and their seven-month-old son Lincoln, whom they dubbed "Hallie"—and detached to inactive duty on 15 December 1954.[7]

Rockwell returned to Maine and tried to earn enough money to support his family. He attacked that task with his usual gusto and eclecticism. He tinkered with several inventions, including a boxlike television-channel selector that displayed advertising and electronic toy dueling guns. He tried his hand at freelance writing, making a few sales and accumulating an impressive number of rejections.[8]

His greatest success was with a new publication he created and designed for the wives of U.S. servicemen. Rockwell's idea was to distribute the magazine free to service wives, which would give it an enormous circulation base and make it a desired venue for advertisers. The venture was too big for him to handle alone and too costly for him to consider financing, so he reluctantly sought partners and investors. He moved his family from Maine to Washington, D.C., the logical home for *U.S. Lady.* The first issue of the magazine was published in September 1955.[9] The magazine appeared headed for success, but Rockwell had a falling out with his partners and financial backers and sold his interest in the publication he had created.

After losing control of *U.S. Lady,* Rockwell worked briefly as an independent contractor for William F. Buckley Jr.'s *National Review,* promoting subscriptions on college campuses. This peripheral relationship with Buckley, which lasted less than six months, formed the basis of Rockwell's later exaggerated claim of intimacy with Buckley.[10] Rockwell then launched Rockwell Promotions, a one-man public relations and advertising firm, but was able to secure few clients.[11] He was under enormous financial and emotional pressure. The birth of his second child with Thora, Jeannie Margaret, and the burden of alimony and child support payments for Judith and her three daughters, kept Link and Thora living hand-to-mouth. In 1957, in desperation, he tried to use Thora's family connections to secure a 7Up bottling franchise and distributorship in Iceland. He even violated his long-held aversion to working for someone else by applying for a job with a large New York public relations firm. But he was unable to secure the 7Up franchise and the public relations firm didn't hire him either.[12]

During his first years in Washington, from 1955 to 1957, Rockwell moved among increasingly conservative political groups until he found a home on the farthest fringe of the right wing. In the wake of Senator Joe McCarthy's 1954 Senate censure, Washington was not particularly hospitable to the far right. Merwin K. Hart, Billy James Hargis, and Carl McIntire were active but virtually invisible. Willis Carto launched his right-wing magazine *Right* in late 1955 and formed the Liberty Lobby to promote his extreme anticommunist and anti-Semitic views in 1957. But the period "marked a low point in the activities of the extreme right in America," and that void was no more pronounced than in the nation's capital.[13] Rockwell saw this situation as both an economic opportunity and a chance to secure a forum for his right-wing views. He was not yet an open Nazi, still reluctant to make that final break with respectability, but his expressed views were on the farthest edge of what could be considered mainstream right-wing politics. He found work in 1956 as an organizer for Robert Snowden's Americans for Constitutional Action (and was fired within a year for "insubordination"), and he wrote a few pieces for Russell Maguire's *American Mercury*. He also tried to mobilize extreme conservative groups under a prestigious-sounding umbrella, The American Federation of Conservative Organizations, but failed to attract the support he believed the idea deserved. In reality, Rockwell was the founder, chairman, and only member.[14]

Rockwell regarded virtually all contemporary right-wing groups as too tame and timid to capture the imagination of the American public. He believed that right-wing leaders—including Hart, Hargis, McIntire, Maguire, and Carto on the fringe and William F. Buckley Jr., Douglas MacArthur, and the die-hard segregationist bloc in Congress closer to the political mainstream—secretly shared his conspiratorial and anti-Semitic views. Rockwell further believed that only their fear of Jewish retribution prevented these right-wing leaders from exposing the Jewish conspiracy for world domination that was so obvious to him. He was convinced that by stepping forward and openly challenging the

Jewish cabal, he would give voice to a large but silent and leaderless segment of the political right.

The more Rockwell thought about this strategy, the more he convinced himself of its validity. He believed that America's right-wing leaders understood the nature and extent of the "Jewish conspiracy" but were too timid to confront the Jews directly. Their timidity, Rockwell reasoned, made their frustrated followers susceptible to the allure of an outspoken new leader who was bold enough to openly attack American Jews. Even Robert Welch's stridently anticommunist John Birch Society failed to address the true nature of "the enemy" to Rockwell's satisfaction. Welch attacked communists but did not openly connect international communism to international Jewry, a connection Rockwell regarded as essential to expose the Jewish-communist threat to the United States. He attributed Welch's failure to expose communism as a Jewish plot for world domination to intimidation by powerful American Jews. To Rockwell, Welch—whom he always referred to as "Rabbit Welch"—was a despicable coward who understood the role of the Jews in communist aggression but shrank from confronting them.

The year 1958 was Rockwell's watershed year, when he crossed his personal political Rubicon, broke with all other fringe groups, openly proclaimed himself a Nazi and an adherent of Adolf Hitler's National Socialism, and formed the American Nazi party. In 1958 he met the two most influential men in his early career as a Nazi: DeWest Hooker and Harold Noel Arrowsmith Jr. Hooker convinced Rockwell that the only effective way to combat the "Jewish conspiracy" was openly, as a Nazi; Arrowsmith provided the funding for Rockwell to become a full-time anti-Semitic agitator. Rockwell made Hooker's acquaintance through the *American Mercury*'s Russell Maguire. Hooker was descended from a very old and very wealthy New York family, and he used his inheritance freely to advance his political ideas. He was handsome, sophisticated, elegant, a graduate of Cornell University, and forty years old, exactly Rockwell's age. The FBI regarded Hooker as one of the most active pro-Nazi anti-Semites within the fringe right and followed with special interest his recruitment of New York City youth for his Nazi-front National Youth League. To Rockwell, Hooker was the ideal Aryan: imperious, intelligent, athletic, and a "fighting, tough, all-out Nazi." After their meeting, Rockwell said, his "life changed permanently." Hooker convinced him that the other fringe-right groups who used code words for their anti-Semitism and racism and thus lacked the courage to face "the enemy" directly would never prevail. Only as an open and defiant Nazi, Hooker told Rockwell, could he win the power he craved. Hooker gave Rockwell the inspiration to "come out" as a Nazi. Harold Noel Arrowsmith Jr. gave him the means to do so.[15]

Arrowsmith was the son and grandson of distinguished and well-respected Episcopal ministers, one of two sons born to the Reverend Harold Noel Arrowsmith Sr. and Frances Swayne Cook Arrowsmith. Reverend Arrowsmith served as canon of the Cathedral Church of the Incarnation in Baltimore, Maryland, for thirty-five years (1916–51). During his tenure, he supervised the completion of the cathedral and was one of the most honored and revered men in Baltimore.[16] Harold Jr. did not follow his father into the church. Instead, he made his fortune in business, retired young, and devoted his life to amateur anthropology, eugenics, racism, and anti-Semitism. In the spring of 1950 he founded the National Committee to Free America from Jewish Domination, a paper organization that primarily printed and distributed anti-Semitic hate literature. In the early 1950s Arrowsmith donated heavily to the International Association for the Advancement of Ethnology and Eugenics, a respectable group of scholars and scientists working to gather scientific data to bolster the segregationist position in the *Brown v. Board of Education* case. In the late 1950s he associated with Salem Bader's Arab-Asian Institute and, for a time, was a registered agent for the government of Saudi Arabia.[17]

In April 1958, William Scott Stephenson, owner and editor of the prosegregationist newspaper *The Virginian,* introduced Arrowsmith to Rockwell. Arrowsmith was looking for a flashy writer to help him revive the dormant National Committee to Free America from Jewish Domination. Rockwell had written a few articles for *The Virginian,* but his erratic and volatile temperament made Stephenson nervous. Rockwell and Arrowsmith seemed a perfect match. Arrowsmith had money, which Rockwell desperately needed, and Rockwell had the guts and glitz to take Arrowsmith's anti-Semitic crusade to the streets. Arrowsmith was a strange, small man with an effeminate manner and delicate hands and feet, short but quite round and soft. He seemed almost fragile. But when he spoke of the Jews, his eyes narrowed and his voice hardened. Rockwell described him as "an exterminationist first, last and always." According to Rockwell, Arrowsmith maintained that Jews were subhuman and that "you are not massacring people when you are massacring Jews."[18]

On 10 May 1958 Rockwell and Arrowsmith left Stephenson's headquarters in Newport News, Virginia, together and drove to Washington, D.C., where Arrowsmith set up Rockwell in a small suburban house with a printing press and free rein to "drive the Jews mad." Arrowsmith funded Rockwell's first overt anti-Semitic act, picketing the White House in protest of President Eisenhower's pro-Israeli policies, and made plans to accelerate their attack on the Jews. Rockwell later claimed that Arrowsmith grew impatient with him because he wanted more physically violent acts against Jewish targets. Within less than five months Rockwell and Arrowsmith were feuding and Arrowsmith withdrew further funding. Rockwell taunted Arrowsmith as "a weakling and a sissy." By September 1958 the breach between the two men was permanent. Arrowsmith's role in Rockwell's career was short-lived but extremely important. Rockwell had become a professional hatemonger, a role he would never relinquish.[19]

Rockwell was now a full-time anti-Semitic agitator looking for a vehicle for his political views and a new patron to finance his activities. He was an open, though not yet public, Nazi. Within the racist right wing his views and allegiance to Hitler-style nazism were well known, but his public activities, such as his picketing of the White House under Arrowsmith's sponsorship in late July 1958, did not flaunt the swastika or otherwise indicate a direct connection to nazism. Although the signs he carried displayed such ethnic slurs as "kikes" to refer to Jews, they ostensibly focused on "treason," not race. But on 12 October 1958, George Lincoln Rockwell was publicly outed as a Nazi. That night the explosion from a crude bomb ripped through the oldest Jewish synagogue in Atlanta, Georgia, the Hebrew Benevolent Congregation, known locally as "the Temple." Initial press reports linked Rockwell to the atrocity.[20]

Earlier that year, Rockwell had a hand in the formation of a new anti-Semitic and racist party in Georgia, the National States Rights party. The founders, Jesse B. Stoner and Edward R. Fields, assembled many of the budding luminaries of the racist fringe—Ned Dupes, Connie Lynch, Gordon Winrod, Wallace Allen, George Bright, James K. Warner, Matt Koehl, Emory Burke, and George Lincoln Rockwell—to launch their new party. Rockwell's National Committee to Free America from Jewish Domination supplied the Atlanta-based NSRP with anti-Semitic literature, signs, and stickers, and Rockwell advised the NSRP's organizers on strategy and tactics. Friendships and allegiances formed that would endure. Warner would later become the first national secretary of Rockwell's American Nazi party; Koehl would be the last.

A particularly strong bond formed quickly between Rockwell and Emory Burke, a veteran of the Georgia race wars. Prior to World War II, Burke was an active fascist and admirer of Hitler's Nazi regime. During the war, the FBI closely monitored Burke, suspecting him of pro-German sympathies. In 1946 he was one of the three cofounders, along with Homer L. Loomis and John H. Zimmerlee, of the first openly neo-Nazi organization in postwar America, the Columbians.[21] Burke headed the Atlanta Police Department's list of suspects in the Temple bombing. While searching his home the day after the bombing, police found a cache of letters from Rockwell to Burke. Although the letters were ambiguous, some sentences and phrases were interpreted as linking Rockwell with the bombing. The FBI already suspected Rockwell's involvement but couldn't tie him directly to the crime. Although the Atlanta police did not have enough evidence to arrest Rockwell, they released the letters—and their thinly veiled suspicions—to the national press.[22]

The Atlanta synagogue bombing drew national attention, and Rockwell's name figured prominently in reports that identified him as a radical Nazi.[23] Even Doc Rockwell was sufficiently shaken by the press reports published in the New England papers to divert attention, for a brief time, from his own life to the activities of his errant son. To Claire, Rockwell's outing came "like a bombshell" with the publicity over the Atlanta synagogue attack. The family was mindful of—and disturbed by—Link's increasingly radical politics, but most of them, with the apparent exception of his brother, Bobby, were unaware of the full extent of his radicalization. His sister, Priscilla, remembers the traumatic first days after the initial news reports, stating that the family was "horrified. . . . we wanted to crawl in a hole and hide. . . . it was a nightmare."[24]

Hardest hit by Rockwell's sudden notoriety was his brother. Bobby was unlike his unconventional older brother in almost every way. He maintained an affection for Link even though they'd had little real contact since Link's return from Iceland. A rising young New England businessman with a growing family, Bobby suffered greatly when the Rockwell name was publicly linked with a terrorist bombing, anti-Semitic hate groups, fringe conspiracies, and *Nazis.* His own reputation and his children's security weighed heavily on his mind in the days after the Atlanta bombing. Foremost, however, was a genuine concern for his brother's mental state. Bobby wrote Link and Thora a long and earnest letter eight days after the bombing in which he recounted the emotional damage Link's public activities wrought on a private and respectable family.

Bobby tried to reason with Link, drawing on whatever vestiges of fraternal attachment remained between the quiet and adoring younger brother and the bold and daring older brother, the exuberant daredevil Bobby referred to in their youth as "the King of Ethiopia." He carefully approached the subject of Link's mental health, raising concerns that had built over a period of more than a decade during which Link's behavior became increasingly erratic and his attachment to reality, in Bobby's view, increasingly tenuous. Bobby moved gingerly to the heart of his plea: a proposal that Link immediately place himself under psychiatric care. He tried to soften the suggestion by reminding Link that their father had repeatedly sought psychiatric counseling throughout his life. Although he had a growing family to support and could ill afford additional financial obligations, Bobby offered to help pay for Link's psychiatric treatment and to solicit support—probably from the deepest pocket in the Rockwell clan, Doc himself—to pay any bills for extended care. Bobby understood that in Link's current mental state, if his suspicion of clinical paranoia was correct, Link needed the strongest inducement possible if there was any hope he would respond. He tried to explain the signs of the paranoia he suspected. He cited for Link, and probably more for Thora, a definition from a psychology textbook of paranoia as "a psychosis which develops relatively late in life and is highly monosymptomatic in that the patient has a systematized set of delusions of persecution which are usually balanced by delusions of grandeur." Trying to force a decision from Link, Bobby gave his brother a proposal and an ultimatum: he, Bobby, would help if Link would abandon all political activity and racist associations, devote his talents and energies to reviving his flagging printing business, and submit willingly to extended and intensive therapy. If Link rejected this proposal, Bobby wrote, he would have no choice but to sever all contact with him. Bobby concluded his letter on a hopeful note, pledging his immediate help if only Link would reach out and grasp the hand being extended.[25]

Bobby's anguish in his letter is palpable. He was genuinely and lovingly concerned about his brother, which is why Link's response devastated him. In a rambling, four-page letter, Link mocked Bobby's concern, ranting about the "conspiracy" of powerful forces committed to his destruction—the press, the police, and the Jews, always the Jews—and, in a scathing final page, attacked Bobby's sincerity and his motives. Link rejected Bobby's suggestion that he seek psychiatric treatment and verbally assaulted the loving brother who sought to help him.[26]

There is no extant record of an independent reply to Bobby from Thora, but the fact remains that by December 1958 she had separated from Rockwell and returned to Iceland with her children. Her uncle, who was at this time the Icelandic ambassador to the United States, expedited their departure. The loss of his second family drove Rockwell to the bottle and into a deep depression. He turned to his mother for comfort. Claire was the only one close to him who was not judgmental, who loved him unconditionally, and he revealed his innermost fears and pains to her. He wrote to Claire shortly after Thora and the children left, detailing his misery and his despair. Rockwell tried to make his mother understand his turn to the political fringe as the action of a patriot who saw dangers to the nation that others ignored. His view of himself, as revealed to Claire, was of a man on a mission, a man of almost mystical destiny. He vowed that one day, if they both survived, Claire would understand and would even be proud of him.[27]

With his wife and children gone, Rockwell was alone with his thoughts and delusions. He saw a world of danger and conspiracy, a world filled with enemies determined to neutralize him and overrun the country he loved. He replayed his conversations with DeWest Hooker, over and over, in his mind and concluded that all subtlety and subterfuge was counterproductive. It was only as an open Nazi that he saw any opportunity to mobilize his race and seize political power in the United States before it was too late. "I tried and nobody paid attention to me," he reasoned, "but no one can ignore Nazis marching in the street."[28] By the end of 1958, Rockwell was displaying a huge Nazi banner in his home and had recruited the first three stormtroopers—J. V. Kenneth Morgan, Eugene Collton, and Louis Yalacki—for his new American Nazi party.[29]

With no reason to believe that any philosophical affinity existed between them, Rockwell tried to enlist the support of the most prominent conservative he knew: William F. Buckley Jr. He drew on their brief acquaintance of several years prior, when Rockwell was a contract subscription salesman for Buckley's *National Review,* to send Buckley the first issue of several anti-Semitic ANP flyers and pamphlets. Buckley's reply was prompt and unequivocal: "the things you sent me physically appalled me. . . . I can only pray that some day they will sicken you too."[30] Rockwell persisted for years in trying to enlist Buckley's support, convinced, with no scintilla of evidence and in the face of Buckley's painfully clear rejections, that Buckley was secretly sympathetic to his cause.[31]

Throughout 1959 Rockwell tried to reconcile with Thora, but her family was determined that she and the children would have no more to do with the volatile American Nazi. In December 1959, almost precisely one year from the day she returned to Iceland, Thora wrote to Link, inviting him to visit her. His hopes soared. He scraped together the money for plane fare and left his fledgling party in the hands of James K. Warner, the ANP's national secretary. Warner, who had joined the party that fall, had no doubt that "if Rockwell's wife had agreed to let him stay in Iceland he would have deserted the party." He recalls heavy bouts of drinking by Rockwell during late 1959, all connected to his inability to accept the loss of Thora and their children. Rockwell alternated between a macho posture—"he bragged about how he used to treat her like a dog and how he kept her in her place"—and maudlin fits of weeping. By the time he received Thora's letter, his drinking had become frighteningly regular, with shots of whiskey before speaking in public and long drinks of iced vodka during his speeches.[32]

Unfortunately for Rockwell, divorce, not reconciliation, had prompted Thora's letter. His trip to Iceland was a disaster. Her family carefully controlled the visit and limited his access to her. After his return to Virginia, Link wrote to his mother that despite his offer to abandon politics and settle in Iceland, Thora still rejected him. He was despondent. In the year since their separation, he'd clung to the hope that somehow he would find a way to win her back.

The trip to Iceland shattered any such illusion. He wrote again to Claire of the physical pain caused by the loss of Thora and their children. Claire soothed her son as best she could through her letters. When his letters to her took a worrisome turn—declaring that without Thora he had nothing worth living for and threatening suicide—she made plans to visit him in Virginia.

Before Claire could make the trip, however, the tone of Link's letters changed dramatically. What he called his "fight" would sustain him, he assured her, and would absorb the pain he felt, converting it to anger against his enemies. On the last day of 1959—and the first day of his renewed commitment to "the fight"—Rockwell wrote to his mother of his destiny. She would, he promised, be proud of her firstborn son. His pain turned outward, Rockwell would make his enemies pay for all that had gone so wrong in his life.[33]

4 THE ANP'S MEMBERS, FOLLOWERS, FUNDING

*My co-workers are unbelievably ... stupid. . . . What a cross to
bear! Sometimes it is even a relief to talk to a vicious and hateful . . . Jew, after suffering with these pitiful "patriots."*
—George Lincoln Rockwell, 1964

The FBI kept the vehicle Rockwell created for his politi-
cal ambitions under close surveillance from its inception, believing that the
American Nazi party, "though small in numbers," was a "dangerous organization" capable, "psychologically and physically," of violence against Jews and
blacks. They had no doubt that Rockwell's Nazis would "follow through with
their obnoxious objectives of liquidating all whom they consider inferior," given
the opportunity to do so. Rockwell was characterized by the FBI as a man of
"unleashed invectives and vitriolic language," one whose "tongue and pen are
jagged weapons." FBI monitors believed that Rockwell meant to make good
on his threats of "gas chambers, hangings, depriving citizens of their homes
and heritage," and they reported that a small revolutionary cadre of fanatical
supporters—well armed with "revolvers, automatic pistols, shotguns, and
rifles"—were prepared to do Rockwell's bidding. Rockwell targeted 1972 as
the year he and his party would come to power. He accurately predicted the
race riots of the mid-1960s and believed those incidents would intensify until
the end of the decade, when economic chaos, fueled by runaway inflation in
the early 1970s, would force the American people to turn to a strong leader
to restore order. Rockwell believed he would be that leader.[1]

Contrary to FBI fears of potential violence, Rockwell's strategy was psychological and political, not terroristic. He planned to agitate Jews and blacks
to force them, by their reaction to him, to give his movement the publicity it
needed to grow. Once he had gathered around himself a hard-core following,
he would be prepared to exploit the chaos he predicted. He also expected that
in 1972 he would be elected president of the United States. As president, he
would implement the ANP's platform: namely, the execution of all those who
were Marxist-Zionist traitors—he variously estimated this meant 80–95 per-

cent of U.S. Jews; removal of all "disloyal Jews" from positions of influence in the media, government, education, and the legal system; and "the establishment of an International Treason Tribunal to investigate, try, and publicly hang, in front of the U.S. Capitol, all non-Jews who are convicted of having consciously acted as fronts for Jewish treason."[2] He further intended to "encourage" all African Americans to emigrate to Africa. Those who refused would be forcibly removed from their homes and restricted to "relocation centers" in desolate areas of the United States, where they would remain, stripped of their citizenship, as wards of the government. Rockwell skirted the issue of his personal role in a Nazi America, paying lip service to the U.S. Constitution and denying dictatorial ambitions, but he made it clear that divergent views would not be tolerated under ANP rule. Among party faithful he was less circumspect: "We favor dictatorship—our own."[3] Fortunately, he failed to garner the numerical strength or financial support to implement his plans.

George Lincoln Rockwell never released specific ANP membership figures, but contemporary newspaper accounts seldom counted more than a hundred active members. Most agreed with a British newspaper's assessment at the time of Rockwell's death that the American Nazi party "has no measurable political voice in the United States."[4] Rockwell's following in New Hampshire was so small, in fact, that he couldn't obtain the 100 signatures necessary to qualify for a place on the 1964 New Hampshire presidential primary ballot, his first foray into electoral politics that he believed would lead, in 1972, to utlimate victory. William Loeb, the archconservative publisher of the *Manchester Union Leader,* wrote: "Frankly, we were surprised, for one would expect that Rockwell's henchmen could have found 50 drunks [in each of New Hampshire's two congressional districts] who would sign their name to anything for 'whiskey money.'"[5] Loeb's surprise was understandable. Rockwell, the consummate salesman, always seemed more formidable than the size of his following implied. Even for his funeral, which his successor, Matt Koehl, tried to turn into a martyr's rally, fewer than fifty Nazi loyalists showed up. Virtually all contemporary assessments of ANP numerical strength concur with Alex Haley's opinion that "Rockwell could not be called a spokesman for any socially or politically significant minority; indeed, his fanatical following is both motley and minuscule."[6] Consider too Ernest Volkman's evaluation that "Rockwell's efforts in this country to create a large national Nazi movement [failed]. . . . At its height, Rockwell's movement was never able to attract more than about five hundred hard-core followers."[7] But "Rockwell's flamboyant personality and his clever if venomous stunts" produced both headlines and the illusion that the American Nazi Party was much larger than it actually was.[8]

In 1965, the California Department of Justice investigated the ANP as part of a broader confidential investigation of extremist right-wing groups. The purpose of the study was to determine the potential of any extremist group to engage in acts of violence within California. The Department of Justice found that Rockwell's Arlington, Virginia, headquarters was seldom staffed with more than two dozen stormtroopers and that "at any given time Rockwell could mobilize less than 150 Stormtroopers nationwide." According to this investigation, the ANP's Western Division, the focus of Rockwell's intense organizational efforts for almost two years, "has never been represented by more than a handful of members [usually about a dozen]." In addition to noting the ANP's numerical weakness, the report comments on the quality of the few troops Rockwell had in California, describing them as "the misfits and maladjusted of society." Indeed, almost half of the ANP's Western Division stormtroopers had felony arrest records or histories of institutionalization for mental illness.[9]

Jewish community organizations, especially the American Jewish Committee and the Anti-Defamation League of B'nai B'rith, conducted continuous surveillance of the ANP. Their intelligence reports provide the most reliable assessment of Rockwell's following from the beginning of his public career in late 1958 until his death. In early 1960, the AJC obtained a copy of a deposition given by Rockwell in a lawsuit filed against him by Harold Noel Arrowsmith Jr., his erstwhile financial patron, who had broken with him in late 1959. In the deposition, Rockwell admitted that "the number of people that I can muster to perform an operation in this country . . . I would say is about 500, but those people are not party members. Our party is very small."[10] Later that same year, the Jewish Community Council of Greater Washington, a coalition of Jewish community organizations in the Washington, D.C., metropolitan area, advised its members that "Rockwell's following is negligible. . . . His hard core of followers consists of some 30 to 50 persons. . . . He may have another few odd-dozen scattered elsewhere. He himself has admitted that the individuals behind him are 'very small in number.' He has said that his group has 'grown' to 30."[11] Robert J. Greene, of the AJC's Washington, D.C., staff, reported that "the Arlington[, Virginia,] police specialist on Rockwell . . . [has] never indicated that Rockwell had more than forty or forty-five adherents."[12] In 1962, on the anniversary of the ANP's founding, the American Jewish Committee reported to its members: "Today, the American Nazi Party remains the same shabby, small-time enterprise, embracing no more than 50 stormtroopers."[13]

The Anti-Defamation League's independent surveillance and analysis of the ANP concurred with that of the AJC. In late 1963, the ADL reported to its members that the ANP had not grown to any measurable degree: "George Lincoln Rockwell . . . remains a nuisance, but is not a menace. . . . Rockwell has not been able to expand his movement and seems destined to remain a mere pimple on the American body politic." The ADL observed no more than fifty individuals in intermittent residence at the party's barracks in Arlington. The report concluded that "Rockwell has not succeeded in organizing anything that resembles a movement. . . . He has perhaps a few hundred sympathizers or supporters scattered around the country."[14]

By early 1964, the AJC estimated Rockwell's following at fewer than sixty persons. According to various Jewish community organizations, that number continued to fluctuate throughout Rockwell's career, depending on events and publicity. The faces change as disaffected Nazis were replaced by new recruits, but the ANP never achieved substantially greater numbers than it attracted during the first few years of its existence.

Although Rockwell jealously guarded ANP membership information, statements by several former Rockwell followers verified these AJC and ADL estimates. After he broke with Rockwell in 1961, James K. Warner, former ANP national secretary and one of Rockwell's closest early advisers, wrote that "[the American Nazi party] in the U.S. numbers less than 25 active members and some 15 inactive members. In most of his operations [Rockwell] gathers all the anti-Jewish people in the Washington, D.C. area . . . and uses them to make his party look bigger." Hal Kaiser, who joined the party in 1961, rising to the rank of lieutenant, places party membership at the time of Rockwell's death at about 200 regulars.[15]

R. E. Cooper was a Rockwell supporter who joined the renamed National Socialist White People's party a little more than two years after Rockwell's death. Matt Koehl, Rockwell's successor, named Cooper business manager of the NSWPP in 1970, giving Cooper daily access to the party's membership lists and records. According to Cooper, the NSWPP maintained separate mailing lists for three categories of supporters: official party members (persons who had filed formal applications to join the party and were accepted as members); official supporters (persons who were not official party members but who regularly made small monthly financial donations to the party); and the party newspaper mailing list (persons who subscribed to the party newspaper but were neither party members nor regular financial contributors). Cooper says that the NSWPP had approximately 100 official party members in 1970, two and a half years after Rockwell's death, which is generally within the range of all estimates of ANP membership under Rockwell. Cooper also estimates that the NSWPP official supporters list contained between 600 and 800 names and that there were approximately 2,500 names on the party newspaper mailing list.[16] Since criteria for inclusion on the ANP's (or the NSWPP's) official supporters list or newspaper mailing list were not clearly defined, these numbers are a less reliable indicator than actual party membership, which required specific application, review, and acceptance procedures in both the ANP and its successor organization. In terms of both party membership—which no reliable source places above 200 individuals—and the less reliable category of ANP supporters—which probably never numbered more than a few thousand individuals—the number of people who were attracted to the ANP message, in a nation as large as the United States, was statistically insignificant. As the Anti-Defamation League noted after Rockwell's death, "Rockwell—skilled performer though he was in gaining national notoriety—was never more than the 'Commander' of a small and tatterdemalion group. . . . Rockwell had become a national figure, but he was never able to marshal a significant following."[17]

American Nazi party funding, like membership information, was closely held by Rockwell and a few intimates. Reliable contemporary descriptions of ANP facilities and resources, however, allow a fairly accurate assessment of the movement's financial strength. Tony Ulasewicz monitored Rockwell's activities for the New York City Police Department from 1958 to 1967. During 1960 and 1961, Rockwell's street demonstrations and violent confrontations with Jewish groups in New York and Washington, D.C., received constant press attention and fostered the impression of a large and growing movement. In late 1961, Ulasewicz visited ANP headquarters in Arlington, Virginia, and found a "grubby haunted house. . . . [Rockwell's] glowing, published accounts of his party's progress had been nothing more than a pack of lies. As I looked around, I noticed that bullet holes punctured all the walls of his house. . . . I also saw a stack of unpaid bills high on a table. Rockwell's electricity had been turned off, and he used kerosene lamps to light the place. . . . Whatever Hitler's ghost had promised Rockwell, it hadn't yet arrived."[18]

Rockwell encouraged the impression that he had a wide base of small contributors and an eager cadre of wealthy patrons, which drew the attention of the U.S. Jewish community. A well-funded American Nazi party, indicative of broad-based support for Nazi intentions, would have posed a physical threat to U.S. Jews, and Jewish community organizations regarded it as critical to accurately determine the extent and nature of Rockwell's funding. In early 1960 the issue of Rockwell's financial status was the subject of an exchange of intelligence between Roy H. Millenson and Edwin J. Lucas, top officials of the American Jewish Committee. Based on the confidential deposition the AJC had been able to obtain, Millenson reported: "In response to a question as to how he financed himself, Rockwell said he just isn't doing it. He is not paying his bills and is in serious financial difficulty continually. This has been the case," Millenson concluded, "since he . . . went into politics about three years ago."[19]

Not completely satisfied, an AJC agent infiltrated ANP headquarters for a firsthand look. The agent described "a wooden house, in very bad condition. . . . There is no running water; they have to pass [water] in from the outside; and so the cups are passed from the kitchen to be washed; the renovation job Rockwell once had planned never panned out. . . . Upstairs there are other rooms—the troopers' rooms, four cots (many of them sleep on the floor); there were no sheets on the cots; everything looked and smelled unclean; . . . all very depressing."[20] After receiving a copy of the report, Isaac Frank, executive director of the Jewish Community Council of Greater Washington, reassured the member organizations of his coalition that "[Rockwell] gets a trickle of money and is always on the verge of being broke. . . . Rockwell's so-called 'American Nazi Party' is an insignificant handful that has managed to keep afloat by 'smart' opportunism and a faculty for making noise and stirring up trouble and creating disorder."[21]

In early 1961 the AJC's Robert J. Greene saw virtually no change in the ANP's financial condition. He wrote that "[Rockwell's] men are living in a most marginal fashion" and that Rockwell himself "is consistently late in meeting alimony payments to his first . . . wife."[22] By 1963 ANP fund-raising had improved slightly but was still marginal. The ADL found that the American Nazi party's annual gross income was no more than $20,000 and that Rockwell had asked his stormtroopers to find jobs and turn over their paychecks to the party. Still, their living conditions did not improve much: "Plumbing at [ANP] headquarters is faulty, and hot water is in short supply. Troopers are often ordered to make necessary repairs since the Party treasury cannot stand the strain of a regular plumber's services. The electrical system is likewise faulty and troopers must also make needed repairs. . . . The rations are skimpy, unappetizing and monotonous. Some troopers have reported eating canned hash for days on end. At other times, the rations include cat food. At still other times, the diet has been a thin stew made from chicken necks." An ADL informant reported: "The party was, as usual, behind in paying its telephone bill and fear was expressed that the phone company would remove the two phones in the headquarters and the one in the barracks."[23]

The dismal picture of Rockwell's American Nazi party based on Jewish community organizations' surveillance is one of a group barely surviving, with its members living at a subsistence level. It is an image of the ANP that Rockwell did not want broadcast and one that he actively sought to suppress. But his private letters reveal a relentless burden of poverty experienced by the ANP that occasionally eased but never fully lifted. Writing to his mother in December 1959, Rockwell complained of the menial jobs he held for food money while he pursued his political goals. Claire Rockwell sent her son cash from time to time to help him make ends meet. As late as mid-1963, Rockwell depended on his mother's largesse for such items as emergency dental work, since he didn't have the fifty dollars a Washington dentist demanded in advance.

Throughout 1960 and 1961, Rockwell repeatedly appealed for funds from sympathizers. During the winter of 1960, he mailed a desperate plea to people who had previously contributed to the ANP, claiming that "[stormtroopers] ARE EATING STALE BREAD AND 10 CENT-A-POUND MEAT INTENDED FOR DOGS! . . . . they can't fight because they are hungry and COLD, . . . we have no money for the heat bill."[24] Rockwell raised enough money from this appeal to make it through that winter, but as winter approached the following year, his party was still surviving only "from miracle to miracle."[25] The ANP's fortunes did not improve appreciably with time. Lee Larson, an ANP storm-trooper from 1964 to 1966, recalls an organization that was "under-staffed, under-trained, and under-funded," with members living in a "residence [that] was in sorry shape."[26]

Rockwell's extensive private correspondence with Bruno Ludtke, ideologue of the neo-Nazi movement in post–World War II West Germany, reveals Rockwell's continual frustration with his party's desperate lack of funds. On Christmas morning in 1963, Rockwell wrote to Ludtke of the ANP's desperate struggle and of the cold and hunger he and his followers had to endure. The following summer the constant struggle for funds to sustain the ANP was still a major component of his letters to Ludtke. Even as late as 1966, Rockwell's letters reflected his anguish over the ANP's lack of funds. He wrote to Ludtke that the never-ending struggle to keep the American Nazi party viable was eating away at his health and strength. Sixteen months before his death, Rockwell complained bitterly to Ludtke that his followers were literally without food to eat.[27] The Rockwell-Ludtke correspondence confirms the information accumulated by AJC and ADL surveillance regarding ANP funding. Because of the legal situation in West Germany at the time, Ludtke was operating underground and could provide Rockwell with little assistance, so it is unlikely that Rockwell was trying to appeal to Ludtke for funds.

Other unpublished Rockwell correspondence confirms that the American Nazi party was continually on the verge of bankruptcy. From 1964 to 1966, the critical lack of funds was a constant theme of his letters to supporters and followers.[28] In August 1966, Rockwell angrily rejected a request from his second-in-command, Matt Koehl, for additional staff, citing a lack of necessities at ANP headquarters and Rockwell's own unmet need for clerical and administrative assistance. An exasperated Rockwell berated Koehl for demanding money for personnel when there wasn't enough money for food and other necessities for ANP stormtroopers.[29] Edward R. Fields of the National States Rights party recalls that "[Rockwell] lived in abject poverty. There was often no food to eat up there [at ANP headquarters]. The cars he drove were just junk. . . . It was a very tough battle. He never had any money."[30]

From 1964 to 1966, Rockwell's financial troubles were compounded by continuing difficulties with the U.S. Internal Revenue Service. In 1964, Rockwell wrote to the IRS district director who was handling his case of his inability to make any tax payments. He claimed that he was only barely keeping up with court-mandated child support payments by disposing of his personal property at local pawnshops.[31] A year later, Rockwell was still battling with the IRS and, in a letter to that agency, referred to an earlier IRS audit that verified his lack of funds to justify his request for additional time to pay back taxes.[32] It was a battle he lost. The IRS held a public auction on 18 February 1966 at which the ANP's first headquarters on Randolph Street in Arlington and all its contents were auctioned to satisfy a tax lien.

Rockwell and his party lived hand-to-mouth from beginning to end. He drew on the generosity of a limited number of patrons at critical points in his career—financial "angels" who provided periodic infusions of cash or other support to help him avoid the total collapse of his movement—but they did not provide continuing funding to any significant degree. These patrons were not connected with any other right-wing political group, and none of the major contributors to mainstream right-wing groups also funded Rockwell and the ANP.

As described earlier, Rockwell's move into flagrant anti-Semitic hatemongering was initially underwritten by Harold Noel Arrowsmith Jr. In a letter to his brother, Robert, in October 1958, Rockwell identified Arrowsmith as the man who provided him with $20,000 worth of support that enabled him to launch his public career.[33] Arrowsmith's backing was primarily in the form of the use of a house in Arlington and a secondhand printing press, plus about $2,500 in cash. But their relationship ended after a few months, and by late 1959 Arrowsmith had gone to court to evict Rockwell from the house in Arlington and recover his printing equipment. By the end of 1960, Rockwell had a new patron.

Floyd Fleming of Arlington, Virginia, was a long-time racist who, with John Kasper, organized the northern Virginia chapter of the White Citizens Council in 1956.[34] Fleming bought a house at 928 North Randolph Street in Arlington that became the new headquarters for the American Nazi party and Rockwell's home.[35] Fleming and his wife, Emma, were of modest means (he was a sign painter, she was a housewife), but they remained regular contributors to Rockwell and his party even after the house they bought for him was seized by the IRS and sold for back taxes in 1966. A reconstruction of the Flemings' total contributions to Rockwell and the ANP is not possible from existing sources, but it was probably between $35,000 and $50,000 from January 1960 to August 1967.

In 1964, Rockwell met his third and last major patron, Robert Surrey of Dallas, Texas. Surrey was co-owner of a modest but prosperous local printing company. His partner was a former U.S. Army major general, Edwin A. Walker. Surrey and his wife, Mary, who was Walker's personal secretary, tried to enlist the reactionary general for Rockwell's cause but failed. Mary Surrey left Walker's employ in anger after the general refused to join her and her husband as Rockwell followers. Robert Surrey, who went by the code name "Max Amann"—taken from the name of a prominent German publisher who was one of Adolf Hitler's earliest supporters—remained a Rockwell loyalist to the end, but he left the party after a dispute with Matt Koehl, Rockwell's successor. In June 1968, Surrey mailed a memorandum to the people on the ANP mailing list (as Rockwell's printer, he had a copy of the list) in which he attacked Koehl's failure to maintain Rockwell's direction. In that memo Surrey referred to the extent of his financial contribution to the party: "my wife and I . . . took money from our own pocket . . . [and] used our own money for bails and fines for the Stormtroopers; we contributed our home as an office and warehouse for the [ANP] Order Department; we filled the orders, answered the letters of inquiry, and kept things running on a day to day basis; and we raised better than $20,000 in a three year period for the Party."[36]

Rockwell repeatedly made cryptic references to "our backers in Dallas," fostering the illusion of major financial patrons in that region, which was well known in the 1960s for its right-wing sympathizers and its rich oilmen who were willing to put their money behind their reactionary politics. But the fact is that Rockwell's Dallas operation consisted of Robert and Mary Surrey and seven to ten other middle-class Texans. As the *Dallas Times-Herald* reported, "Rockwell's claim that a building had been purchased in Oak Cliff . . . can't be substantiated. . . . The Dallas Nazis couldn't buy a building in Oak Cliff, or anywhere else for that matter, right now. They're broke. They have had financial problems from their start. . . . The local party's sole source of income is contributions and dues from the members. There are no big money contributors in the background. . . . So far, authoritative sources report, the Nazis have been thoroughly unsuccessful in tapping any of the rich 'angels' who have helped finance past extremist activities in Dallas." The only suggestion of a possible subsidy of Rockwell's activities in Texas by a wealthy patron appeared in a book on the right wing published a few years after his death that quoted Minuteman leader Robert DePugh as stating that Rockwell got money from Clint Murchison Sr., a Dallas multimillionaire. That contention, while possible, cannot be verified from existing sources.[37]

Several other individuals came through with financial gifts for Rockwell from time to time when his party fell on particularly hard times, but none, with the possible exception of Mr. and Mrs. George Ware of Kentucky, were consistent patrons like the Flemings and the Surreys or had the timely impact of Harold

Noel Arrowsmith Jr. The only other individual who made significant and regular financial contributions to Rockwell was Ray York of California, who contributed approximately $25,000 in cash, services, and rent-free use of his property between 1962 and 1967. Rockwell was introduced to York by Robert Surrey.

In his memoirs, Tony Ulasewicz suggests that Rockwell may have received periodic funding from anti-Israeli Arab or Middle Eastern countries through their United Nations delegations, but he offers no concrete evidence to substantiate the claim. Ulasewicz's only reference to a specific individual in his book is his mention of several public statements by Egyptian President Gamal Abdel Nasser praising Rockwell "for his anti-Zionist campaign."[38] Nasser's name also surfaces in the previously cited deposition from the Arrowsmith-Rockwell litigation in which Rockwell states that "Arrowsmith had brought a man described as the head of Nasser's secret service to see him on July 29 or 30, 1958."[39] It's possible that Rockwell occasionally received some money from anti-Israeli states in the Middle East, but the precise origin of that funding, or its extent, cannot be verified from existing sources. The constant state of poverty in which Rockwell and the ANP existed—a circumstance that is amply documented—suggests that any funding he may have received from foreign nations was not substantial enough to measurably affect his operation.

Rockwell always believed that the wealthy individuals who regularly subsidized conservative and right-wing political candidates and causes shared his hate of the Jews and would support him financially once they understood that he was an uncompromising enemy of the Jews. He chased this illusion, without success, to the end of his life. According to a party secretary and early Rockwell aide, James K. Warner, Rockwell "kept sending letters to . . . patriotic millionaires in the U.S., but they would have nothing to do with him and the American Nazi Party."[40] By late 1963 the Anti-Defamation League was able to report to its members that "no known or respected person gives [Rockwell] support."[41]

None of Rockwell's major patrons—Arrowsmith, Fleming, York, or Surrey—were as wealthy as or had the stature of those individuals who regularly contributed to the "more respectable" right-wing extremist groups. There is no evidence that either of the era's major benefactors of extremist causes— H. L. Hunt (who contributed approximately $1 million a year to radical right-wing causes) and Hugh R. Cullen (who was believed to be the most generous patron of radical right-wing causes in the nation)—ever contributed financially to George Lincoln Rockwell or the American Nazi party. There is also no evidence that any of the more than two dozen wealthy U.S. industrialists who were the prime national benefactors of extremist right-wing politics in the United States in the early 1960s ever contributed to Rockwell or the ANP. Rockwell's failure to attract such support was a major source of frustration throughout his career—though he never lost faith that he would eventually find the right issue, or touch the right nerve, that would energize his country's ruling elite and unlock their purses. What he didn't appear to understand was that his use of Nazi symbols and terminology made him and his party anathema among virtually all wealthy U.S. right-wing extremists. They, like the public at large, shunned him.

5 AGITATING FOR POWER

I was born to be a revolutionary.
—George Lincoln Rockwell, 1963

Rockwell's strategy to win a mass following and, eventually, political power rested on the provocation of his enemies through the dissemination of "vicious, repulsive, and unrestrained" hate literature and the staging of flamboyant street rallies and demonstrations.[1] He believed that American Jews controlled the U.S. media (as well as government, banking, and commerce) and would conspire to smother his movement with an impenetrable news blackout unless his actions were so outrageous that it would be impossible to isolate his conduct from the public. Rockwell also had little regard for the intelligence and discernment of "the masses" and believed that any appeal but one packaged in the most simplistic and cartoonish antics would fail to hold the public's attention. He believed that those he considered the twentieth century's most enlightened race leaders—Henry Ford, Charles A. Lindbergh, Charles E. Coughlin, Joseph McCarthy—were subverted by the Jews, whom he repeatedly characterized as sneaks and liars. Rockwell saw "Jewish power" as virtually unrestrained.

To break the hold of that power, Rockwell plotted to win over the masses of people who "read comic books, . . . [watch] TV, . . . [and] read dime novels and pulp." Before they could be educated, Rockwell believed that such people first "must be entertained." The political message they needed to hear "must be sugar-coated and easy" because the people he "need[ed] to win [over] won't study." Rockwell was convinced that to gain political power his message must reach people with limited attention spans and frames of reference, "not book-readers, not deep-thinkers." He directed his message to the listener's emotions, rather than to his or her intellect, through the promotion of issues that he considered to be viscerally appealing to the masses. He stressed putting an end to socializing between the races and protecting white homes and families, and especially white women, from predatory blacks. These overt appeals to racism were perfect for his strategy because, according to Rockwell, "people hate niggers and are afraid of them."[2]

African Americans were an appealing target because Rockwell believed the vast majority of America's white citizens shared his disdain for blacks. To Rockwell, blacks were an irritant; by contrast, Jews were the enemy, and to defeat that enemy Rockwell sought a weakness, a fatal flaw, an Achilles' heel. He believed that the strength of the Jews was in their ability to be cold and calculating in pursuit of their aims but that the flagrant display of the swastika put them off balance and made them vulnerable. Nothing, Rockwell boasted to the leaders of his American Nazi party, works as well as a "full Nazi uniform in front of a bunch of Jews." The swastika on uniforms and banners, he believed, "paralyzes" Jews while enraging them and forces them into revealing their true selves, by which they "convict themselves before the mob."[3] Even though the swastika was anathema to the vast majority of postwar Americans and a "wedge" separating Rockwell from "much of the extreme right wing," he regarded its use as central to his overall strategy.[4] That strategy depended on the unfolding of a precise scenario: the enlistment of a small, "revolutionary cadre of fighters"; public agitation by outrageous means to compel media coverage; disruption of the Jewish "ruling clique's" equanimity through the use of the swastika; mobilization of the white masses following race riots that would lead to race war (which Rockwell predicted for 1966) and economic collapse due to runaway inflation (which Rockwell predicted for 1970); and, finally, Rockwell's election as president of the United States in 1972. Rockwell believed that chaos in the streets and on Wall Street would drive the nation's economic elite to support him, so that he might protect their fortunes from a Jewish-led communist takeover. "When these rich people feel that clammy communist hand on their wallet, and when they want somebody to get that hairy hand off their wallet," he predicted, "they're gonna come looking for somebody [who will] fight."[5]

Rockwell consistently overestimated the extent and depth of his support among public officials, military leaders, police officers, and the general public. For example, he invariably interpreted comments and actions of individual antiblack or anti-Semitic police officers—and there were many—as indicative of widespread support for his political ambitions among all police officers.[6] He came to believe his own propaganda early in his career, which fed an unrealistic assessment of the progress of his movement and set a pattern for self-delusion thereafter. Rockwell told so many different stories to so many different people that the distinction between propaganda and reality—perhaps even to Rockwell himself—was often blurred. He had the ability to believe, with fervor, what he was saying at any given time and to believe, with equal fervor, the opposite "truth" at a subsequent time. "Any lie that tells the truth, I'm for it!" he once said.[7] The assumption, of course, is that Rockwell held the "truth" in clear sight, even if it was hidden from others.

Rockwell's first major foray into public agitation as an Nazi came in the spring and summer of 1960 in Washington, D.C., and New York City. He planned public events to "aggravate the Jews so bad" that they would "be compelled to accord him publicity." In March 1960 he announced that he would launch a series of public speeches on the Capitol Mall in Washington during the noon hour, when the Mall was crowded with government workers on their lunch breaks and tourists from all over the United States and the world. He began giving speeches in early April and continued intermittently through early July, when a "riot" between ANP stormtroopers and enraged Jews led to Rockwell's first arrest—and a major publicity splash nationwide.[8]

An even larger staged event in New York City in June made Rockwell the most prominent anti-Semitic hatemonger in the United States. New York, at the time the largest city in the nation, was the center of electronic and print media and home to the country's largest concentration of Jews, including many survivors of the Holocaust. Rockwell applied for a permit to stage an ANP-sponsored Independence Day rally in Union Square. Jewish community organizations, supported by veterans' groups, opposed the issuance of the permit and prevailed upon Mayor Robert F. Wagner Jr. to deny permission to Rockwell to use city property for such an event. The American Civil Liberties Union came to Rockwell's defense on the grounds that denial of the permit abridged his right to free speech. The conflict reached a crescendo on 22 June, when a riot broke out in the rotunda of the state supreme court building in New York City. Rockwell made inflammatory remarks to the assembled media, sparking an attack by 200 anti-Nazi demonstrators. He left the city under police protection and was condemned by the mayor as "a half-penny Hitler" who intentionally incited "riot and disorder."[9]

In early July Rockwell wrote to his mother, exulting over what he regarded as back-to-back triumphs in Washington and New York. He assured her that police in both cities were surreptitiously sympathetic to him and that the masses of ordinary citizens secretly supported his cause. The tone of the news coverage of his demonstrations—invariably condemnatory of him and his actions—mattered little to Rockwell, for he believed that any publicity served his purpose. He urged his mother to ignore what she read in the newspapers because news accounts written in the Jewish-controlled print media invariably lied about him and the level of his public support. As he had many time before, he assured her that in the end he would triumph and that she would be proud of him.[10]

Rockwell used his elevated profile to press his newly recruited supporters for funds to accelerate his agitation. Flushed by the "victory" of sudden national notoriety, he revealed the depth of his anti-Semitism. "The ONLY cure for 'Jewitis,'" Rockwell wrote, "is old Doctor Adolf's GAS-CURE!!" He promised—in exchange for a monthly pledge of ten dollars—to "exterminate the swarms of Jewish traitors in our gas-chambers" when his American Nazi party took power in 1972. In exchange for pledges of continuing financial support, Rockwell promised "such a royal FIGHT as you have never seen." With each new pledge, the ANP would be better able to afford "HUNDREDS OF THOUSANDS OF PROPAGANDA LEAFLETS, instead of ten or a dozen thousand," and he would be able to increase the number and intensity of street demonstrations. He concluded that "the many wealthy individuals in America who want what we are doing but still can't believe it can be done will be convinced, and some REAL money can become available."[11]

One unintended and unwelcome consequence of Rockwell's growing celebrity had already occurred, on 1 February 1960, when the Department of the Navy revoked his commission in the reserves following a hearing in Washington. He was charged with activities that "openly espoused race and religious hatred," with using his rank in printed matter distributed to the public "fostering race and religious hatred," and with compromising his ability to command men of "races and religions at which [his] propaganda is aimed." Rockwell refuted each charge at length. He loved the navy and valued his status as an officer; and it is not unlikely that he also needed the monthly stipend the position provided. But none of that seemed to matter once he realized that he could gain publicity by portraying his discharge as persecution by high-ranking Jews. During his testimony, which he turned into a vitriolic attack on Jews in influential positions who sought to harm him, he made specific mention of Anna M. Rosenberg, the assistant secretary of defense for manpower calling her a "traitor." He urged the review board to "show the manipulators and subvertors, the traitors and the liars that the blood of our fighting forefathers still flows in our veins, and we will no longer bow before threats and pressure." The board voted unanimously against him and ordered his discharge.[12]

The early 1960s also saw the continuation of the fractiousness that marked Rockwell's relationship with other leaders of the racist right, none of whom seemed capable of working cooperatively for any length of time. Rockwell had already broken with a number of his early colleagues and patrons—notably, Arrowsmith, Stephenson, and Maguire—and in 1960 he added Gerald L. K. Smith to that list, followed in 1964 by Edward R. Fields and Jesse B. Stoner. For the remainder of his career, Rockwell's costly and acrimonious feuds with Fields and Stoner diverted scarce resources and energy from the ANP.[13] The longest-running and most costly feud involved litigation Rockwell brought against Edward R. Fields of the National States Rights party because Fields wrote in the NSRP's paper that Rockwell clandestinely fed right-wing secrets to Drew Pearson in exchange for publicity—virtually all of it negative—in Pearson's nationally syndicated newspaper column. Although the charges were probably true, Fields could not prove them and eventually had to pay a small cash settlement and print a retraction.[14]

In 1961, the ANP suffered its first major setback with the defection of its national secretary, James K. Warner. One of Rockwell's first recruits, Warner was an adept administrator and filled an organizational void created by Rockwell's chronic inattention to detail. Warner brought order to Rockwell's files and assisted with fund-raising and membership recruitment. The reason for the break is not clear, but it probably retarded the party's growth to some degree, if for no other reason than Warner was the most organized officer among the small core of party regulars. Of course, in absolute numbers the ANP never exceeded 200 members before or after Warner, and the impact of his defection must be measured in that context. But for Rockwell personally the break with Warner took its toll because he was forced to assume administrative duties for which he was ill suited. The gap left by Warner's departure was not adequately filled until Matt Koehl took over as the party's chief administrative officer in early 1963.

Warner's break with Rockwell was bitter. In a short, self-published book written in 1961, Warner made charges against Rockwell that would be used by Rockwell's enemies in the right wing for the rest of his career. Among the charges were laziness, duplicity, insincerity, greed, and cowardice. Warner's Rockwell "acted like a mad man tearing the envelopes" and packages received in the mail "looking for cash"; he sat around or slept most of the day, avoiding any physical work at the headquarters and barracks; he took "the choicest food" and left "the scraps for everyone else"; he manipulated people and led them to the brink of danger but avoided the physical combat to which he so willingly committed his stormtroopers—such as the riot on the Capital Mall on 3 July 1960, during which, according to Warner, Rockwell hid behind the speaker's platform.[15] The veracity of Warner's charges are difficult to verify. Similar charges appear throughout Rockwell's career, from various sources, but those may well be restatements of Warner's charges. Regardless of the specifics, the vitriolic nature of Warner's break with Rockwell—neither the last nor the most bitter within Rockwell's inner circle—points out a critical flaw in the American Nazi party: the inability of its founder to maintain a core of officers committed over time to the attainment of the long-range goals of the organization. Rockwell's personality and the character of individuals drawn to racist fringe groups guaranteed a fractiousness that doomed the ANP, making it little more than a vehicle for George Lincoln Rockwell's ambitions and visions.

Despite the defections and the feuds, the heady events of 1960 served to inflate Rockwell's natural optimism. He became a magnet for the disaffected, and his party grew. Rockwell the showman concocted imaginative new stunts to keep his name before the public. He and his stormtroopers picketed the opening of the movie *Exodus* in several East Coast cities; stormtroopers drove a "Hate Bus" to New Orleans to mock the Freedom Riders struggling to integrate public transportation in the South; and he enlisted racist singers and musicians to perform at fund-raisers he referred to as "Hate-o-nannies." The ANP also coordinated the indoctrination and training of recruits at its chapter offices in Chicago, Los Angeles, and Dallas.[16]

As Rockwell's notoriety increased, so did his estrangement from his family. In early 1961 he wrote a four-page letter to his mother, his sister, and his brother to explain and justify his actions. He began the letter on a conciliatory note and apologized for putting the family in an awkward position because of his activities. He assured them that his actions were not ego-driven but were carefully planned and designed to force an unsympathetic press to give coverage to his views. Still deeply mourning the departure of his second wife, Thora, and his children, Rockwell reminded his family of the tremendous price he'd already paid to advance his political views. But just when the letter seemed the most rational, Rockwell proceeded to lash out at his father, angrily rejecting Doc's dismissal of his political activities as mere publicity stunts with no political substance. In what must have been a chilling passage to Bobby, who feared that his brother's delusions indicated a growing detachment from reality, the commander of a handful of malcontents and misfits asserted that he was the leader of a "huge but hidden movement." In words that jump off the page with anger, Rockwell shouts at his family that his command of a powerful global movement is proof that he is neither a failure nor insane. Still smarting from Bobby's suggestion in 1958 that his behavior was abnormal and that he should seek psychiatric care, Rockwell closed the letter with a defiance that may have masked a subliminal plea for help, taunting Bobby and the family to dispute his "facts" and disprove the logic of his arguments.[17]

Later that year Rockwell again wrote to his mother—who by mid-1961 was the only family member still on speaking terms with him. He clung to the connection she provided to the family while alternating between expressions of sadness over the estrangement and vicious attacks on Bobby, whom he irrationally accused of cowardice and duplicity. He opened his heart to his mother about his continuing anguish over the breakup of his second marriage and told her that he believed in an eventual reconciliation. Remarkably, he saw his political triumph as the key to winning back his family on his terms.[18]

The year 1962 was an active one for Rockwell. In January, hoping to replicate his media success of 1960, he applied for a permit to hold a Nazi rally in New York City's Union Square on Hitler's birthday, 20 April, which was also Good Friday and the second day of the Passover. He was again blocked by city officials, but this time Jewish community organizations were determined to deny Rockwell a publicity bonanza. They kept their protests to a minimum, and Rockwell's protests and taunting passed largely unnoticed. The strategy of "quarantine," developed by the American Jewish Committee's Solomon Andhil Fineberg, which was to minimize Rockwell's manipulation of the media for the rest of his career, was tested successfully. The next month, Rockwell changed tactics and scored another publicity coup. He made contact with the Nation of Islam leader Elijah Muhammad and exploited their common desire for racial segregation to wrangle an invitation to address the 1962 national convention of the NOI at Muhammad's Chicago Temple of Islam. Rockwell drew nationwide headlines with his description of Muhammad as the "Adolf Hitler of the black man." At midyear Rockwell was again in the news when he traveled to England to meet with the British Nazi leader Colin Jordan and form the World Union of National Socialists. His deportation from England as an "undesirable" drew international press coverage.[19]

Rockwell believed that 1963 would be a breakthrough year for him and the American Nazi party. The event he decided to take advantage of was Martin Luther King Jr.'s "March on Washington," planned for 28 August. Rockwell hoped to harness white racism to propel himself to national prominence, and he believed that he could do that by establishing himself as the white alternative to Dr. King. Rockwell drew on his powers as an orator and a crafter of vivid racist images to bring to the surface the crudest instincts and deepest fears among rural and small-town white people throughout Virginia, hoping to rally them to his side against the "black hordes" being aroused by Jewish-communist agitators. He implored racist whites to join him in Washington to demonstrate against King's march. He appealed to their patriotism—raising the specter of black mobs overrunning Congress—and to their prejudices—referring to King as "Martin Luther Coon" and to King's aide Bayard Rustin as a "queer." He also appealed to his audience's fear of communism, painting a shocking verbal picture of the "Soviet America" that was in their future unless they followed him in active resistance. The crowds were larger and more enthusiastic—and less derisive—than Rockwell was used to, leading him to confidently predict a throng of 10,000 counterdemonstrators on the day of the march.[20]

The logistics gave Rockwell trouble from the start. He applied for a demonstration permit through the Washington, D.C., Police Department, once again mistakingly assuming that he had friends and supporters in high places within the department. His letters to police officials were filled with unreciprocated expressions of camaraderie and racist statements about King's "nigger army." In one letter, Rockwell wrote to a District Police captain about their presumed common interest in thwarting King. While King may not have been popular with Washington, D.C., police officers—in 1963 the force was very white and very southern—their approach to dealing with him was certainly nothing like the approach Rockwell was proposing. His application was denied, as was an application he filed with the National Park Service.[21]

In an attempt to get King's permit canceled, Rockwell appealed to powerful segregationist congressmen whom he believed, again mistakenly, would be *for* him because they were *against* King. Repeated letters—in which he again referred to King as "Martin Luther Coon"—visits, and calls went for naught. The segregationist bloc in Congress wanted no part of George Lincoln Rockwell.[22] He was even rebuffed by the White Citizens' Council of New Orleans when he attempted to forge an alliance with that racist organization to disrupt King's march.[23] As 28 August drew closer, Rockwell sensed that any momentum he'd generated for a counterdemonstration was faltering. He feared that a poor turnout—any number substantially below the 10,000 he'd promised—would expose the shallowness of his support. In desperation he wrote to the two most prominent segregationists of that era—Alabama Governor George C. Wallace and Mississippi Governor Ross Barnett—and begged them for a commitment to speak at his counterdemonstration. To each he wrote: "Will you SPEAK, sir? I do not care how you denounce me. . . . In fact, I recommend it. I will even turn the demonstration over to you, and suffer the label 'chicken' in the interests of our Race and our Nation."[24]

No record of their replies exist, if in fact either Wallace or Barnett ever answered Rockwell's embarrassing plea. On 28 August 1963, fewer than ninety people showed up for Rockwell's counterdemonstration—less than one-tenth of 1 percent of his estimate. An undetermined number of those in attendance were surveillance officers from local police, federal law enforcement agencies, and Jewish community organizations. Although Rockwell didn't realize it, then, his power to shake and shock, to draw media attention and crowds with his antics, had already peaked. He would continue agitation for almost five more years, and he would pass on a significant intellectual and strategic legacy to the next generation of hatemongers, but George Lincoln Rockwell's slim and brief potential to become a meaningful force in American politics withered on the steps of the Lincoln Memorial in the late summer of 1963. He became an inconsequential figure, overshadowed by Martin Luther King Jr.'s noble words and nobler dreams.

6

QUARANTINE: LEASHING THE BEAST

The problem of building a political organization . . . in spite of the enemy's utter mastery of all means of communicating with the masses, is . . . first the problem of reaching the masses —any way at all. It does not matter how you reach them at first, so long as they come to know of you and the fact that you are at the opposite pole from those in power.
—George Lincoln Rockwell, 1961

Although Rockwell ridiculed and disparaged African Americans and homosexuals, his most vitriolic and consistent attacks focused on the Jews. "To Jew traitors," he warned, "we are deadly, and we openly inform them we will stuff them in the gas chambers in 1972 when we are elected to power."[1] The American Jewish community, with the memory of the Holocaust still so fresh, could not easily dismiss or ignore Rockwell. Certainly, it would respond, but the form that response would take engendered prolonged and bitter debate among the major American Jewish community organizations.

In the 1940s, Dr. Solomon Andhil Fineberg of the American Jewish Committee devised a strategy of containment against that era's most flagrant anti-Semite, Gerald L. K. Smith. Fineberg initially called that strategy "dynamic silence," or the "silent treatment."[2] He later renamed it "quarantine," a term he believed more accurately described the process.[3] The quarantine strategy included two key components: coordination among major American Jewish community organizations to minimize public confrontations between an anti-Semite and his or her opponents in order to deny the anti-Semite a dramatic event that would invite publicity; and the dissemination of information on the background and tactics of the anti-Semite to the news media in an attempt to convince the media that, in the absence of a violent confrontation between an anti-Semite and his or her adversaries, there was little newsworthy in what the anti-Semite had to say.[4] The strategy intended to "prevent the rabble-rouser from becoming a serious public menace by depriving him of the publicity he needs to increase his audience."[5] Fineberg lobbied extensively within the Jewish community for acceptance of his strategy, and on 17 December 1947, despite serious misgivings, the National Community Relations Advisory Council, which was the interagency federation of all major national American

Jewish community organizations, officially adopted quarantine as the endorsed strategy for dealing with Gerald L. K. Smith and other hatemongers.[6] Although quarantine contributed to Smith's decline in the late 1940s, that lesson had to be relearned a decade later.[7]

In the fall of 1958, under the financial patronage of Harold Noel Arrowsmith Jr., Rockwell used the tactic of overt anti-Semitism—the screaming of insults—to attract attention to the newly revived National Committee to Free America from Jewish Domination. As an adman and showman in his own right, he understood that the emerging techniques of advertising and public relations, used to sell products and package ideas, could also be applied to politics and public issues. Rockwell had a press agent's knack for sensing the right phrase, the right gesture, the right symbolic action to compel press attention. "George Lincoln Rockwell's talent was that he knew what would make people hate him. . . . [He] had an inordinate capacity for finding out what would make people the angriest and exploiting it."[8] In an interview given toward the end of his career, he admitted: "When I was in the advertising game, we used to use nude women. Now I use the swastika and storm troopers. You use what brings them in."[9]

Rockwell was unlike any anti-Semite the American Jewish community had faced before. He didn't attempt to hide his anti-Semitism, to cleverly conceal it within code phrases. Instead, he spoke openly of his admiration for Adolf Hitler. He flaunted the swastika. He spoke of trials and gas chambers. He was the dark rider on a pale horse who galloped through every immigrant Jew's nightmares. A frightened and angry American Jewish community turned to its national organizations to find a way to combat the tall, handsome, dark-eyed, telegenic crusader who said without shame: "I like Jews. I'll be very sorry when we've killed the last of them."[10]

By mid-1960 Rockwell was the most-publicized, best-known anti-Semite in the nation. He boasted of a significant following and claimed the tacit support of "millions" of Americans. To Jewish immigrants who still bore the physical and emotional scars of the Holocaust, it seemed as though their nightmare had followed them to America. Rockwell's wild rantings about a "Jewish conspiracy to destroy our beloved American Republic, our precious freedoms, and even our very genes and chromosomes" had a hauntingly familiar ring.[11] His calculated use of the words "gas chambers" and "gassing" in connection with how America should deal with "Jewish traitors" evoked horrible images for a people to whom those images were recent and real. American Jews pressured the major national organizations serving the Jewish community—the American Jewish Committee, the American Jewish Congress, the Anti-Defamation League of B'nai B'rith, the Jewish War Veterans of the United States—to respond. But Jewish leaders were seriously divided on *how* to respond. Many urged public demonstrations and counterpublicity. Fineberg, who was head of the AJC's community relations division, argued that the quarantine strategy remained the most potent weapon available against hatemongers. He and his assistant, Isaiah Terman, reminded the AJC leadership, many of whom were not in positions of authority a decade earlier, of how quarantine had been used successfully against Gerald L. K. Smith.[12] Fineberg believed quarantine to be the perfect antidote to Rockwell's brand of hatemongering, but he had to convince his associates and the American Jewish community as a whole that quarantine was not an outdated approach to a new situation.

Rockwell wanted the American Jewish community to respond to him in order to create the newsworthy incidents that would feed his movement's growth. William L. Pierce, one of Rockwell's closest advisers, wrote that Rockwell "concentrated the activities of his small group . . . under circumstances especially chosen to provoke violent opposition—anything and everything . . . to gain mass publicity, to become generally recognized as *the* opponent of the Jews."[13] Rockwell adopted the swastika as the symbol of his party because of its effect on Jews. "Upon seeing [the swastika] Jews lost their cold, calculating reasoning abilities and became hysterical, screaming with fear and rage at the American Nazi Party. This reaction led Jews to unwittingly aid the movement: while moving to stamp out Nazism, they were forced to give the party free publicity."[14]

Fineberg countered that since hatemongers use language specifically designed to provoke a violent reaction, the quarantine strategy must first convince the hatemonger's targets to avoid public confrontations, because violent confrontation itself compels news coverage and publicity. He adapted quarantine to "three publics"—the anti-Semitic public, the Jewish public, and the general public—and to the press serving each of these.[15] As much as possible, Fineberg isolated the anti-Semitic public from information on Rockwell to prevent their gathering to his cause; he controlled the spread of rumors about Rockwell's activities within the Jewish community and encouraged restraint in the community's reaction to Rockwell; and he presented to the general public a picture of Rockwell as, at best, a curiosity without standing or substance. Local AJC members carried out much of the work with the press on a one-to-one basis, meeting individually with local media leaders. In late 1958, for example, AJC member Harold Wolozin met with Phil Stern, editor of the *Northern Virginia Sun*. Rockwell's Arlington headquarters was within the *Sun*'s circulation area, and the newspaper gave him a great deal of early publicity. Wolozin reported to Fineberg that Stern agreed "that his paper gave Rockwell publicity [and] . . . that this was most welcome to the guy, and that it is undesirable to give him any more. . . . I hope that Stern is not just being agreeable, but I think not and I do feel that he is most interested in the quarantine approach."[16]

Wolozin's letter sheds light on how the strategy worked at its most basic level. The temptation always existed to cross the line by using coercion or economic threats to force editors to comply. Fineberg recognized that such tactics were imprudent and dangerous. The Wolozin letter and other correspondence on subsequent media contacts suggest that persuasion, not coercion, was the tactic most commonly employed. However, it would be naïve to assume that the absence of such overt tactics implies that economic or political pressure was always absent from these exchanges. Rockwell's political heirs, particularly Matt Koehl, have suggested that a sophisticated and elaborate economic boycott existed but that all records of its existence have been purged from the remaining documentary evidence; they also maintain that a conspiracy of silence was successfully engineered to prevent any mention of the boycott in the contemporary press. Koehl's speculation is not supported by verifiable evidence.

In March 1960, Rockwell wrote a letter to the editor of the *Washington Post* announcing plans to speak on the Capitol Mall on Sunday, 3 April 1960. He warned that "some citizens have been threatening us with violence and forcible suppression of our peaceful right to address our fellow Americans according to the law."[17] But Rockwell had no interest in avoiding violence; instead, he had a vital stake in promoting it. Following the Capitol Mall speech, he mailed a letter to his supporters and financial patrons that told a different story. He confided his intention to "PROVOKE and AGGRAVATE the Jew traitors BEYOND ENDURANCE. We not only knew they would attack, but we sought their attack. . . . [O]ur activity has been successful beyond our wildest dreams, and all of it has been aimed not at education or 'waking people up,' but at gaining POWER. . . . and then, and only then can we exterminate the swarms of Jewish traitors in our gas chambers."[18]

As discussed earlier, Rockwell's plan to hold a Fourth of July 1960 rally in New York City set off a storm of protest within the Jewish community and gained him much-needed publicity. Despite Fineberg's best efforts, the quarantine broke down with precisely the outcome he feared. When Rockwell was denied a permit to speak, his cause became the cause of free speech. His name appeared in the newspapers almost daily, as his appeal made its way through the courts. On 22 June 1960, an enraged mob, including many survivors of Nazi concentration camps, attacked him, but he was saved from serious injury by the quick action of the police. The leadership of the American Jewish Committee moved to contain the damage and, if possible, salvage the quarantine before the situation got completely out of control. The AJC's executive vice president, John Slawson, advised the Executive Board that "Rockwell's device for winning public attention . . . proved to be a cunning and effective means of overcoming the quarantine. . . . He repeatedly said publicly that he would goad Jews into publicizing him. It is not surprising that many Jews, with memories of Hitler still strongly in mind, would react emotionally rather than pragmatically on hearing of swastika-studded uniforms and the advocacy of gas chambers."[19] David McReynolds, writing in the *Village Voice,* said that the way Rockwell was handled in New York "did more to promote anti-Semitism than anything Rockwell himself could possibly have said in Union Square on July 4. . . . Rockwell is not yet a serious political force. But I am afraid that if we give the professional anti-bigots enough time they may yet turn Mr. Rockwell and his tiny band into a real movement."[20]

Pressure mounted within the Jewish community to abandon quarantine. "[The] fact that Rockwell has already received publicity does not mean that quarantine is no longer feasible," Slawson told the AJC Executive Board. "Further publicity will only prolong Rockwell's moment in the sun and give him access to audiences he could never otherwise command. Denial of undue publicity will relegate him to the obscurity from which he came."[21] Rockwell vowed to endure any hardship for the opportunity to explain his program to the people of New York. But months later, when the New York State Court of Appeals overturned the city's denial of his permit to speak, Rockwell "never even bothered to pick up the permit."[22] The issue had slipped to the back pages of the newspapers, and Rockwell was already looking for "new worlds to inflame."[23]

In addition to bringing Rockwell much-needed publicity, incidents like the New York altercation had a beneficial effect on the American Nazi party's finances. Tony Ulasewicz, the New York City policeman who shielded Rockwell during the harrowing near-riot in the state supreme court building, remembered seeing "two big mail sacks full of letters" at ANP headquarters after a particular incident.[24] "Rockwell needed the publicity to get his contributions in," Ulasewicz said.[25] "To get around some of his financial difficulties, Rockwell described how he randomly picked targets for his rallies. Once he publicly announced that he was coming, the public's fur, as he put it, would stand on end. Local newspapers, radio and television would give him just enough publicity to guarantee the delivery of four or five sacks of mail to his doorstep. . . . Rockwell said he received a lot of 'atta boy, George' letters with dollar bills folded up inside the envelope. He said that just the threat of his coming was good for a couple of grand."[26]

In the aftermath of the events in New York, Rockwell taunted Fineberg over the breakdown of quarantine and boasted about the ANP's victory: "the Jewish councils have spent millions of dollars to spread the word among the Jews to ignore us. But the hordes of guilty little sinners can't do it! When they see that Swastika and hear us praising Adolf Hitler and describing the gas chambers for traitors, they become the screaming, wild ghetto Jews who have eternally blown up their victories at the last moment by their insane passions of hate and revenge. The result is the lifeblood of a political movement: *publicity!*"[27]

Meanwhile, Fineberg methodically repaired the quarantine coalition. Supporters wrote articles for the Jewish press on the reasons for the quarantine and the soundness of the strategy: "Rockwell has great difficulty in raising the funds to keep his hate leaflets printed and circulated. He appeals also for funds to keep his group alive. . . . Without publicity, Rockwell cannot raise the necessary funds to maintain himself and his group. . . . [The] most effective . . . way of combating the Rockwell menace is to literally starve him out. Quarantine can be made effective. If we deny him publicity, we deny him money."[28]

Rockwell accelerated his agitation in Washington, D.C., where regular appearances on the Capitol Mall drew increasing attention from militant members of the Jewish War Veterans, hoping to duplicate his New York publicity bonanza. James K. Warner, an ANP participant in those incidents, later recalled: "Every week before going to the Mall, Link would rehearse the men and tell them to agitate the jews as much as possible. . . . [On 3 July 1960] over 300 jews showed up for the speech while we only had 11 men there. Link wanted to provoke them into battle and said so several times."[29] Rockwell's agitation on the Mall succeeded, although on a smaller scale. Violent confrontations between ANP stormtroopers and Jewish War Veterans members made national headlines, which prompted Fineberg to work harder to bring recalcitrant members of Washington's Jewish community into agreement on quarantine. By the end of 1960 the clashes and the headlines ceased. Rockwell felt the effect of dwindling publicity: "Three years ago we announced our plans to 'aggravate the Jews so bad' that they would react irrationally and FORCE the publicity which the 'quarantine' or 'silent treatment' has denied to all other outfits who have tried to expose the Jew and his treason. Without publicity, attempts to expose the Jew . . . are reduced to the pitiful private meetings of people who already know 'the score', and the eternal game of passing 'literature' around to the same gang of frustrated people year after year."[30]

No evidence exists that Rockwell and Fineberg ever met face to face, but each man clearly understood the other's strategies and the stakes of their battle. In a letter to his mother and sister in early 1961, Rockwell described how he saw the struggle: "I have used the dramatic Nazi method to put the press manipulators in an impossible position. If they try to suppress the news of us . . . they find that too many people begin to get wise to this dishonest use of our national information media. It is utterly impossible for them to hide or ignore NAZIS marching in the streets."[31] Still, what Rockwell called the "paper curtain" slowly and effectively descended on him and his activities as the Jewish War Veterans in Washington withdrew from any further violent confrontations with the Nazis, and the national media, in the absence of such confrontations, ignored Rockwell. He tried to convince his stagnant party that its message was getting through, that the tactic of agitation, which had worked so well in the past, still worked. But his words carried more bravado than fact: "For three years we have forcefully exposed the Jew liars and traitors to the point at which they react irrationally and stupidly. With our fight to speak in [New York City's] red Union Square . . . we have utterly smashed their despicable 'silent treatment.' The big Jews have been telling their lesser brethren that . . . we would disappear if ignored. . . . The Jew press manipulators are finally unable to pretend any longer we are only lunatics, cowards, profiteers or hoodlums. They know now that white gentiles are *winning* for the first time in fifty years!"[32]

Many people within the AJC and the American Jewish community at large felt that the New York and Washington breaches had so compromised the quarantine that a new strategy was necessary. In the summer of 1961, Fineberg wrote to Roy Millenson of the AJC: "I hear again and again—at AJC, even— from my closest colleagues, 'Too late for quarantine.' That is preposterous."[33] He always viewed the quarantine as relative, measuring the amount of publicity given against the potential for such publicity. The ideal, of course, was an absence of publicity; but since reality seldom matches the ideal in any human endeavor, a quarantine that minimized Rockwell's publicity was the goal. Quarantine worked as a continuing process with periods of both relative success and failure, and the failures did not—should not—invalidate the strategy. AJC staff and members continued working with newspaper editors to minimize Rockwell's coverage. Sometimes those efforts were fruitless, as in the case with the *Virginian Pilot*, which ran a major profile of Rockwell and the ANP on 17 September 1961, despite personal entreaties from the AJC's Robert J. Greene.[34] But the strategy worked well enough to force Rockwell to seek new ways to get himself noticed.

In late 1961, Rockwell heard rumors that several politicians and Jewish leaders were urging an investigation of the American Nazi party for possible placement on the U.S. attorney general's list of subversive organizations. He challenged the Department of Justice to investigate the ANP, writing that "we openly demand and heartily welcome any and all investigations and hearings and stand ready to prove beyond any question of a doubt that the American

Nazi Party, its doctrines and tenets, advocate nothing more than the eternal protection of our United States of America, and our sacred white race."[35] Of course, Rockwell understood the publicity value of having the ANP as the center of attention at a congressional hearing and the opportunity to appear before a congressional committee in full Nazi regalia to defend the patriotism of his party and to attack the Jews.[36] Fineberg recognized the trap Rockwell was setting. "Rockwell cannot be put on the Attorney General's list without a hearing," he wrote to New York Senator Kenneth B. Keating. "He would gladly welcome that hearing. . . . I believe that the Attorney General is wise in not tangling with him. There is only one possible way to be rid of Rockwell, and that is quarantine."[37] Not long thereafter, U.S. Attorney General Robert F. Kennedy suspended further investigation of the American Nazi party.[38]

The year 1961 marked the end of significant debate within the American Jewish community on the role of quarantine in the community's fight against Rockwell and the American Nazi party. There would be subsequent breaches of the quarantine, and some groups within the American Jewish community— most notably the Jewish War Veterans—remained reluctant partners in the quarantine coalition; but after 1961 quarantine was never again seriously questioned as the consensus strategy in dealing with Rockwell. Both aspects of quarantine—maintaining nonconfrontational solidarity within the Jewish community and lobbying the mass media for minimal coverage of Rockwell—required Fineberg's constant attention. Throughout 1962 Rockwell probed for a way to engage Jewish opponents in violent street action. He had isolated successes, but in general American Jews refused to respond. Rockwell visited Los Angeles in March 1962 to stimulate interest in the creation of an ANP western chapter and to explore possible future street actions. His visit went virtually unmentioned in the media.[39] In August 1962, Fineberg wrote an urgent letter to Jules Cohen of the Philadelphia Jewish Community Relations Council, which was about to repeat the New York debacle by instituting legal action to deny Rockwell a permit to speak in that city. Fineberg reminded Cohen of quarantine's success during Rockwell's national tour and urged Cohen to abandon any attempt to restrict Rockwell's right to speak, arguing that Rockwell "made a tour of the United States these past five months that netted him practically nothing. . . . [The] police were kept informed of Rockwell's movements, which is part of quarantine; the mass media were tipped off discretely to give him no publicity unless there [was] public disorder, another feature of quarantine, and there were no disorders. . . . Quarantine was clamped down perfectly on Rockwell again and again. . . . That Rockwell does not have twenty or thirty die-hards in every sizable American city is due, I believe, to the work that has been done to quarantine him." Fineberg then went to the heart of the matter, Philadelphia's potential break with a successful strategy: "The present position of the Philadelphia JCRC is a departure from quarantine. It means that you risk Rockwell's getting civil libertarians' support all the way to the Supreme Court and the publicity attendant thereon. Without quarantine, any anti-Semite could become a national figure in a short time. He need only be dramatic and have plenty of opposition."[40] Fineberg's counsel prevailed. The JCRC dropped its legal action and restrained the Philadelphia Jewish community so that Rockwell's initial success in engaging violent opposition on the streets of that city was short-lived.

By the end of 1962, Fineberg reported to John Slawson, his immediate superior at the AJC, that "despite the tremendous publicity Rockwell has received in New York, Boston, Washington, D.C., and a few other cities, the difficulties he created were greatly curtailed by AJC's efforts. . . . Rockwell has visited many cities where he has no or very few followers. We have been able . . . to keep quarantine clamped on Rockwell's activities many times."[41] Although neither Rockwell nor Fineberg realized it at the time, their battle had effectively concluded. Rockwell's national tour, undertaken with much optimism, was a dismal failure. He found no national constituency anxious to embrace him; and, more important, he found no corner of the nation where Fineberg's quarantine could not reach him. From 1963 until his death in 1967, Rockwell tried new ways to break the quarantine, new gimmicks to attract publicity, but he never achieved the dramatic media breakthrough he sought. There remained for him long periods of frustration broken by occasional dramatic successes—such as a well-publicized riot at the Shrine Auditorium in Los Angeles in the spring of 1963 and his parasitic attachment to the violent anti–open housing marches in Chicago in the fall of 1966. But each localized success was eventually contained by the effective application of quarantine.

In 1963 Rockwell discovered the college lecture circuit, which provided his most consistent source of publicity and a steady income for the remainder of his career. Fineberg and the promoters of quarantine considered the possible effects of this new phase of Rockwell's activity, but Fineberg did not see college campuses as fertile ground for ANP recruitment. Although the American Jewish Committee still regarded the maintenance of a quarantine with appropriate seriousness, a staff memo about Rockwell's college lectures carried a hint of lightheartedness not seen in earlier AJC documents: "With all his recent activity, [Rockwell] is likely to be introduced next as 'that well-known college lecturer.' At any rate, we are trying to work through the various responsible student organizations to dissuade campus groups from inviting him to speak on the grounds that he adds nothing, but detracts a great deal. . . . I hope now that spring is here, a young student's heart will turn to thoughts of you-know-what rather than our friend, the Nazi."[42]

Rockwell's college appearances occasionally drew large crowds and publicity, and Fineberg maintained close surveillance of his activities and tried to minimize both, but Rockwell's concentration on this activity, and his corresponding deemphasis of violent street demonstrations, represented his tacit surrender in the arena Fineberg feared most.[43] This is not to suggest that Rockwell totally abandoned either his attempts to instigate street violence or his dream of a mass following, but the fact is that from 1963 until his death in 1967 Rockwell increasingly turned to the college podium, not the streetcorner, as his preferred platform from which to broadcast his message. Fineberg's quarantine often made even that platform an uncomfortable, frustrating place. For example, toward the end of his career, Rockwell spoke at Wake Forest University, a North Carolina school with only fourteen Jewish students. Rabbi David Rose and other members of the local chapter of the Anti-Defamation League of B'nai B'rith prepared for Rockwell's coming by providing local media and college officials with background information on Rockwell, emphasizing his need for publicity. "Rockwell arrived. He spoke. There was no cheering, no jeering, no demonstrations, no anything—not even when he concluded his speech and stood staring expectantly at the audience. Finally, one of the few Negro students at the college broke the silence. "I'd rather be a citizen of the United States the way it is than have it changed the way you want it,' he said. . . . The student turned and left the auditorium—followed by the Wake Forest football team and the rest of the audience. There was no newspaper publicity about Rockwell's appearance, no follow-ups by the college. To everyone, except Rockwell, it was as though it had never happened."[44]

Building and maintaining a consensus supporting quarantine within the American Jewish community constituted Fineberg's most difficult and persistent challenge. He understood that continuing support for quarantine by the Jewish press, far more influential in the immigrant Jewish community than the mainstream American press, was critical. He assiduously courted the Jewish press, urging editors to keep Rockwell's threat in perspective. In early 1960, he assured Boris Smolar of the Jewish Telegraphic Agency that "even with all the publicity that certain people in Washington are giving him, Mr. Rockwell is too incompetent, too inept and too stupid to build a dangerous anti-Semitic organization. His effect upon public opinion has been nil. . . . Any worthless bum who wanted to turn anti-Semitic could do about as well as Rockwell. He ought to be Quarantined, *und fertig.*"[45]

At first, many Jewish newspapers, including the influential *Examiner* of Brooklyn, New York, rejected Fineberg's assurances and dismissed the quarantine as "ineffectual."[46] J. I. Fishbein, editor of the most influential Jewish newspaper outside New York City, *The Sentinel* of Chicago, had long been skeptical of quarantine, even writing editorials against the strategy in the late

1940s, when it was first used against Gerald L. K. Smith. Fineberg knew he had to convince Fishbein (who printed descriptions in *The Sentinel* of this new application of quarantine as "the ostrich response") that in this case quarantine was both practical and effective.[47] Fineberg worked on Fishbein, visiting him on a number of occasions to reason and argue with him. By the end of 1960 Fishbein became an influential convert whose support had come at a crucial time. The Jewish War Veterans were confronting every American Nazi party demonstration with a show of greater force, and the resulting outbreaks of violence gave Rockwell and the ANP important early publicity. In a critical editorial, Fishbein sided with Fineberg against the JWV: "let us assume that a melee had broken out in which the J.W.V. had 'mixed it up' with Rockwell and his 'boys.' Would not this have given the self-styled American Nazi 'leader' the publicity he so badly wants since no paper could have possibly buried such a story? And would it not have made of him a martyr, alienating many people who disapprove of others taking the law into their own hands?"[48] Fishbein proved to be a powerful link to working-class and immigrant Jews, someone who sided with Fineberg whenever the JWV broke with the nonconfrontational aspect of the quarantine strategy.[49]

Every opportunity was taken to protect quarantine within the Jewish press. When a letter criticizing quarantine appeared in the *Jewish National Post,* Fineberg not only contacted the editor but also wrote a personal reply to the letter writer: "I don't know whether I shall be able to make you understand that trying to deal with a man like Rockwell by any method but quarantine is like trying to nail cranberry jelly to the wall or trying to wrap fire in paper."[50] He also responded when any Jewish newspaper editorialized against quarantine or questioned its continued validity.[51]

Fineberg paid special attention to *Aufbau,* a German-language Jewish newspaper whose editor, Manfred George, was skeptical of quarantine. He met with George and reported the results to his AJC team: "I visited Manfred George . . . a week ago and explained to him the need to quarantine Rockwell. . . . The result was this extremely satisfactory article, 'Don't Fall for Rockwell,' in which the readers of *Aufbau* are cautioned to stay away from Rockwell's meetings."[52] Before publishing the article, George had sent a translation of it to Fineberg for his comments, along with a letter that read in part: "I think that your arguments are very valid as you can see from the article. I made full use of it."[53] In the article George wrote: "What Rockwell wants is obvious. No one can perform a better service for Rockwell when he comes to New York for his April 20th appearance (Hitler's birthday, Good Friday and second day of Passover) than to let the occasion degenerate into a sizable brawl. Rockwell has the right to speak, and while speaking will have police protection. The only way to defeat Rockwell is to leave him without an audience. Everything else only serves him and his ambitions."[54]

By early 1962, near unanimity in support of quarantine existed in the Jewish press, including influential Jewish college newspapers. A prominent AJC emissary had visited the student editor of Yeshiva University's *Commentator* for example, and convinced him to promote the quarantine strategy to the paper's potentially volatile student readers.[55] Yiddish-, German-, and English-language Jewish newspapers across the country all helped to minimize violent confrontation between American Jews and Rockwell's stormtroopers and, by keeping their readers aware of Rockwell's activities, helped to prevent the spread of fear and anger within the Jewish community that Rockwell was counting on.

Despite the efforts of Fineberg and others, groups that only nominally supported quarantine periodically broke ranks. Whether such breaches were due to divided opinion on quarantine within the leadership of these organizations or to a perceived need by the leaders to protect themselves and their institutions from the frustration of their own members is not clear. But their actions caused the chief of the AJC's Washington office, Robert J. Greene, to express his anger in a memo to the staff at the New York office: "In the course of the past nine months, unilateral and publicized moves without warning by sister agencies has [*sic*] contributed to confusion and bungled situations. . . . I could cite chapter and verse on how the campaign has suffered from 'loners' and 'grandstanders.'" Greene was able to conclude, however, that the "sister agencies" have "come back to the AJC method."[56] While Fineberg never lost patience with those who did not understand quarantine, he showed less patience with a lack of understanding among the Jewish leadership. He didn't seem to fully appreciate the dilemma facing the AJC's top leaders, Edwin Lukas and John Slawson, who sometimes had to tolerate, without challenge, the actions of their counterparts from other organizations in order to hold the Jewish coalition together.

Fineberg's frustration surfaced in a letter to Greene, his colleague and friend: "Apparently the quarantine treatment is on the rocks, and I shall probably have to write a new book and many articles before I can get it readopted. It happens to be the *only method* that can have any chance of success against this type of vermin. But evidently even the American Jewish Committee has tossed it away."[57] Still, Fineberg didn't allow his frustration with these occasional setbacks to interfere with his efforts on behalf of quarantine. Whenever and wherever a crack appeared in the quarantine, he moved to repair it. When Rockwell moved into Cleveland, Ohio, a city with a large Jewish population, some Jewish leaders in that city panicked and called for direct action in contradiction to the principles of quarantine. The situation quickly became volatile. Fineberg wrote a long letter to Alan D. Kandel, the head of the Jewish Community Federation of Cleveland. "There are certain people who will not understand the fallacy of falling into Rockwell's trap no matter what we say or do," Fineberg reasoned. "I hope that the Cleveland Council can keep your community calm and make the Jewish citizens there realize that it is infinitely better to create a desirable situation than to relieve heated emotions. Otherwise you may have Mr. Rockwell as a regular visitor, a celebrity about town. I know of no way to prevent this but quarantine."[58]

One of the major advantages Rockwell held in his strategic duel with Fineberg was the ability to choose the battlefield. When quarantine worked in one city, Rockwell moved to another. When one mode of instigation failed, Rockwell tried another. He probed for weaknesses in the Jewish coalition, and when his probe revealed a weakness, he directed his efforts there. When he found that the small Jewish community in Richmond, Virginia, was considering direct action to keep him from speaking in their city, he stepped up his efforts to speak there. The AJC dispatched Robert J. Greene to assist the Richmond Jewish community. He brought along the message that the AJC did not "encourage any of its members or staff to initiate or to join with others in seeking to prevent Rockwell from holding public meetings. . . . Certainly we would want to discourage any overt effort to prevent Rockwell's meetings, or to create disturbances at them—in the manner of the JWV [Jewish War Veterans] people in Washington. It is our belief . . . that left to his own self-corrosive devices, the sheer absurdity of this sick buffoon would . . . so quickly discredit him in the eyes of a Christian audience he would, before long, seek still another community in which to peddle his pathological poison."[59] The reference to "the JWV people in Washington" reflected a major and continuing concern among quarantine proponents as to how the volatile Jewish veterans should be handled. The AJC, through its Washington chapter, tried to reach as many of the individual veterans among its own members as possible, telling them: "Understandably, with the memory of the six million, it is difficult to explain AJC strategy and a true appraisal of the problem to Jewry. Sadly, too little was done . . . to interpret this phenomenon to Jews and discourage them from falling into the trap which Rockwell candidly declared he was setting. . . . [Past] errors need not foredoom the future. Rockwell is not achieving his goals and, with perhaps a wiser Jewish community's cooperation, quarantine . . . can restore perspective to the treatment of this ugly intrusion upon our community life."[60]

JWV members had created problems for quarantine from the beginning. After the altercation surrounding the denial of Rockwell's permit to speak in New York City on the Fourth of July, Fineberg appealed to the head of the

Jewish War Veterans, Joseph F. Barr, in an attempt to get him to restrain JWV members. Nominally, Barr endorsed quarantine, but he was either unable or unwilling to convince a substantial portion of his organization's membership to comply with the strategy.[61] In November 1960, the JWV chapter in Chicago threatened to break ranks on quarantine, and Fineberg again appealed to Barr.[62]

While dissenting groups of Jewish veterans took to the streets to oppose Rockwell, the Anti-Defamation League of B'nai B'rith presented even more serious problems for the proponents of quarantine during 1960 and 1961. The ADL pursued legal action against Rockwell and the American Nazi party to prevent him from speaking or holding public rallies. Fineberg believed that the ADL's legal action brought to Rockwell's side civil libertarian allies who would normally have shunned him. He was also convinced that the publicity surrounding a legal controversy over the right to speak was more beneficial to Rockwell than publicity from street violence. Robert J. Greene complained in a letter to Fineberg that "Rockwell, like Hitler, laid his blueprint before us and . . . it called for baiting us to 'take in his laundry' by setting up our own clamor. . . . [The] pursuit of our goals were [*sic*] constantly undercut by the ADL efforts."[63] Fineberg worked the ADL leadership assiduously, and by mid-1961 it ended its legal challenges to Rockwell's right to speak, falling in step, albeit reluctantly, with Fineberg's quarantine strategy.

In 1961 Rockwell launched a new program: picketing *Exodus*, a Hollywood movie about the founding of the modern state of Israel. His first attempt, in Boston, was a great success: a hostile crowd gathered and a riot ensued. Local Jewish leaders tried to impose quarantine but failed.[64] Rockwell was thus convinced that if he could repeat his Boston success in other cities, quarantine might well be abandoned entirely, so he moved on to Detroit. Fineberg, working through the Jewish Community Council of Metropolitan Detroit, called a meeting of the local chapters of all major Jewish community organizations—the American Jewish Committee, the Anti-Defamation League of B'nai B'rith, the Jewish War Veterans, the American Jewish Congress, and the Jewish Labor Committee. At that meeting, "agreement was easily reached that our ultimate goal was total insulation if such was possible. That is, to have his coming and going completely unmarked by any commotion or publicity." Even the JWV agreed to avoid a street confrontation with the Rockwell pickets. In fact, the JWV contacted the local chapter of the American Legion (an organization that participated in the ill-conceived anti-Rockwell demonstration in Boston) and secured its cooperation. The Detroit community coalition then approached the local news media and "in each instance, the reaction was the one sought—namely that advance publicity would not be used. We understood and could not argue with the proposition that *if* something newsworthy broke, these media would have to take notice."[65]

The coalition—and the quarantine—held. Rockwell's picketing of *Exodus* in Detroit proceeded without incident and virtually without notice. The two experiences—Boston and Detroit—showed the national Jewish leadership the advantage of quarantine over street action and marked the beginning of the actual solidification of the American Jewish community behind quarantine. This is not to suggest that there were no further breaches in quarantine, for there were, or that local Jewish groups did not lose patience with the strategy, for several did. But the momentum within the American Jewish community clearly had shifted toward the proponents of quarantine and away from its detractors.

The ability to recognize such a shift in momentum is one benefit of hindsight. At the time, the acceptance of quarantine as the consensus strategy was not obvious at all to those on the front line of the battle. In late April 1961, Robert J. Greene, who was closest to the front line of the strategic struggle with Rockwell, still saw the "failure" of his organization to constrain dissidents within the Jewish community as the most significant threat to quarantine's success. "Here . . . is where . . . we have failed," Greene complained. "We . . . have not been able to convince enough members of the Jewish community enough times to ignore what New York's Mayor Wagner properly called a 'half-penny Hitler,' and thus surely condemn him to the obscurity he so richly deserves."[66] Recognized or not, the momentum had, in fact, shifted to quarantine in early 1961. By late spring of that year, Jewish organizations throughout the country contacted Fineberg and the AJC for advice on the implementation of quarantine in their communities and to report on Rockwell's visit to their communities. Fineberg's office became, in effect, the national clearinghouse for quarantine.[67]

The last organizations within the Jewish community to abandon street demonstrations against Rockwell were those often most susceptible to Rockwell's provocations—that is, those groups representing Nazi concentration camp survivors. Fineberg personally worked within those organizations so that, by mid-1962, they also accepted the course he advocated.[68] With their acquiescence, effective unanimity within the American Jewish community on the application of quarantine against George Lincoln Rockwell and the American Nazi party prevailed. Applying quarantine on a day-to-day basis remained a major focus of Fineberg's work until Rockwell's death in August 1967. After 1962, Fineberg did so with the full support and cooperation of a unified American Jewish community. Although no more than a relationship of association between Rockwell's peak of notoriety and the universal acceptance of quarantine as the Jewish community's oppositional strategy at the end of 1962 is possible, the two are probably not unrelated.

In one of Rockwell's earliest flyers, which he distributed in Washington, D.C., during his 1960 street rallies, he attacked the "Jewish 'Paper Curtain' of iron press control" and complained that "the Jew aim was NOT to give any publicity to real Nazis, to help them grow as all publicity always helps us, no matter how they smear us, lie or ridicule us."[69] In the spring of 1961, American Jewish Committee intelligence revealed that "Rockwell is reported to be shaken by his recent failures in the picketing of 'Exodus,' and is also reported to feel that the presence of too many police have kept Jews from demonstrating. Reportedly, he has sent his lieutenant, [J. V. Kenneth] Morgan, to the police to ask for less protection."[70] The report verified Rockwell's reliance on a Jewish reaction as essential to his publicity goals. In mid-1962, with quarantine being applied in full force by a unified American Jewish community, Rockwell devoted almost an entire issue of his party newsletter, *The Rockwell Report,* to ridiculing the strategy. But his bravado belied his frustration with quarantine's effects, and his words were intended to goad an elusive enemy into the streets. "Sometimes it is just plain FUN to be a Nazi!" Rockwell wrote. "Watching the Jew liars and schemers crawling around on the floor, looking for new dark corners in which to hide is always amusing. And when they are as pompous and stupid as 'Dr.' S. Andhil Fineberg, there just ain't words to describe the pleasure of watching him trying to 'lead' his fellow Hebrews out of the growing wilderness of Nazism." Rockwell hoped to lure militant Jews away from Fineberg and back into the streets. "Three years ago S. Andhil pompously counselled his fellow Jews to 'ignore Rockwell and he will go away like all the others have.' The 'Dr.' set himself up as the originator of what he calls the 'quarantine' treatment of bigots—but what is actually the same old censorship of ideas practiced by all tyrants; and the lovers of free speech then went round to the press, TV, etc. and handed down the Solomonic orders that us Nazis were not to be mentioned even if we ran up the White House lawn naked." Rockwell concluded ominously: "S. Andhil and his fellow Jew ostriches put their long noses together under the sand and assure each other over and over that by exposing their Jew bottoms to the well-placed kicks of the Nazis they will tire us out. . . . [But] I can't help feel sorry for people whose only defense against the leader of an outraged people . . . is to try to giggle while the gas chambers are assembled and tested."[71] Fineberg ignored the bait.

In his private correspondence, Rockwell agonized over how to break the quarantine. To Bruno Ludtke, a German Nazi and Rockwell confidant, he wrote: "you should realize that the Jews have read *Mein Kampf* and studied Hitler's success exhaustively. They are not stupid. They have applied forces which are particularly designed to prevent any repetition of Hitler's methods. I must constantly devise new and shocking and surprising weapons with which to strike at the Jews."[72] His exasperation with the impact of quarantine on the ANP surfaced in a letter to his chief administrative officer, Matt Koehl. "Surely you are aware of the capabilities of the Jews," Rockwell wrote in 1966, "and know what the . . . 'blackout' does to us. . . . There are endless ways they are quietly bleeding us to death. . . . They came out and FOUGHT Hitler. You know damned well that they won't DO that for us, today. Instead they get us fighting each OTHER with the damnable pressure of the darkness and poverty."[73]

Rockwell knew that to have any chance to win power, he needed social unrest and emotional turmoil. He believed that emotionally agitated people were the most vulnerable to manipulation. "You can never convert people's attitudes by lecturing and reasoning," he said. "Attitudes can only be changed through 'emotional engineering.' This is the key thing. It doesn't matter what the emotion is: love, fear, hatred. As long as there is an emotion in a person, I can change him. When I agitate in uniform, I want people to hate me. I want them emotionally worked up."[74] Quarantine denied him that opportunity. Fineberg believed that the "damnable pressure of the darkness and poverty" protected his people from any chance for Rockwell's "emotional engineering" to succeed. Within a year, Rockwell's attacks on quarantine grew more strident, and he made quarantine a free speech issue. In doing so, Rockwell identified the strategy's unresolved dilemma.

Rockwell struck a raw nerve when he attacked quarantine as a free speech issue. "I can FORCE the Jews to drop their lovable pose as humanitarian 'liberals,'" he wrote, "and reveal themselves in all their ferocity as the original old-testament TERRORISTS who call down the very wrath of heaven on their enemies, burn books, suppress free speech, preach unbounded HATE of anybody with whom they disagree and terrorize even the most idealistic 'liberals' who imagine the Jews mean what they preach about 'free speech.' What honest 'liberal' can fail to note the demand by the Jews that I be 'QUARANTINED'—and then begin to wonder what is the difference between the 'quarantine' and the 'censorship' of the Soviets. And if I can be 'quarantined,' then so can ANY-BODY. Who is to decide who gets 'quarantined'?"[75]

The quarantine employed against Rockwell and the American Nazi party raised significant questions about the limits of political speech in a free society. While few civil libertarians would defend the content of Rockwell's message, virtually all defended his right to deliver it. But Fineberg believed that some circumstances—few and limited—allowed political speech to be muted for a greater good. He argued that certain categories of political speech, especially hateful and hurtful speech aimed at a targeted minority, could be effectively restrained without damaging the essential nature of a free society.

These contending viewpoints engage a larger issue. If a free society accepts any limitation on free speech, who will be entrusted with the responsibility to determine which speech is "hurtful and hateful" and should be suppressed? Fineberg never addressed the question of how limitations on political speech would be determined in instances other than the quarantine of George Lincoln Rockwell and the American Nazi party. He also did not address the larger question of whether any suppression of political speech establishes a dangerous precedent. Instead, he focused on quarantine and defended his strategy as not only necessary but within the bounds of the American constitutional tradition of free speech.

Not everyone agreed. In 1965, Ben H. Bagdikian criticized the quarantine of Rockwell as "a quarantine under the best possible conditions of a subject odious to most Americans. But the quarantine is still pernicious."[76] He contended that Washington newspapers "apply a special test for hard news about Nazi activities" and that while theirs "is not an absolute quarantine," Rockwell and the ANP get "special handling, with the conscious objective of denying the Nazis publicity and minimizing their impact."[77] Bagdikian claimed that while not actually suppressing all news about Rockwell and the ANP, the editors applied different standards to Rockwell and the ANP than they did to other political figures and organizations. They consciously tried to "run news of the Nazis as little as possible," and when they did run it they tried to "minimize any advantage to the Nazis."[78] In doing so, Bagdikian asserted, the editors who embraced the quarantine of Rockwell followed the same path as those segregationist editors who, during the civil rights struggle of the 1950s and 1960s, "censored out news of integrationist agitation, believing they were doing it for the good of the community."[79] Bagdikian agreed that the right to free speech protected the demagogue, but he argued that excluding the demagogue from such protection jeopardized free speech for everyone. He also disputed Fineberg's contention that actions planned solely to capture media attention are, by definition, unworthy of news coverage. "How can the editor ignore all planned events?" Bagdikian argued. "If he did there would be almost no political news, because if there is one thing a politician plots day and night it is how to exploit the news process, and this goes from the President down to Rockwell."[80]

Bagdikian contended that placing moral judgments on the reporting of public events was an inappropriate function for editors and reporters. "When [a reporter] begins to filter what he sees and reports through a concern whether the reader will react 'correctly' he has ceased being a reporter."[81] A *New York*

Post editorial expressed similar sentiments on the heels of Rockwell's aborted attempt to hold a rally at Union Square on 4 July 1960: "We believe the Bill of Rights covers all forms of political madness; that the test of men's devotion to it comes when they are forced to endure the sound of loathsome voices."[82]

Fineberg understood the dilemma his strategy engendered, although he never addressed it directly or reconciled it adequately. Publicly, he maintained that there existed no conflict between quarantine and free speech. He tried to reconcile quarantine with adherence to the principles of free speech in *Deflating the Professional Bigot,* a pamphlet that was the most widely circulated AJC quarantine document during the Rockwell years.[83] But Fineberg's critics held that his recognition of the principles of free speech amounted to little more than lip service to principles he skirted in practice.

Although the American Jewish community never adequately addressed quarantine's free speech dilemma, there is a sizable body of evidence that the community's leaders could not, and did not, escape a significant degree of anguish over this sensitive issue. At a multiagency strategy session in early 1961, at the most critical period of Rockwell's campaign of public provocation—at a time when no one could predict the outcome of the Jewish community's struggle to contain him—the discussion centered on the protection of Rockwell's constitutional rights. At this strategy session, attended by high-level representatives of all national Jewish community organizations, the need to contain Rockwell was the obvious objective, but the participants addressed the need to do so within the law and with respect for Rockwell's right of free speech. This concern was so important to them that the discussion comprised the bulk of the notes recorded at this confidential gathering.[84] The notes that survive from that meeting reveal an almost surreal scene in which Jewish leaders, one after the other, speak up for Rockwell's right to advocate their execution and the gassing of their people.

The American Jewish community's leaders were torn by conflicting demands: the perceived need to respond in an effective manner to thwart Rockwell and a deeply held respect for the principle of free speech. What resulted was a continual reiteration of the community's adherence to the *principle* of free speech—a virtual civil libertarian mantra—without ever really subjecting quarantine to more than a superficial test of its compatibility with the practical application of that principle. No matter how quarantine's proponents attempted to reconcile the strategy with the principle of free speech, there remained an unresolved conflict between the principle and the practice.

Quarantine bound George Lincoln Rockwell and Solomon Andhill Fineberg together in an association neither sought and neither wanted. Yet it forced the two men together in a struggle neither could abandon. Each helped define the other by testing the other's fundamental character in the heat and noise of a critical struggle. For Rockwell, the battle over quarantine was his personal Waterloo. He fought other battles and had a lasting impact on those who shared his obsession, but Fineberg's quarantine leashed him. Rockwell lived with, but never shed, its restraints.

7

THE SCORNED

*Outside of niggers and Jews, I never met anyone who didn't love
the Commander.*
—former ANP stormtrooper, 1991

By more than any other measure, Rockwell defined him-
self by what he was not. The essence of his life's work was to marginalize, per-
secute, and, if given the opportunity, exterminate those he scorned: Jews,
blacks, and homosexuals. But in Rockwell's pantheon of enemies, only one held
center stage: the Jew. In his view, Jews were the cunning force behind world
communism; they manipulated blacks to further their own communist interests and pulled the strings on every center of power in America. Ultimately,
wittingly or unwittingly, all his enemies, including "liberals" and "queers,"
served the ruling Jews. Rockwell confided to Bruno Ludtke that a leader of
genius reduces many enemies to one in the mind of his followers. Rockwell
did just that. The enemy was always the cunning and manipulative Jew. The
"lesser" or "inferior" peoples were always his pawns.[1]

A clever man, Rockwell usually qualified his talk of "executions" and "gas
chambers" with references to "Jew-*traitors*" rather than just to "Jews." But the
preponderance of the evidence clearly suggests that the distinction was more
a prudent semanticism than a real difference to Rockwell. Genocide, with
whatever linguistic justifications accompany it, was not unthinkable in a
Rockwell-led America.

Rockwell believed in a Jewish-orchestrated conspiracy to enslave the white
race. This conspiracy contained a distinct religious or supernatural element
in that Jews, in Rockwell's view, were a satanic breed of subhumans.[2] They
wove their cabalistic powers around a naïve and distracted white race and
plotted the permanent domination of that naturally superior race by contami-
nating its blood with that of the black race, which was a genetically inferior
human subspecies. In this scenario, blood takes on a distinctly mystical quality. A mere drop of Jewish or black blood degrades and pollutes a member of

the white race beyond redemption. Much of Rockwell's thinking in this regard, which is standard American racism of a rather pedestrian variety, mirrors the rhetoric of an early political influence, retired Admiral John G. Crommelin, a perennial candidate for local, state, and federal public office in Alabama and a well-known racist. Rockwell admired Crommelin's racial views, not to mention his military stature, and became involved in his first political campaign during Crommelin's Alabama gubernatorial bid in 1958. Contamination of Aryan blood as a strategy of Jewish domination was a consistent theme in Crommelin's campaigns. He often spoke of "the satanic plot to mix the blood of the white man with the Negro" as being "financed and directed by the Communist-Jewish conspiracy."[3] Rockwell, a political strategist rather than an innovative thinker, lifted much of Crommelin's theoretical framework and made it his own.

The blood contamination issue—which has no scientific validity whatsoever—regularly arose when Rockwell's racial position was disputed. Whenever challengers referred to the accomplishments, in all fields, of African Americans as de facto proof of the ridiculousness of Rockwell's claim, he customarily replied, "I've not seen very many Congo black gorilla-type Negroes who have achieved anything"—thereby dismissing each example to the contrary as the result of the beneficial and uplifting influence of white blood in a racially mixed person. For Rockwell, droplets of blood had the near-magical power to debase the purest Aryan while uplifting the most depraved African American. For pure "gorilla-type Negroes"—to Rockwell, the majority of African Americans—he had nothing but unalloyed disdain. He regarded any attempt at social integration of the races to be odious. "I like to see monkeys at the zoo," he said, "but I don't think they should be sitting around a banquet table." He attacked social welfare programs as promoting "the boom of little black bastards."[4] He ridiculed African-American music and dance as "degenerate" and likened all mid-60s dances—specifically "the frug, the monkey, and the watusi"—as "anarchy through culture." He derided African-American teenagers, and the white teenagers who "copied" them, who could be seen "jumping around like animals in the jungle." And he linked that "cultural degradation" to rampant inner-city crime and Castro-sponsored urban terrorism, all presumed to have been instigated by Jewish agents of "cultural anarchy, like Benny Goodman."[5]

As with all of Rockwell's public positions, it is difficult to discern—amid the posturing, the demagoguery, and the flim-flam of the con man—just what his true intentions were regarding African Americans. His attitude toward them is indisputably one of contempt and disdain, but he tried, however ineptly, to conceal the depth of that contempt by feigning a paternal concern for them. The American Nazi party's "official" position proffered "no animosity toward the Negro." Rockwell proposed a "voluntary" resettlement of African Americans to Africa with generous funding of the colony by a Nazi-led U.S. government.[6] He claimed that he intended to divert the "billions of dollars we're wasting on foreign aid" to assist "American Negroes" in building their own nation in Africa. He claimed that this resettlement plan would benefit African Americans since a "pure black Congo Negro" couldn't hope to compete successfully in white society. He admitted that blacks had a "rotten situation" in America and insisted that the only solution was to "separate them" from the white race.[7]

Off the record, and within the confines of private ANP gatherings, Rockwell's paternalism toward African Americans was less evident. He predicted that his followers' children "[would] be forced to exterminate swarms of wild niggers until all of them are finally corralled in Africa."[8] To Bruno Ludtke, Rockwell confided that his ultimate goal upon achieving political power in the United States was the forced deportation of African Americans to Africa. He admitted that his public position of advocating voluntary emigration was merely a ruse to temper African American opposition until he seized power. In an unusual disagreement with his closest confidant, Rockwell dismissed any attempt by Ludtke to advise him on how to handle African Americans. He reminded Ludtke that "you have few nigger Germans to deal with," whereas he had to contend with "millions of these semi-apes."[9]

Rockwell believed that a race war was imminent. He expressed horror at the prospect of interracial carnage on American soil but actually welcomed it as a necessary element of the social chaos that would sweep him to power. "Commander Rockwell was POSITIVE," a follower wrote, "that the Blacks were going to go on an all-out rampage before the decade of the Sixties was out, and touch off the race war that so many talked about in those days." To a boyhood friend not involved in ANP politics, Rockwell confided: "I am . . . convinced that the world is building to a RACE WAR, in which we are outnumbered ten to one, we are divided and decadent, while the colored races are hard and getting harder."[10] The terror of that race war, Rockwell believed, would drive the American people to him as the only politician tough enough to protect their interests. For Rockwell, the coming race war was but one battle in the larger war with the Jews. In that battle, white Americans would face the "mutiny of the scum of the world led by the Jews." He characterized the racial unrest of the 1960s, which he saw as a prelude to the wider conflagration, as "Jew brains directing nigger bodies" in a "revolt of the 'untermenschen.'"[11] He warned his followers never to forget that "nigger agitators" always work "under the direction of . . . criminal Jews" and that "the savage, stupid mobs of black jungle animals, now raging and terrorizing White Men and Women in our streets [are] a result of Jew agitation."[12]

Rockwell's obsession with Jewish cunning occasionally—and bizarrely—intersected with his lurid fascination with interracial sex. "More and more I am seeing the results of the combination of a Jew brain injected into the gorilla-like body of the African," Rockwell told his followers. "From the loins of Jewish girls under blankets with savage African Negroes . . . are crawling a generation of these gorilla-bodies implanted with Jewish brains. Nothing from outer-space or the Black Lagoon could be more terrible."[13]

As part of his constant search for issues, and angles, to exploit, in 1963 Rockwell tried to rally mainstream support against home rule for the District of Columbia, a city with an African-American majority, on the grounds that "the very capital of White, Western, Christian civilization" should not be under the control of "a group of Negroes."[14] The issue never caught on for him. He had far greater success in Chicago in 1966 when—from 20 August to 10 September—he shadowed Martin Luther King Jr.'s open housing marches with street demonstrations and invective-laden harangues that inflamed the racial turmoil in that suffering city and kept his name in the headlines. Rockwell was arrested twice and reaped more precious publicity than during any comparable period in his public career.[15]

Rockwell loathed King and always referred to him, in public and in writing, as "Martin Luther Coon." Whether he believed it or not, he ardently asserted that King was a dupe of the communists, a pawn of the communists, a communist himself.[16] On two occasions Rockwell instigated physical assaults on King, and one of Rockwell's most faithful and fanatical followers considered assassinating the civil rights leader. On 28 September 1962, King was speaking before the Southern Christian Leadership Conference in Birmingham, Alabama—the first integrated public meeting ever held in that city—when a young white man calmly walked across the stage. When King turned to face him as he reached the podium, believing him to be a messenger, the young man lashed out with his fist, striking King below the left eye. King staggered backward and the assailant hit him again, on the side of the face, then twice more from behind. King was spun around by the force of the blows.

The large crowd, at first transfixed in horror at the scene, suddenly erupted in shrieks and cries of outrage as the man hit King again and again. Several aides and people from the audience jumped onto the stage and rushed to help King. Witnesses reported a strange occurrence as the rescuers moved toward the attacker. After absorbing a particularly savage blow, King stood facing his assailant and dropped his hands. Septima Clark, a journalist who witnessed the events from her seat in the first row, said that King turned his open hands out "like a newborn baby" and faced his attacker with a look of "transcendent calm." That action momentarily froze all participants, including the attacker. One of King's aides rushed the man as the angry crowd surged forward. But King prevented the mob from harming his attacker. "Don't touch him! Don't touch him!" King admonished. "We have to pray for him." From that moment on, Septima Clark, who had cynically suspected that King's advocacy of non-violence was the result of "slow calculation," believed instead that it "was the response of his quickest instinct."[17]

Rockwell awarded Roy James, King's assailant and an American Nazi party stormtrooper, the ANP's highest honor, the Order of Adolf Hitler Silver Medal. The citation Rockwell presented to James praised him for his "heroic deed" of attacking the nation's leading "communist-nigger agitator."[18]

On 18 January 1965, Martin Luther King Jr. led a voter registration march to the Selma, Alabama, courthouse steps, where he made a brief speech. Afterward, King and his aides checked into Selma's celebrated Hotel Albert and became the first African Americans to stay as registered guests at the venerable antebellum hotel, a slave-built southern landmark and "symbol of white supremacy." As King crossed the opulent lobby, a man—later identified by Wilson Baker, Selma's commissioner of public safety, as a local member of the ANP—walked up to King and punched him in the face. Police subdued the assailant before he could continue his attack. As they dragged the man away, a white woman stood on a lobby chair, pointed at King, and screamed to white onlookers: "Get him! Get him!"[19]

Although not present during the attack on King, Rockwell was conspicuous in the crowd of onlookers during King's march and met with Selma's ANP members, presumably including King's assailant, that morning. King's chief aide, the Reverend Ralph Abernathy, reported that King noticed Rockwell in the crowd and went over to him after his speech. No record exists of what was said during the only face-to-face meeting between the two. Abernathy was startled to learn that King had invited Rockwell to address an SCLC rally in Selma the next evening. Whatever Rockwell may have said to King at the hotel, he did not speak at the rally.[20]

Later that year, Karl R. Allen, the ANP's deputy commander, disrupted a King speech in Danville, Virginia. Allen jumped onto the stage and screamed racial epithets at King, although he did not physically assault him. Rockwell praised Allen's actions in the party newsletter.[21] A top Rockwell aide and ANP captain, Ralph P. Forbes, who headed the party's Western Division, considered assassinating King in 1964 or 1965. An FBI informant reported that Forbes confided to party members: "If I thought killing . . . Martin Luther King would solve the nigger problems I wouldn't hesitate to do it, . . . but I don't think it would accomplish anything but make a martyr out of him."[22] Forbes revered Rockwell, remaining active in racist activities and elevating Rockwell to near-sainthood after his death. One of the few ANP leaders to remain loyal to Rockwell throughout Rockwell's entire public career, Forbes was the storm-trooper Rockwell most often chose for sensitive and dangerous assignments. While there is no extant documentation that Forbes ever discussed the possible assassination of King with Rockwell, their relationship makes it unbelievable that he would have contemplated such drastic action without consulting Rockwell.

Nothing—not his obsessive hatred of Jews nor his attempts to dehumanize blacks—matched Rockwell's visceral abhorrence of homosexuals. "If there is anything I would rather gas than Jew Communist traitors," Rockwell wrote to a critic, "it is queer traitors. I despise homosexuals as one despises syphilis germs."[23] Rockwell told intimates that when he took power, "the first item of business"—before dealing with Jews and blacks—"would be the systematic confinement of all homosexuals." His intentions beyond confinement were well understood by his inner circle. Rockwell's propaganda chief, John Patler (later the man convicted of killing Rockwell), told a reporter, "Maybe we'll let the Storm Troopers use them," perhaps revealing far more than he intended.[24]

Homosexuality within the ranks of the ANP was a constant concern to Rockwell and a constant source of speculation among his enemies. "There is a tendency for queers to come here," Rockwell admitted to a hostile interviewer at the ANP's Arlington barracks; then he quickly distanced himself from homosexuals by adding, "because to a queer, this place is as tempting as a girls' school would be to me."[25] According to FBI surveillance, Rockwell's fear of gay stormtroopers was well founded. The ANP's Western Division, particularly, was shaken by the revelation that the unit's chief, Leonard Holstein—who was also half-Jewish—was gay.[26]

Persistent rumors of gays within the ANP's top echelon—primarily centering on Rockwell's chief of staff, Matt Koehl—damaged the party within the racist right wing. When rumors of Koehl's homosexuality first surfaced, one party member wrote to Rockwell that he could "tolerate the reputation of being a fascist" but never "an association" with "queers."[27]

Matt Koehl—born Matthias Koehl Jr. in Milwaukee, Wisconsin, on 22 January 1935—was the son of Hungarian immigrants of German extraction. A sensitive, intelligent boy with more than average musical talent (he played violin with the Milwaukee Civic Opera Association as a young man), Koehl clashed violently with his rough-hewn immigrant father but had a deep affection for, and was particularly devoted to, his soft-spoken mother. By age thirteen he had a reputation in his neighborhood as a vocal anti-Semite, and at seventeen he regularly distributed anti-Semitic propaganda in Milwaukee for Conde McGinley, an East Coast–based anti-Semitic agitator. Koehl attended the University of Wisconsin for three years, majoring in journalism, but didn't graduate.

Prior to enlisting in the U.S. Marine Corps, where he spent two years on active duty and six years in the reserves, Koehl moved to New York City and joined James Madole's National Renaissance party, one of the first postwar proto-Nazi groups operating in the United States. Always fascinated with insignia and uniforms, Koehl organized the NRP's "elite guard," which served as a security corps for Madole and as a show unit on ceremonial occasions. After his discharge from active duty with the marines, Koehl joined a small group in Chicago that mass mailed anti-Semitic tracts. By 1957 he had moved comfortably within the small circle of American racist leaders. That year, hoping to exploit the elevated racial tensions in the South over the forced integration of the Little Rock, Arkansas, public schools, Koehl joined forces with Emory Burke, Dan Kurtz, Wallace Allen, Ned Dupes, John Kasper, and Edward R. Fields to organize the United White party in Knoxville, Tennessee. The following year, the UWP was absorbed by Fields and Jesse B. Stoner's National States Rights party.

Through Fields and the NSRP, Koehl met George Lincoln Rockwell in 1958, shortly before the Atlanta synagogue bombing and Rockwell's emergence as an open Nazi (see chapter 3). Koehl and Rockwell became fast friends. Their personalities complemented each other. Rockwell—dashing, outgoing, outspoken, bold, brimming with schemes and plans—was a leader looking for a movement; he found in Koehl—introverted and adept at the detail work Rockwell despised—a Martin Bormann craving an Adolf Hitler. During the summer of 1958, Rockwell and Koehl worked together on Crommelin's Alabama gubernatorial campaign. They stayed in close contact after the campaign, and in 1962 Koehl joined the American Nazi party as head of its new Chicago unit. In February 1963, Rockwell transferred Koehl to ANP headquarters in Arlington, Virginia, to bring administrative order to the chaos he generated. By late that year Rockwell promoted Koehl to the rank of major and named him national secretary—the party's chief administrative officer—a post that had been vacant since James K. Warner's 1961 defection.[28]

The allegations within the racist right of Koehl's homosexuality center primarily around an accusation that in 1951, as a sixteen-year-old member of the Committee to Free Ezra Pound, he engaged in homosexual activities with two older gay committee members, Eustace Mullins and Edward Fleckstein. His enemies on the right also claim that Koehl participated with Mullins and Fleckstein in the homosexual rape of a fifteen-year-old male. Those same enemies—primarily Rickey E. Cooper, a onetime Koehl aide and current head of the Nazi National Socialist Vanguard—further allege that Crommelin discovered Koehl and another male—*not* Rockwell—engaged in a homosexual act in his basement during the 1958 gubernatorial campaign and banned the two men from his house, his sight, and his organization. These accusations, although quite persistent and specific, are undocumented. Charges of homosexuality against Koehl, which dogged him throughout his career with Rockwell, never involved alleged incidents after 1958.[29]

True or not, the allegations disturbed Rockwell. According to Herbert Hillary Booker, an on-again, off-again stormtrooper and distant Rockwell relative, at one point Rockwell tried to dispel the rumors by bringing a woman from Cleveland to Arlington to help his embattled aide improve his "womanless image." The woman, a widow with four children, was a pure Aryan and a devoted Nazi. She dutifully made herself available to Matt Koehl, but Koehl ignored her. Rockwell's vision of a bevy of Teutonic babies as testament to Koehl's heterosexuality obviously did not appeal to Koehl.[30]

Speculation persisted throughout Rockwell's career, and after his death, about his own sexual orientation. There is no evidence that he ever engaged in anything but heterosexual relations. Rockwell was the subject of intense scrutiny and surveillance by government and private agencies throughout his public career; had any incidents of homosexuality in Rockwell's life been detected, those agencies would have had no reason to conceal them. Without digressing into a psychological analysis, suffice it to say that Rockwell's emphatic and frequent affirmations of his own masculinity raise questions about the state of his subconscious. "Any pansy can be a pink," he wrote, "[but] it takes a MAN to be a Nazi." He also asserted that "any man who didn't vigorously enjoy normal sex could never be a National Socialist," and he vigorously contested anyone who publicly questioned his exclusive attraction to women. Still, someone who knew him well wrote: "Rockwell . . . had a fixation on homosexuality and tried to tar all his opponents with that brush. He said that he had problems with that in his own organization. . . . [He] was so rabid on the point that I often wondered if he were not himself so inclined." And in a curious letter to his mother, the one person with whom he shared his innermost thoughts, Rockwell confessed on the eve of his incarceration in Chicago that "the bad part, of course, is the possibility of being thrown into that vile jail with all the colored brothers eagerly awaiting to make 'love' to me." That would seem to be a curious fear for a strapping 6'3", 185-pound, relatively young and fit man.[31]

Inseparable from Rockwell's insecurity about homosexuals and homosexuality is his view of women. He constantly related "manliness" to strength and power and frequently asserted that "a man who won't fuck won't fight." His views reflected Nietzsche's, that "man should be educated and trained for war and woman for the recreation of the warrior." Any suggestion in opposition to this cosmic order infuriated Rockwell: "When a nation gets to the point when the men ain't men, and the women ain't women, and you can't tell the difference anymore, it's on the way down the drain!"[32]

Women played no leadership role in Rockwell's American Nazi party. According to James K. Warner, Rockwell believed that "woman's place is in the kitchen and the bedroom" and that women "have no place in politics." At first, Rockwell was against even allowing women to join the ANP, but he changed his mind on that score because income was scarce and he couldn't afford to turn down anyone who was willing to pay dues. In his personal view, Rockwell believed that "women should be trained like dogs." According to Warner, under a Rockwell-led Nazi regime "women [would] be reduced to serfdom with no rights at all."[33]

"Our kind of people, Nazis, are, by nature, masculine, virile and tend to be quite extreme in these characteristics," Rockwell explained. Party literature often described "the masses" as "feminine" and subconsciously craving male domination. "The masses say no," the ANP leaders instructed recruits, "but what they mean is force me to say yes to what I really want but won't admit." Rockwell viewed the masses as he viewed all women: indecisive but ultimately submissive and compliant in the face of superior (male) force. The masses are, he wrote, "completely, hopelessly female in their approach to 'reason,' and always, *always* prefer strength to 'rightness.'" In this regard, Rockwell's depiction of the swastika was almost phallic: "When [the masses] say 'no' to our Swastika . . . they are only the eternal female saying 'no,' but meaning: 'If you accept my 'no,' then you are a weakling and have no right to my favors. Let us see if you have the manhood and strength and genius to *make* me say 'yes.'"[34] To his mother, Rockwell raged at those who go "against any MAN who stands up and says, thinks and does MASCULINE AGGRESSIVE things, instead of . . . simpering, feminine stuff." For Rockwell, aggression was masculine and being seen as unmanly by the world, or even by his mother, was his greatest fear.

George Lovejoy "Doc" Rockwell.

Rockwell at nine months. His beautiful mother, Claire, was the one constant in his life.

Rockwell, the navy aviator, sought a combat assignment at the completion of flight training.

Claire Schade Rockwell visited her son before he shipped out to the Pacific during World War II.

Rockwell preparing for a television appearance during the 1965 race for governor of Virginia.

Rockwell (left, behind the sign) picketing the White House in 1958. Harold Noel Arrowsmith Jr., Rockwell's first financial patron, is on the right.

Rockwell (center) was the international commander of the World Union of National Socialists.

"Hatemonger Hill," the ANP headquarters in Arlington, Virginia.

Rockwell (left of the podium) at a rally on the Mall in Washington, D.C., hoping to incite violence and garner some much-needed publicity.

Rockwell's hard-core followers seldom numbered more than twenty-five.

Rockwell preparing for a speech on the college lecture circuit.

An avid sailor, Rockwell was most at peace when at sea. This photograph was taken while he was sailing on Chesapeake Bay just two weeks before his death.

The only known group photo of the participants at the 1962 Cotswold Conference that organized the WUNS. In the second row are Rockwell (second from the right), Colin Jordan (second from the left), and Bruno Ludtke (first from the right). The mystical Savitri Devi is in the center of the front row.

Rockwell was assassinated on 25 August 1967 in the parking lot of a laundromat in Arlington, Virginia, by John Patler, his erstwhile protégé.

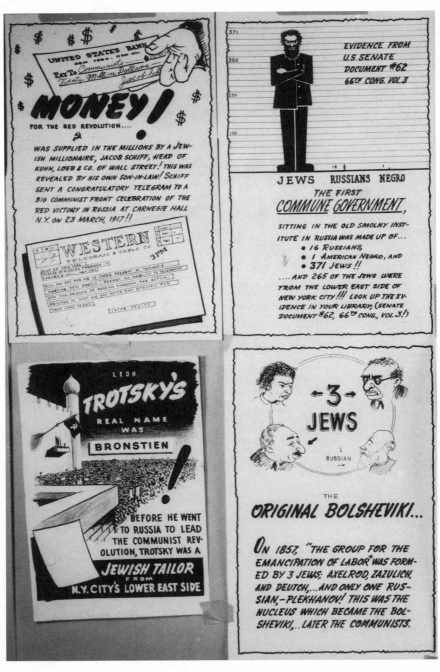

Rockwell, a talented artist, produced most of the illustrations for the ANP's hate literature.

OULINAOV (LENIN) ←

BRONSTIEN
(TROTSKY) →

APFELBAUM,
(ZINOVIEV)

**THE FIRST
"POLITBURO"**

(OCT. CENTRAL COMMITTEE)
TROTSKY'S BOOK, "STALIN"
LISTS THE FIRST RULERS
OF RED RUSSIA. COUNT
THE JEWS!... 75%.
....CHECK THE BOOK!

ROSENFELD, (KAMENEV)

I HATE THE CATHOLICS!

I HATE THE
DAMN
NIGGERS!

THESE ARE →

BIGOTS......

..They deserve your _CONTEMPT_!

They hate whole groups which are
different from themselves.....just because they are different. There is
no reason or excuse for their stupid intolerance! To hate a man because of religion or skin-color is
silly.......and DANGEROUS!!

IN 1907

IN LONDON..
the SOCIAL-DEMOCRATIC PARTY

HELD A GIANT UNIFICATION CONGRESS OF
WORLD COMMUNIST FORCES. ALL OF THE
LEADERS EXCEPT 3 WERE JEWS!! IN-
CLUDED WERE TROTSKY (BRONSTIEN),
LUXEMBERG, MARTOV (TSEDERBAUM), DAN,
(GURVICH), ABRAMOVITCH, DANIEVSKY, ZIN-
OVIEV (APFELBAUM), KAMENEV. (ROSENFELD),
LIEBER, ...ALL JEWS!!

HE
HAS
CHECKED

He isn't prejudiced against any-
body because of _RELIGION_ or _COL-
OR,_ .....but he has checked all the
facts, and _knows_ large numbers of
Jews are working fanatically to
SMASH _HIS_ _SOCIETY_! ..He knows
it is not "prejudice" or "intolerance"
to expose the _TRUTH_ about people
who are trying to hurt you! ...He
wants _YOU_ to judge whether these
facts are true.... by checking!!

COMMUNISM IS MASTERMINDED BY **JEWS**

THIS MAN IS.....

<u>NOT</u> A BIGOT

He is <u>not</u> saying "<u>All</u> Jews are Communists"...or "<u>All</u> Communists are Jews." Many Jews are fine, patriotic Americans!

But it is not intolerant or bigotted to say "Communism is masterminded by Jews"....This man knows it is a simple, honest, *FACT!*..

It is <u>not</u> "Hate"..or "Anti-Semitism!"

...HE DOESN'T WANT TO SHOOT ANYBODY!

He knows that there is a diabolical plot to make a slave out of him. But he believes,—with Henry Ford, that <u>NO</u> plot can succeed if the intended victim knows what the plotters are up to, ... and *WHO* they are!

He is sure Americans have nothing to fear from Communism, once they know Communism is part of a plot which is *MASTERMINDED* by Jews.

YOU CAN'T LEARN THE TRUTH *from* NEWSPAPERS, RADIO, BOOKS, etc.

N.B.C., C.B.S., *and* A.B.C. are all Jew-owned! M.G.M., Paramount, Loews, Warner Bros. and 20th Century-Fox are Jewish firms! The N.Y. Times, Washington Post, St. Louis Dispatch, N.Y. Post, Look, Quick, U.S. News, ...all are Jew-owned....*ALL* major public information sources are directly or indirectly Jew-controlled!...If you don't believe that,...<u>check</u> the *FACTS* in the following pages. Then ask yourself why you've never heard of them before ???

KARL MARX,
Father of Communism

Karl Marx was a Jewish-German,. and Fredrich Engle's, Co-founder of Communism, was another Jew. They organized in theory the bitterness and hate which boiled in Europe's Jewish Ghettoes. The Jewish Encyclopedia frankly admits that the "Social-Revolutionary Party" had its roots in Russia's Jewish "Pale-of-Settlement".

8 THE WORLD UNION OF NATIONAL SOCIALISTS

The LAST TIME our leader [Adolf Hitler] showed the way to victory in one single area of the earth. "Today Germany!" he predicted[,] "TOMORROW THE WORLD!!" Now it is TOMORROW! Now is the time, White Men! THIS TIME THE WORLD!
—George Lincoln Rockwell, 1961

On 25 August 1992—the twenty-fifth anniversary of Rockwell's death—Nazi leaders from all over Europe gathered at a secret location to pay homage to his memory and reaffirm their commitment to his vision of a worldwide National Socialist revival. For them, Rockwell was the "great founding figure" of reborn National Socialism through the international organization he had created—the World Union of National Socialists (WUNS). The gathering concluded with the adoption of a WUNS "Declaration of Principles" based on a solemn code "set forth by Lincoln Rockwell upon the revival of the National Socialist movement after World War II."[1]

"From the beginning," according to William L. Pierce, "Rockwell had understood the necessity for the National Socialist movement eventually to operate from a worldwide basis," for Rockwell's final objective "was the establishment of an Aryan world order."[2] He envisioned the "liberation" of Germany through a Nazi political triumph in the United States and the domination of the world through an Anglo-German-American Nazi axis.[3] Beginning in 1958 and 1959, concurrent with his emergence as a self-proclaimed Nazi, Rockwell probed potential foreign allies for the establishment of a transnational political network. He made several efforts to contact Egyptian president Nasser and other enemies of Israel in the Middle East in an attempt to forge a political alliance based on anti-Zionism and anti-Semitism. His efforts proved unsuccessful.[4]

In early 1959, Rockwell began formulating plans for a worldwide network of National Socialists to implement an international Nazi revival. He created a new organization, which he initially called the World Union of Free Enterprise National Socialists (WUFENS), later shortened to the World Union of National Socialists (WUNS). By 1961 he had made contact with Colin Jordan, leader of the British National Socialist Movement (and chief right-wing rival of Sir Oswald Mosley's British Union of Fascists). Jordan shared Rockwell's racist and anti-Semitic views as well as his impatience with right wingers and fellow racists who were reluctant to take bold action and risk public censure. Rockwell and Jordan formed a solid friendship that lasted until Rockwell's death. Jordan introduced Rockwell to European Nazis who were tentatively emerging from their postwar camouflage. Jordan had a strong and lasting impact on WUNS and on Rockwell due to his loyalty, his tenacious devotion to "the Cause," and his organizational skills. But two European Nazis Jordan brought to Rockwell had an even more profound influence on Rockwell's intellectual development as a National Socialist: Savitri Devi and Bruno Ludtke.

Savitri Devi was born Maximiani Portas in Lyons, France, on 30 September 1905. A chemist by training, with an earned doctorate, Devi was a savant and mystic by inclination. In 1932 she moved to India to study ancient Aryan philosophy and rituals; while there, she adopted the name Savitri Devi, after the Aryan sun goddess. The circumstances of her conversion to National Socialism are unclear, but by 1935 she was a devotee of Adolf Hitler and a staunch Nazi. She was "active in Axis circles in India" prior to and during World War II. After Devi returned to Europe following the war, Allied authorities imprisoned her for her wartime activities and her persistent defense of National Socialism in postwar West Germany. A lean, intense woman with wrinkled, leathery skin and piercing ice-blue eyes, Devi mesmerized Rockwell when they met in England in 1962, after corresponding for two years. Her incisive mind and mystical visions of a Nazi resurrection appealed to Rockwell, as did her direct connection to Hitler's Third Reich.[5]

Even more than Colin Jordan or Savitri Devi, perhaps more than any other single person, Bruno Ludtke influenced Rockwell's thinking on National Socialism's revival as a world political movement. Devoted to Rockwell to the brink of sycophancy, Ludtke played to Rockwell's vanity and sense of destiny in a voluminous personal correspondence that lasted from 1960 until Rockwell's death in 1967. To Ludtke, the German Reich of 1933–45 was only a prelude to the worldwide National Socialist empire of the future—and in his opinion, Rockwell held the key to that future. In a letter to a close Rockwell aide, which Rockwell was sure to see, Ludtke described the American Nazi party founder as the most important National Socialist since Adolf Hitler and Hitler's heir among the true believers. In Rockwell, Ludtke saw the strong leader with a clear vision, the man who would replace the Führer. He wrote of the future of the Aryan race being in Rockwell's hands. He might also have added that with Rockwell rode his last chance to play a leadership role in a National Socialist world.[6]

Bruno Armin Ludtke was born on 15 November 1926 in Hamburg on the

Elbe, since 1938 a part of Greater Hamburg. His parents, members of the conservative Christian Church of God, raised him in a stern Christian Fundamentalist household. As devoted members of a peculiar religious sect, the Ludtkes were always outsiders in their own mostly Lutheran community. Ludtke's father, a vehement anti-Nazi, clashed with his young son who, from an early age, idolized Adolf Hitler. In 1940, at the age of fourteen, Ludtke joined the Hitler-Jügend (Hitler Youth) over his father's objections. From that point on, Ludtke and his father seldom spoke to each other. Ludtke's attempt to enlist in the SS in 1943 failed because of his poor health. But as the Soviet winter consumed the mighty German army on the Russian steppes, the Wehrmacht lowered its physical standards and called Ludtke to service in October 1944.

Ludtke served in Denmark until the war's end, when he relocated to Cologne to study engineering. Married and divorced within a three-month span in 1953, he supported his former wife and the son she later gave birth to by working as an engineer. In 1960 he lost his job and moved to Frankfurt, where he found temporary work as an Olivetti office machines salesman. In deteriorating health—he suffered from multiple sclerosis—and often unemployed, Ludtke barely eked out enough of a living to support his Cologne family and his second wife, whom he had married in 1956, and their four daughters. Still, he could not let go of the passion he held for Adolf Hitler and Hitler's dream of a racially pure National Socialist world. Until introduced to Rockwell by Savitri Devi, Ludtke had no outlet for his passion and little hope that he would live to see a Nazi resurgence. Through Rockwell, Ludtke's hopes soared.[7]

Rockwell's treasured connection to nazism's past glories, Ludtke constantly and willingly reassured Rockwell of his place as Hitler's heir and of the inevitability of his triumph. A theorist and philosopher, he patiently instructed Rockwell in the subtleties of National Socialism and in the history of Hitler's rise to power in Germany. Rockwell needed to hear that Hitler's earlier travails in Germany paralleled his own in America, and Ludtke, sensing that need, eagerly met it. Ludtke, who grappled with his father's ghost as fiercely as Rockwell grappled with Doc Rockwell's disapproval throughout his own life, sought reconciliation through Rockwell. On his deathbed, Ludtke's father shared a "dream" with his son that the young man would one day be the leader of Germany. Ludtke confided to Rockwell that in the end his father believed in his prophetic dreams as firmly as he believed in his Bible. Whether the elder Ludtke's dream emanated from a feverish delirium or from a deep-seated desire to reconcile with his rebellious and enigmatic son did not matter. What was important was Bruno Ludtke's belief that his triumph was preordained and that, through his triumph, reconciliation with his father was possible. Rockwell was the catalyst for Ludtke's political destiny and his personal redemption.[8]

Ludtke advised Rockwell on strategy and bolstered his courage. "Illegal things must be done, but never spoken of," he cautioned. Of Ludtke, Rockwell, and Jordan—whom Ludtke proudly referred to as "Hitler's sons"—Ludtke was in the most precarious position because Nazi advocacy, recruitment, and agitation were illegal in postwar West Germany. Ludtke paid the price for his activities by numerous arrests and long periods of incarceration, which encouraged and inspired Rockwell to persevere.[9] Ludtke's letters from prison gave Rockwell solace in his darkest moments, relieving his sense of isolated suffering and giving him hope that his sacrifices were not folly.

Whenever Rockwell neared the end of his ability to absorb more loss and loneliness, Ludtke seemed to sense that his friend—who was both his leader and his protégé—needed an exemplar during a crisis of spirit. In one particularly instructive letter, Ludtke described a recent time in prison when the stress of prosecution and incarceration seemed almost unbearable. At that moment, Ludtke wrote to Rockwell, he "died." His metaphorical death brought visions of a poignant scene, which he described for Rockwell—and with it came a valuable lesson on survival and triumph. Ludtke wrote of a triumphant death, visualized while lying on his cot in an isolated prison cell. In "death" Ludtke was not a prisoner but the glorified leader of the renewed German Reich. He described the ceremony of his state funeral in great detail: the vast, flag-draped hall, the solemn music, the honor guard of SS officers, and—at the center of the fantasy— Rockwell himself, at Ludtke's side, ready to receive the mantle of leadership and the sacred commission to carry on the glory of the Reich. When Ludtke awoke from the dream-trance, all fatigue had disappeared and he was prepared to carry on through the dark days of the present toward the glorious and triumphant light of the future.[10]

Whenever Rockwell's enthusiasm for the struggle waned, Ludtke painted marvelously detailed pictures, glorious fantasies, of what awaited them in victory. He wrote in minute detail of the capital they would build, of a government complex dominated by "Adolf Hitler-Square," of "Lincoln Rockwell-Hall," which would accommodate 20,000 people for huge rallies. He described a great "Empire-Library" to house the artifacts and records of the struggle and a gigantic edifice, the "Reichshof—the seat of the Commander and his Deputy," designed to dwarf the Pentagon, the White House, or any existing or imagined seat of power. Ludtke coaxed Rockwell to imagine granite towers topped with eagles and swastikas, great halls, and beautiful monuments, all built to glorify the Nazi past and—not incidentally—to immortalize George Lincoln Rockwell.[11]

Ludtke fed Rockwell stories of the glory of life in Hitler's Reich as a form of psychic nourishment and Rockwell responded enthusiastically. He wrote to Ludtke, in response to a particularly graphic description of Hitler's National Socialist paradise, that if he had the choice, he would return in time to experience the glory of Hitler's Reich himself, even if it meant dying with the Führer in 1945. Overwhelmed by Ludtke's exaggerated images of life in Nazi Germany, Rockwell lamented that he might never live to see America replicate the "heaven" Germany must have been under Hitler.[12]

Rockwell, in turn, confided to Ludtke about his loneliness and how much he missed his second wife and their children. Like a father-confessor, Ludtke encouraged sexual abstinence as noble and necessary in the life of a great warrior.[13] Throughout their association, Ludtke remained Rockwell's most loyal disciple, his most trusted confidant, his staunchest defender, and his truest believer.

Ludtke understood the centrality of the strong leader to Nazi philosophy. For him, Rockwell *was* that leader, and any attack on Rockwell betrayed the movement. Early in their association, Ludtke warned Rockwell that the movement could not tolerate heresy in any form or any challenge to, or deviation from, the positions taken by its leader. He warned that the movement must have but "one point of crystallization," one leader: Rockwell himself.[14] Ludtke advocated Rockwell's supremacy to Colin Jordan, their partner in the international Nazi triumvirate and Rockwell's senior as a National Socialist revolutionist. He argued to Jordan that Arlington, Virginia, not London, would be the center of the revived Nazi Reich, and he demanded Jordan's unconditional subordination to Rockwell's authority.

At first, Jordan feared that anti-American bias among defeated European Nazis would diminish Rockwell's effectiveness as the international leader of a resurgent National Socialism. Ludtke allayed Jordan's fears and established the strategic tone for responding to that objection among other National Socialists. According to Ludtke, they should emphasize a common Aryan National Socialist union of the future and downplay national identities entirely. Ludtke reassured Jordan that once Rockwell seized power in America, he would establish a National Socialist World Senate—Ludtke's idea—to internationalize the movement. But he warned that until European National Socialists accepted Rockwell's leadership and built up his international authority, their movement would stagnate.[15]

Ludtke demanded one hierarchy, one movement, one leader. By organizing, plotting, recruiting, and cajoling among the small circle of postwar European National Socialists, Ludtke helped deliver a unified Europe to his new American fuehrer. He condemned any European National Socialist movement that did not subordinate itself to the international movement's sole legitimate leader: George Lincoln Rockwell. He worked assiduously among his fellow

Europeans to affiliate national Nazi movements with WUNS, Rockwell's creation, as an affirmation of orthodoxy.[16] Ludtke's forceful personality, his iron will, the persuasiveness of his logic, the volume of his contacts, and the inspirational example of his willingness to suffer imprisonment and deprivation for the cause magnified his influence with Rockwell. He led no stormtroopers, headed no formal organization in Germany, and had no great resources to command. His power was that of the relentless fanatic in a movement built on possibilities and dreams.

In July 1962, Rockwell secretly traveled to England, via Ireland, to attend a clandestine meeting of National Socialist leaders from seven nations—the United States, Great Britain, West Germany, France, Austria, Ireland, and Belgium—in the remote countryside of the Cotswold hills of Gloucestershire. It was Rockwell's first face-to-face meeting with his host, Colin Jordan, his mentor, Bruno Ludtke, and the mysterious and hypnotic Savitri Devi. The preparatory work and initial contacts hardly anticipated the bond forged among those gathered at Cotswold. At that brief six-day conference, the participants drafted a consensus document, the Cotswold Agreements, that laid out a plan for National Socialist world revolution and the "final settlement of the Jewish problem." They also formed an organization, the World Union of National Socialists (WUNS), to implement the Cotswold plan.[17] Rockwell and Jordan left Cotswold as "co-leaders" of the movement, with Jordan in an honorific pro tempore superior position because of his seniority. But Rockwell clearly dominated the gathering. Within months Rockwell was the commander of WUNS in name as well as fact.[18]

The Cotswold Agreements were a bold statement that announced the formation of a "monolithic, combat efficient, international political apparatus to combat and utterly destroy the International Jewish Communist and Zionist apparatus of treason and subversion." WUNS pledged "an eventual world ORDER, based on RACE" and—using deliberate phrasing that conjured the unmistakable image of Hitler's failed "Final Solution"—a "final settlement of the Jewish problem." The Cotswold Agreements served as the WUNS constitution, and in defining the criteria for recognition of national affiliates, they stipulated that "no organization or individual failing to acknowledge the spiritual leadership of Adolf Hitler" would be admitted to membership.[19]

British authorities deported Rockwell from England on 9 August 1962 (unable to obtain a visa, he had entered the country illegally). News coverage of the Cotswold Conference focused on the photogenic and quotable young American Nazi, making Rockwell an international celebrity and the focus of intensified scrutiny by American and European law enforcement agencies.

Following the Cotswold Conference, the West German government, which

vigorously investigated any resurgence of National Socialism, focused its at-
tention on Bruno Ludtke. Feeling pressure from police agencies in the United
States and West Germany, Rockwell and Ludtke publicly represented the
Cotswold Agreements as a working draft rather than a legal document.
Rockwell, who always cooperated with the FBI and believed—rightly or not—
that the agency's director, J. Edgar Hoover, secretly sympathized with most
of his aims, now fed false information to the FBI about the nature of the
Cotswold Agreements because he feared prosecution under federal law re-
quiring the registration of an agent of a foreign country or political organization. Shortly after returning to the United States from England, Rockwell
wrote confidentially to Ludtke that the Cotswold Agreements should never
be referred to as anything but a proposed draft because he was convinced that
if he took a single order from Colin Jordan, federal law enforcement agents
in the United States would prosecute him as an unregistered agent of a foreign political party. His fears may have rested on tenuous legal ground, but
they were nonetheless real to him.

Ludtke had even more to fear. To alleviate legal pressure on himself and
other German National Socialists, he consistently maintained a tactical denial
that the Cotswold Agreements were anything more than a provisional draft.
Such denials enabled him to evade "the present prohibitory laws" on National
Socialist political activity in West Germany.[20] In reality, of course, the Cotswold
Agreements fully defined WUNS's structure and program and were honored
and enforced within the closed international Nazi community.

Operating exclusively by mail, Rockwell supervised Jordan's organizational
efforts at WUNS's European headquarters in England and encouraged the
formation of WUNS chapters through direct contact with potential Nazi leaders throughout the world. By 1965 the World Union of National Socialists had
operative chapters in nineteen countries. Throughout late 1962 and 1963,
Jordan faced prosecution and intermittent imprisonment in England for his
Nazi activities. He continued his WUNS efforts from Aylesbury Prison through
surrogates, primarily his chief deputy, John Tyndall, top aides Denis Pirie and
Peter Ling, and his wife, a beautiful aristocratic French Nazi named Françoise
Dior, the Comtesse R. H. de Caumont La Force. Jordan was able to maintain
his correspondence with Rockwell while in prison thanks to his elderly mother,
Bertha Beecham Jordan, who served as his courier, hand-delivering forbidden letters from Rockwell to Jordan and smuggling Jordan's replies out of
prison to send to Rockwell. Surviving letters between Rockwell and Jordan
reveal the toll taken on the movement in both countries by what Jordan and
Rockwell considered "government harassment." One 1963 Rockwell letter
complains that approximately two dozen ANP stormtroopers were in jail or

awaiting trial—a significant portion of Rockwell's total manpower, given what is now known of the limited number of stormtroopers available to him at any one time. As Rockwell confided to Jordan, the ANP had virtually no money and few dependable followers and operated largely on "guts, bluff and faith."[21]

Despite these difficulties, WUNS grew steadily from its founding, largely due to the combined impetus of Jordan's administrative and organizational skills and Rockwell's zealous advocacy. Less than two weeks after the close of the Cotswold Conference, Jordan contacted sympathetic organizations in several countries throughout Europe. By late 1963 WUNS had added chapters in South America—Argentina, Chile, and Uruguay—and in Puerto Rico, Italy, Sweden, Iceland, and Japan. Not all chapters survived, and not all chapters that survived flourished, but within a year and a half of the conference there was a revived Nazi presence, affiliated with WUNS and sworn to George Lincoln Rockwell as its leader, on every inhabited continent.[22] Although unable to provide financial assistance, Rockwell's ANP supplied significant quantities of printed material—books, flyers, pamphlets, posters, and stickers—to WUNS headquarters for distribution to affiliates worldwide.[23]

Few countries would grant Rockwell a visa, and his inability to travel abroad inhibited his capacity to guide WUNS's growth. In the spring of 1966, he complained to Jordan that he couldn't even travel to Canada and that travel outside North America was effectively banned. Directing an international movement in its nascent stages by mail and through proxies was cumbersome. When Yves Jeanne, a French Nazi, moved to replace Jordan as European commander of WUNS in 1964—probably a critical first move in seizing control of the organization from Rockwell—Rockwell had to rely on Bruno Ludtke and Jordan himself to put down the mutiny. Playing the game of internal intrigue with considerable skill, Ludtke verified and solidified Rockwell's support throughout the European chapters before Jordan informed Jeanne that the European command of WUNS was an appointment that could be made, or taken away, only by the international commander, George Lincoln Rockwell. Jordan made sure that Jeanne—and, more important, the other national leaders of WUNS chapters—understood that the challenge had failed. Suppression of this revolt solidified Rockwell's control as "supreme and final" commander.[24]

Rockwell made a concerted effort to locate former Nazis with ties to the Third Reich and incorporate them into WUNS. An intriguing effort in this regard involved Martin Bormann, the highest-ranking official of the Third Reich not accounted for at the end of World War II. If he were still alive, Bormann would be a showpiece of inestimable value and, perhaps, a source of much-needed funding. Although unconvinced of Bormann's potential value to their movement, Ludtke did Rockwell's bidding and exploited every contact available to him in the fugitive Nazi underground. In 1965, Ludtke reported to Rockwell that he had personally heard from a former SS officer that Bormann was still alive. No record exists of further correspondence between Ludtke and Rockwell on this matter, and Ludtke's intelligence seems to have been faulty, but Rockwell's esteem for architects of Hitler's Third Reich remained undiminished.[25]

Of the nineteen WUNS chapters recognized during Rockwell's lifetime, only one operated in the Middle East—in Lebanon—and one in Asia—in Japan. Jordan's wife, Françoise Dior, nurtured the organization of the Lebanese chapter through Antoine Jaouiche, a French expatriate living in Beirut. Rockwell's Japanese contacts actually predated WUNS. By 1960, Rockwell had been in communication with an ultranationalist right-wing group, the Greater Japan Patriotic Society, which advocated Japanese racial purity as a mirror image of Rockwell's doctrine of Aryan racial superiority and employed the swastika as its symbol. In November 1960, a seventeen-year-old society member assassinated the chairman of the Japanese Socialist party and then committed ritual suicide. Although Rockwell probably had nothing to do with the assassination, he praised it lavishly in the ANP newspaper and glorified the young assassin as a National Socialist revolutionary. The Greater Japan Patriotic Society remained in loose affiliation with WUNS, although it is unlikely that its leaders paid much heed to the international aspect of their work. For Rockwell, the society fit into his plans for world governance as his surrogates in an Asian "racial sphere" of command.[26]

WUNS found fertile ground in Scandinavia, forming active chapters in Sweden and Denmark. Rockwell always claimed an active WUNS chapter in Iceland, but no evidence exists to substantiate that claim.[27] WUNS efforts in Africa centered on South Africa, where the most extreme of several white supremacy organizations, the South African Anglo-Norman Union, expressed interest in being designated as South Africa's WUNS affiliate. Its leader, Ray K. Rudman, was skittish, however, about the open use of the swastika and remained on the fringe of WUNS for that reason.[28]

WUNS efforts in South America were most fruitful in Chile and Argentina, where open and active WUNS chapters flourished. In Chile, Franz Pfeiffer, a former SS colonel and the last commander of Hitler's Leibstandarte, drew on large numbers of Nazi exiles to create an active and, in the view of the Chilean government, an extremely dangerous National Socialist party, the Partido Nacionalsocialista Chileno. Pfeiffer impressed Rockwell, and Rockwell suggested to Jordan that Pfeiffer might be a suitable WUNS continental commander for all of South America. Pfeiffer's performance in a potentially devastating crisis particularly stirred Rockwell. Three months after Pfeiffer was named leader of WUNS-Chile, Chilean authorities arrested his closest friend and longtime comrade, Werner Rauff, and extradited him to West Germany on war crimes charges. West Germany accused Rauff, a top wartime aide to Adolf Eichmann, with personally murdering some ninety thousand Jews. Instead of abandoning Rauff, Pfeiffer openly defended him and hired a Chilean lawyer to fight the extradition order. In a letter to Rockwell during the crisis, Pfeiffer hinted that he was also considering employing physical force to free Rauff—which certainly would have further elevated his stature in Rockwell's eyes. In a letter to Ludtke, Rockwell described Pfeiffer as a leader who would "make history" some day.[29] When the Chilean government outlawed Pfeiffer's party and WUNS-Chile in late 1964, Pfeiffer refused to moderate his statements or curtail his activities. He was arrested and jailed in February 1965.[30]

As Chilean authorities shut down WUNS-Chile, Rockwell turned his South American focus to Argentina, where Horst Eichmann, Adolf Eichmann's son, headed the Argentine National Socialist party. Eichmann had a substantial following within the German expatriate community in Argentina and a recognized name worldwide, making him very useful to Rockwell, but he was never as fully loyal to Rockwell as was Franz Pfeiffer. Young Eichmann believed, with good cause, that he had greater visibility among South American Nazis than did Rockwell. In his view, a new fuehrer would more likely emerge from the German enclaves of South America than from suburban Virginia. Rockwell tolerated Eichmann because his name had value, but he never really controlled him. With Franz Pfeiffer in jail, WUNS in South America never reached the potential Rockwell expected of it.[31]

Rockwell's prospects in two promising English-speaking countries—Australia and Canada—were limited by aggressive anti-Nazi governmental action, including vigorous prosecution of WUNS operatives under laws designed to control racist and revolutionary political movements. Australia tantalized Rockwell. He believed it to be fertile ground for his doctrines. Howard Williams, an American living in Australia and a trusted Rockwell disciple, led WUNS's organizational efforts there. On Williams's recommendation, Rockwell named Arthur Smith (a.k.a. Paul Martin) leader of WUNS-Australia, a mysterious career criminal and fanatical Nazi named Briam Raven provided a dimension of physical intimidation to the Australian Nazis' arsenal. But thorough investigation of Nazi activities and effective prosecution of Smith kept the leadership of WUNS-Australia in disarray and, more often than not, in prison, muting any impact Rockwell hoped to have on Australian politics.[32]

Early Rockwell efforts in Canada, from 1961 to 1965, were in cooperation with Andre Bellfeuille's Canadian Nazi party. Rockwell had appointed Bellfeuille's deputy, Janos Pall, the first international secretary of the World Union of Free Enterprise National Socialist, the predecessor organization to WUNS, and Pall had helped Rockwell with the initial organization of WUNS. Bellfeuille's Canadian Nazi party was the first WUNS-Canada chapter.[33] But infighting among the Canadian racist right fragmented the small support base of the movement, and by 1965 Rockwell faced the unpleasant task of choosing among diminished and rival racist groups as the WUNS designate— Bellfeuille's CNP, Jacques Taylor's Canadian National Socialist party, and Don Andrews's Western Guard party. Instead, he took a chance on John Beattie, a dynamic newcomer to the political wars of the racist right. Selecting Beattie as leader of WUNS-Canada—although practical political concerns negated the actual designation of Beattie as such—proved a wise decision. Ludtke, who guided Rockwell to the right choice, said of the young Beattie: "That is the face of the Canadian Hitler."[34]

By early 1966, Beattie had consolidated much of the Canadian racist right around his leadership and was one of the few bright spots in Rockwell's world order. Rockwell met regularly with his protégé and reported on Beattie's progress to Colin Jordan. Rockwell described Beattie's organizational success, careful to stipulate that while Beattie's skills were second to Jordan's—a concession to Jordan's fragile ego—his implementation of their legal, political, and psychological strategies in Canada made Beattie their most useful national agent. Rockwell concluded that Beattie suffered from the usual lack of funds that plagued the movement everywhere but managed to continue the struggle despite adversity.[35]

Europe contained the largest concentration of WUNS chapters, but some, including those in Hungary, Italy, and Switzerland, appear to have been chapters in name only, with no active organization and limited, if any, public programs.[36] Ireland and Spain had moderately active chapters but failed to meet Rockwell's expectations primarily because of strong government opposition. The failure of the Irish National Union particularly disappointed Rockwell. The Irish Nazis had expressed tacit approval of the principles contained in the Cotswold Agreements but refused to endorse them publicly. They pleaded with Colin Jordan to intercede with Rockwell and explain to him that they were too "young and weak" to carry the movement to the streets. Rockwell patiently replied that although he well understood the limitations of emerging national Nazi movements, "the way to get old and strong is not to remain in hiding in cellars." It wasn't until Bernard E. Horgan took command of WUNS-Ireland in 1966 that political and propaganda activities became visible, although they never matched Rockwell's lofty expectations.[37] WUNS-Spain was organized and led by a German expatriate and Third Reich veteran named Friedrich

Kuhfuss. While Kuhfuss remained the de facto leader of the organization, he put forth his deputy, Antonio Madrano, a native Spaniard, as the nominal leader to avoid the appearance of foreign, especially German, intrusion into Spain's internal politics.[38]

England, France, and Belgium boasted the largest, strongest, and most active WUNS chapters in Europe.[39] England's National Socialist Movement, under Colin Jordan, was relentless in the production and distribution of racist and anti-Semitic propaganda, capturing public notice through demonstrations of all sorts and recruiting young members by proselytizing among Britain's disaffected working-class whites. Jordan benefited from a talented and committed cadre of NSM deputies—John Tyndall, Roland Kerr-Ritchie, Denis Pirie, Peter Ling, J. D. F. Knight, and Gordon Hingston—and the active support of his mother and his wife. Still, the English movement was riddled by feuds and infighting, no less fractious and volatile than its American counterpart. Over the course of his career, Jordan fought with everyone he worked with except for his mother and Rockwell. Jealous of his own position and power, virtually to the point of paranoia, he deferred only to Rockwell, and his deference was complete and slavish.[40]

Second only to England among WUNS chapters, and frequently in open competition for European dominance, was the incendiary French National Socialist movement, led by the volatile Yves Jeanne. Even before the Cotswold Conference, Rockwell attempted to foster the emergence of a National Socialist movement in France. Bruno Ludtke believed that France, not England, would be the centerpiece of a Nazi resurgence in Europe, and he pressed that view on Rockwell. Ludtke predicted that the Continental countries—Germany, France, Holland, Belgium, Denmark, Norway, and Sweden— would gradually join with the United States and Iceland in a National Socialist Nordic Confederation but that Great Britain would be the last Jewish stronghold in Europe. In early 1962, Ludtke urged Rockwell to focus the movement's limited resources on France. Even more than in his native Germany, where his activities were closely proscribed, Ludtke took an active hand in encouraging and organizing the movement in France.[41] Two women, Savitri Devi and the Comtesse R. H. de Caumont La Force—prior to her marriage to Colin Jordan—provided the organizational impetus, and probably the funds, to form WUNS-France in 1962. Devi represented France at the Cotswold Conference. Françoise Dior, the privileged daughter of a wealthy and influential family, brought her ample checkbook and connections to the French aristocracy to the effort. She brought into the movement Claude Normand (in reality, Claude Janne, a former Waffen SS officer who commanded a French SS unit on the Eastern Front during World War II and was known in WUNS circles as "the old fighter"). Normand, along with his secretary and confidant, Anne Houel, and his deputy, Raymond Dubois, formed the first leadership cadre of WUNS-France in 1963.[42]

In 1964, Yves Jeanne took control of WUNS-France amid a concerted crackdown on Nazi agitation by the French government. By the summer of that year, government pressure was so intense that Jeanne suspended most party activities. Shortly thereafter, he started moving against his European superior, Colin Jordan, in an attempt to seize control of WUNS-Europe. As discussed earlier, Rockwell backed Jordan and Jeanne's coup failed. He remained affiliated with WUNS until 1966, when the French chapter distanced itself from WUNS under intensified governmental pressure. But his grab for power had permanently split the movement in France, with Savitri Devi siding with Jeanne and Françoise Dior remaining loyal to Jordan, whom she had married in October 1963 (and from whom she was divorced in October 1966).[43]

Yves Jeanne's ambition not only disrupted WUNS efforts in France but in Belgium as well. The first leader of WUNS-Belgium was J. R. Debbaudt, editor of *L'Europe Reele,* a right-wing Brussels newspaper. Debbaudt was intelligent, articulate, and committed to the cause. Like France's Claude Normand—who may have introduced Debbaudt to Colin Jordan—Debbaudt fought for the Third Reich on the Eastern Front as commander of the Walloon Legion of the Waffen SS. Along with his deputies, Nicholas Janssens and Henri Devos, Debbaudt made reasonable headway in locating and recruiting former Nazis and Nazi sympathizers for WUNS.[44] In 1965, Jeanne attempted to consolidate all French-speaking National Socialists under one command, and he proposed to Rockwell and Jordan that command boundaries, which normally followed national boundaries, be altered to incorporate the French-speaking regions of Belgium under his command. Fearful of alienating the most important WUNS chapter in Europe, Rockwell acquiesced.

Infuriated by the usurpation of his command, Debbaudt resigned from WUNS. Rockwell, who was left with no leader in a critical chapter, followed Jordan's recommendation and appointed Rudiger van Sande to fill the vacancy. Van Sande, whose devotion to Rockwell eclipsed his abilities, swept out Debbaudt's carefully constructed team and replaced it with his own—Deputy Leader Eduard Verlinden, Charles Bertrand, Hermann Wachtelaer, and Ronal Hall.[45] Bruno Ludtke did not like or respect van Sande and urged Rockwell to pursue Leon Degrelle, another former Belgian SS officer and a man much like J. R. Debbaudt. Degrelle, an SS Standartenfuehrer, had been decorated for bravery in Russia during World War II, and in Ludtke's view he had the character and the stature to sustain WUNS's momentum in Belgium.

Ignoring Ludtke's advice, Rockwell chose van Sande, head of the Belgian

National Socialist Union, to succeed Debbaudt.[46] Within months of assuming leadership of WUNS-Belgium, van Sande was fired by his German-based employer, Gestetner, Ltd. Belgian police raided his house in the first action of what would become a major acceleration of anti-Nazi actions in Belgium. By late summer 1965, van Sande—unemployed and with a wife and three children to support—found himself the head of a decimated organization, a wrecked shadow of what only months before had been WUNS's showpiece of Europe.

Van Sande's limited abilities— Ludtke judged him a "low-witted man"— were not up to the challenge of rebuilding the party in a hostile political environment. Rockwell relieved him of his command and elevated van Sande's deputy, Eduard Verlinden. But the events of 1966 had left WUNS-Belgium disorganized and ineffective. As in most countries where Rockwell attempted to build the nucleus of a Fourth Reich, his efforts in Belgium were undermined by a devastating combination of incompetent or traitorous subordinates and intense, concerted governmental harassment.[47]

Germany, the Fatherland, the sacred site of the world's only National Socialist state, held a place apart in Rockwell's organization. Anti-Nazi laws, enacted under Allied supervision by the West German government after World War II, were stricter in West Germany than anywhere else in the world, so WUNS activities had to be underground and clandestine. But a worldwide resurgence of National Socialism in which Germany did not figure prominently was unthinkable to Rockwell. In 1961 he had received a letter from a German who had been sent copies of Rockwell's literature by Savitri Devi. That German was Bruno Ludtke, who soon became an ardent Rockwell disciple and his most trusted confidant. Most important to Rockwell's early efforts in Germany was Ludtke's offer to translate ANP literature into German and to distribute that literature among Nazi sympathizers inside Germany. The dissemination of Nazi propaganda was illegal in West Germany at that time, but Ludtke resolutely spread Rockwell's message at great peril to himself. The de facto head of WUNS-Germany, Ludtke maintained close but secret contact with Nazis throughout West Germany. He wrote to Rockwell that, for them, his words were "like the rain, going down to the thirsty ground."[48]

Ludtke worked tirelessly to gather in his former comrades to swell Rockwell's flock, and he offered Rockwell abundant advice on organizing throughout Europe, sending him regular, detailed reports.[49] From 1962 until Rockwell's death in 1967, Ludtke functioned as Rockwell's eyes and ears in Europe, providing Rockwell with more complete and perceptive intelligence than he received from any other source. Ludtke was also Rockwell's inspiration, "nobly" proving that in the spiritual Fatherland, where open expression of National Socialism was banned, it was still possible to defy legal repression.[50]

It is impossible to quantify Ludtke's effectiveness in Germany or to measure the extent of Rockwell's impact on sustaining the flame of National Socialism among the defeated Nazis who still secretly harbored Hitler's dream. But a letter Rockwell received in 1963 from a German citizen may give some clue to the feelings he stirred in a silent and unknown number of Germans. The man wrote after seeing Rockwell on German television: "If Hitler is dead, or if he is still [living] yet, makes no difference, he is still [living] under us for all the Times. 33 years ago I read *Mein Kampf*. It is my bible. Now I read it always yet."[51] That solitary German was able to connect his deepest feelings to others of like mind through Ludtke and Rockwell. Making that connection, for unknown and unknowable numbers of Nazis in postwar Germany and worldwide, kept the flickering flame of Hitler's dream alive.

9

WHITE POWER

*It's hard for me . . . to contradict Hitler on this White Unity busi-
ness, unless we do it intelligently and in a manner to WIN people,
not to piss them off.*
—George Lincoln Rockwell, 1966

The crowd wasn't big, but it was enthusiastic. The people
sat in semicircular rows of chairs and talked excitedly among themselves as they
waited for the man they'd come to hear—George Lincoln Rockwell—to be introduced. They were well dressed and looked prosperous, "comfortably situ-
ated," in the parlance of the time. Some were downright affluent. The audience, white and mostly suburbanites, didn't flinch at the word "nigger." These
were the type of people Rockwell hoped to sway into open support: Birchites,
White Citizens' Council members, the polished, better-educated cousins of
rural Klansmen. He believed that he was close to a major breakthrough in 1965.
The turmoil of the early civil rights movement set people throughout the South
on edge, especially the kind of people sitting that night waiting for Rockwell.
From Montgomery to Little Rock, southerners saw their way of life, their cher-
ished social customs, their inviolate racial prerogatives challenged and dis-
mantled. Black radicals, stirred up by outside agitators and backed up by federal marshals dispatched by northern liberals, were integrating the schools, the
stores, the restaurants, the buses and trains. Few imagined that the South's
peculiar social customs, which had stood as a formidable bulwark of white supremacy since the Redemption of the 1870s, would fall so far, or so fast. The
changes frightened and infuriated them. The kind of people sitting in the audience that evening probably weren't in the crowds that brutalized the Freedom Riders in 1961, or along the dark dirt road of rural Mississippi when Freedom Summer ended for Michael Schwerner, Andrew Goodman, and James
Chaney, but they probably watched from a safe distance and reassured each
other that these troublemakers had gotten what they deserved.

In 1965, Rockwell stood as a candidate for governor of Virginia. The street
demonstrator and self-proclaimed Nazi hadn't changed since he began his

racist agitation in the late 1950s. Maybe the people in his audience hadn't changed all that much either, though they seemed somehow less repelled by his crude racism. They took no offense at his depiction of African Americans as "burr-heads" and were amused when he taunted and ridiculed Martin Luther King Jr., the first native southerner to be honored with the Nobel Peace Prize.

Candidate Rockwell had initiated a subtle but significant political metamorphosis. He referred to Adolf Hitler less frequently, substituting laudatory allusions to George Wallace and Orville Faubus. The swastika was nowhere in sight, save for a small gold lapel pin—and that too would be gone by mid-campaign. American Nazi party stormtroopers, shorn of uniform and swagger, were transformed into neatly dressed, clean-cut "campaign aides." The crowd applauded politely when Rockwell was introduced, smiled and nodded in agreement as he warmed to his theme. Perhaps some were even surprised at how much they agreed with this Nazi.

Rockwell was trying out a new approach he had perfected before audiences of affluent "closet" supporters throughout the South the year before. The lines come smoothly after months of practice. "As Governor of Virginia," he declares, lowering his voice and leaning his lanky frame over the podium, "I [would] have pardon powers. And if one of my men gets carried away and shoots a nigger agitator"—a smile plays on his lips as titters ripple through the crowd—"why I can send for him on the way to the electric chair, pardon him, and have him over for dinner at the Executive Mansion that night!" The applause and hoots are loud and sustained. Rockwell grins. As the din subsides, Rockwell assures the crowd, "We're going to have nice peaceful niggers like we used to in Virginia!"[1]

It is impossible to pinpoint just when Rockwell decided that the road to power was shorter and surer through the exploitation of racial hatred than through anti-Semitism. But in 1965 he moved in that direction. The vehicle he chose to traverse that road was built by grafting a unique twist onto an old theme. Rockwell certainly did not abandon anti-Semitism in 1965 or mute his virulence—"demonic Jews" still held center stage in his personal odeum of evil—but he employed a new strategic emphasis on blacks to exploit the racial tension rapidly rising in America. He had long predicted that race war was inevitable, followed closely by economic chaos as the "manipulators of capital"—the Jews—withdrew their American investments for more secure environs. According to Rockwell, race war and economic cataclysm would destroy the postwar political order as white Americans sought a strong leader to suppress savage blacks and bring order to a ravaged economy. That scenario, he believed, would usher in the Nazi era, with him as its authoritarian white savior. Working Americans, terrorized by rampaging blacks and demoralized by the loss of savings and security, would abandon failed liberal democracy and embrace Rockwell's National Socialist alternative. He was very realistic about the necessity of societal chaos as a precursor to his rise to power. The FBI quotes him as observing to a comrade: "You can't make a revolutionary out of a guy with two cars and an electric lawn mower and a fur toilet seat."[2] When race riots erupted in scores of American cities during the summer of 1965, Rockwell had to believe that his dreams were unfolding at last.

Rockwell had planned his 1965 run for governor of Virginia at least a year in advance. He wrote to Bruno Ludtke in January 1964 that a such a campaign would be a useful tactical device to inflame Jewish opposition, thereby garnering the media attention he believed his movement needed in order to grow.[3] The outbreak of race-based urban violence in the summer of 1965 confirmed, for Rockwell, the fortuitousness of his timing. He used "white unity" as the central motif of his campaign and hammered it home throughout the summer. "There is exactly *one* way for us to win," he told an exuberant crowd in the closing weeks of the campaign, "and that is to fight on racial grounds; to think, to act, above all, to *vote* as *whites* and nothing else."[4] Rockwell anticipated strong black support for the Democratic nominee, Mills Godwin, Virginia's lieutenant governor. Since the Republican party was very weak in Virginia in 1965, Rockwell believed that if he could position himself, an independent candidate, as the only credible advocate of white supremacy, and if the right circumstances polarized the Virginia electorate along racial lines, he stood a chance of winning the election.[5] He expressed the belief that victory in the gubernatorial race was a real possibility to a nonpolitical, longtime friend while his campaign was in its earliest planning stage. Throughout his career, Rockwell steadfastly maintained that the vast majority of American whites secretly agreed with him but lacked the courage to do so openly.[6]

The size and enthusiasm of the crowds he attracted during the campaign surprised and pleased Rockwell. They were minuscule by traditional standards but must have seemed gargantuan to Rockwell when compared to the dozen or so people he was used to addressing. His natural optimism led him to overestimate his chances. When the campaign was just getting underway, Rockwell reported to Colin Jordan that an unidentified Philadelphia radio station estimated that he had a 50-50 chance of winning. He seems to have convinced himself of the accuracy of that unlikely assessment and told Jordan that Mills Godwin, the eventual winner, would be fatally damaged by his support for equal treatment for Virginia's blacks. Dismissing the Republican candidate's chances, Rockwell reasoned that he could possibly, with luck, capture the governorship of Virginia.[7]

When Rockwell wrote to Jordan four months later, in the midst of the campaign, he was not so optimistic. He expressed bitterness over the failure of white supremacists to embrace him as the white alternative to the integrationist Godwin. Instead, they entered a competing racist slate of candidates, which forced those people Rockwell took to be his natural constituency to choose between two candidates. As usual, Rockwell overestimated his acceptability— even to racists—as a political alternative. He complained about having to battle fellow racists in addition to battling "the Jews, niggers and Democrats."[8]

On 3 November 1965, Rockwell picked up approximately 6,500 votes and was not a factor in the outcome of the election. The result shocked and greatly disappointed him; within a matter of days he had written to Bruno Ludtke, sharing with him this latest defeat. Three weeks later, he was putting a positive spin on the results, telling a student audience at the University of North Dakota that "with a budget of $15,000, with a total press blackout, and with a 'Kosher conservative' [splitting the vote] . . . I got 7,000 people to vote for a Nazi."[9] Despite his paltry showing, Rockwell believed he had discovered the key to mass political appeal: white unity in a racially polarized electorate. Of course, this strategy had been practiced by racist southern politicians for generations. Rockwell's innovation was far less significant as a political strategy than as a method for racists to mainstream their political careers.

During 1966, the last full year of his life, Rockwell monitored America's troubled racial landscape for a crisis to exploit, a hatred to aggravate, a strain to intensify. That fall, at Brown University, he again described the scenario that he believed would lead to his rise to power—race riots and economic disruption. With racial conflict seemingly spreading from city to city, he turned to the second ingredient in his prescription: "They have already taken the gold from your paper money. Then they took the silver from your paper money. Now they've taken the silver from your silver and you've got phony money." Rockwell seemed to be predicting, either through astuteness or, more likely, sheer luck, the inflation that would grip the United States in the next decade. "This is what they did in Germany . . . and catastrophic inflation is not far ahead." But Rockwell had a cure for the coming troubles. "When you finally get a good dose of it," he predicted, "when you get all you're going to take of Negroes pushing you, and when you get all you're going to take of rotten, phony money that's worthless, then you're going to be looking for somebody to put a stop to it."[10]

In the summer of 1966, Stokely Carmichael, the fiery leader of the Student Nonviolent Coordinating Committee, coined the phrase "Black Power" to describe the sociopolitical objectives of the militant young blacks who came to maturity as activists in Martin Luther King Jr. civil rights struggles of the past decade. Immediately, Rockwell seized on the political value of positioning himself as Carmichael's opposite. For Rockwell, and for many middle-class white Americans, Stokely Carmichael and his followers embodied the pervasive racist stereotype of aggressive, violence-prone blacks. All the negrophobic mythology crafted over centuries to alienate white Americans from black Americans reinforced that stereotype and allowed demagogues like Rockwell to manipulate myth and fear to their advantage.

As a talented adapter and pitchman, Rockwell had a knack for coming up with the right phrase, the right slogan, the right image in a well-timed publicity campaign. During a few weeks in the summer of 1966, the "Black Power" slogan was ubiquitous in newspapers, magazines, on radio, and on television; it was accompanied in print and on television by Carmichael's intense, angular face and his upthrust, clenched fist. This image energized militant blacks and enraged militant whites. As reaction to Carmichael and the Black Power movement polarized along racial lines, Rockwell recognized his opportunity and seized it. He promoted "White Power" as the antidote to black excesses. By midsummer, the "White Power" counterslogan was taken up by whites, both the fearful and the hateful, across the country.[11]

Had Rockwell done nothing more than create a slogan, even one that would endure long after his death, his impact on the racist right would have been minimal. But, as conceived by Rockwell, "White Power" symbolized a new concept of race unity, one that carried the potential of a new majoritarian movement in U.S. politics. Rockwell had long grappled with the need for National Socialism to broaden its appeal in order to evolve into a viable political movement. In a letter to Bruno Ludtke in early 1965 he wrote that the primary aim of such a movement must be white racial political unity. He identified this strategic initiative as "fundamental" to their success.[12]

Rockwell developed and promoted a concept of white unity based on "pan-white" inclusion.[13] As such, his "white race" differed markedly from Hitler's, which was exclusively Nordic-Germanic, and from the "white race" of most previous and contemporary American white supremacists, which was and is nativist and Protestant. For his part, Rockwell saw a struggle in which "the dark peoples of the earth, led by the Jews" outnumbered "us"—as Rockwell referred to those who were neither "dark" nor Jew—by a "ratio of 7:1." The two forces— Rockwell's "dark people" and "white people"—were locked in a cataclysmic struggle for mastery of the earth. Moreover, survival, not just mastery, was at stake.[14]

Given the dimensions of that struggle, the outnumbered whites, in Rockwell's view, could not afford to exclude anyone who was not clearly of the "dark peoples." In other words, exclusion of Catholics or of Slavs, Greeks, and other foreign-born whites was strategic folly for the beleaguered and outnumbered white race. Especially in the United States, where immigrant "whites" and "whites" of southern or Eastern European extraction outnumbered Anglo-Saxons in many parts of the country, a political movement that did not appeal to them was doomed. By 1965, Rockwell had decided that his task was more complex than Hitler's. Unlike Hitler, who developed the Nazi theories of race in a largely homogeneous prewar Germany, Rockwell had to make his definition of the "white race" more inclusive than Hitler's or reconcile himself to permanent status as a powerless gadfly. Not surprisingly, he chose to deviate from Hitler's racial dogma. In so doing, he created a valuable strategic legacy for future white racists but also caused a painful and costly rift among his hard-core Nazi following.

While the validity of race as a biological construct has many challengers, none deny its power as a sociological concept.[15] As sociological concepts, racial distinctions and race boundaries are time- and culture-bound. Hitler and his Nazi theoreticians dealt with the term "race" in its nineteenth-century context, which was more akin to ethnicity than to the late twentieth-century understanding of the term. They posited a systematic grouping of the earth's "races" within a hierarchical structure in which the Germans—the "master race"—together with their ethnic cousins—northern European Anglo-Saxons and Scandinavians—stood above the less-blessed "races," in descending order: the Mediterranean peoples, the Slavs, the Asiatics, and the blacks. At the very bottom of the hierarchy—even, perhaps, beyond the pale of humanity—was the "Jewish race." For the Nazi true believer, that racial dogma was unalterable and unchallengeable. It was a revealed truth, the acceptance of which defined a Nazi. As Hitler's American heir, Rockwell accepted it and preached it, but by 1965 he had come to view it as a fatal impediment to his political ambition. Perhaps it is a testament to his intellectual flexibility, or merely an insight into his moral rootlessness, but whatever his motivation Rockwell jettisoned Hitler's sacred dogma.

With his recasting of the "white race" to include multitudinous Americans of southern and Eastern European ethnicity, especially the Slavic peoples—Poles and Russians—and the Mediterranean peoples—Italians, Greeks, Spaniards, and Turks—Rockwell brought about a rupture in the American Nazi party. His young propaganda chief, John Patler, was the son of Greek immigrants, Christ and Athena Patsalos. He was short and swarthy, with jet-black hair and dark eyes. Visually, Patler was the antithesis of the Nazi Nordic warrior. His presence in the party's inner circle never sat well with Rockwell's right-hand man, the Germanophilic Matt Koehl. But Rockwell liked Patler, so Patler stayed. Patler defended Rockwell's new expansive definition of the "master race," which convinced Koehl and his supporters that the commander had been influenced by the only party insider who stood to benefit by the heresy. Matt Koehl respected and followed Rockwell, but he worshiped Adolf Hitler. Rockwell's deviation from Hitler's dogma was, to Koehl, an abomination—one that was shared by a small but influential circle within the ANP hierarchy: namely, William L. Pierce, Frank Drager, and Alan Welch. The ANP leadership thus split into two factions in 1965. The "Aryan Unity" faction, led by Koehl, demanded strict adherence to the literal teachings of Hitler on race. They held firmly to Nordic-Germanic racial superiority and regarded "darker" whites like Patler to be inferior. The "White Power" faction, led by Rockwell, was increasingly drawn to the practical considerations of majoritarian politics and unconcerned with the restrictions of dogmatic orthodoxy.

Rockwell could ill afford a rupture in his small party. He demanded that the abrasive Patler not antagonize the Hitler purists. He wrote to Patler, "[Hitler] preached what these guys are hung up on," and instructed him to work "quietly and diplomatically" to heal the schism. At the same time, Rockwell had no intention of retreating from his decision to preach a decidedly non-Hitlerian form of white unity under his new "White Power" banner. Stand firm, he promised Patler, and "we will make White Unity the biggest thing in history."[16] Eventually, Rockwell prevailed. It was, after all, his party. He suppressed Koehl's potential mutiny and led his men to Chicago where, bedecked in their new "White Power" T-shirts, they prepared to confront Martin Luther King and those marching for open housing.[17]

In 1966, Chicago was the largest of America's most segregated northern cities. It was there, in the Polish-American and Italian-American enclaves of the southwest side of Chicago, around Gage and Marquette Parks, that King announced he would lead a demonstration for open housing. "The time for 'creative tension' had arrived in Chicago," he said.[18] By 1966 King's civil rights movement had stalled somewhat, with a number of black leaders whispering that his time had passed. New militant black champions were impatient with King's tactics of passive resistance and argued that he was irrelevant in the hard streets of the nation's urban black ghettos.[19] King went to Chicago to prove them wrong.

Rockwell saw King's march in Chicago as the perfect opportunity to field-test his "White Power" strategy. There was no question that King would meet with local opposition, most likely violent opposition. The people who saw King's presence as a violation of their neighborhood—working-class whites, Poles and Italians, factory hands, steelworkers, housewives—were the people Rockwell hoped to coalesce under his "White Power" banner to form a new racial majority. When King marched on 5 August 1966, the local resistance he encountered, both in magnitude and intensity, shocked even the most battle-hard-ened veterans of the southern civil rights marches. A King aide, Andrew Young, compared what the demonstrators experienced in Chicago with the riots they had survived in the South. "The violence in the South always came from a rabble element," Young said. "But these"—referring to the Gage Park rioters—"were women and children and husbands and wives coming out of their homes and becoming a mob—and in some ways it was far more frightening."[20] More than a thousand local residents pelted King's marchers with bricks and bottles while shouting racist slogans and waving Confederate and Nazi flags. When a rock struck King above his right ear, the crowd cheered. The dominant chant among the whites lining the route of King's march was "White Power." By the time the marchers reached Gage Park, the number of hostile residents had swollen to 2,500. Several ANP banners were visible in the crowd. One woman, a local housewife, was heard to say, "God, I hate niggers and nigger-lovers."[21]

Rockwell was everywhere that day, up and down the route of the march, egging on the crowd, distributing "White Power" T-shirts and posters, climb-ing on the hood of a parked car to exhort the crowd through his bullhorn, di-recting his stormtroopers as they funneled the curious from the side streets to the march route and then on to Gage Park. "I've never seen anything like it," a weary and disheartened King told reporters later. "I've been in many demonstrations all across the South, . . . [and] I have never seen—even in Mississippi and Alabama—mobs as hostile and as hate-filled."[22] King failed in Chicago and Rockwell triumphed, at least on the surface. ANP banners and "White Power" T-shirts and signs were the dominant images conveyed across the nation by the media.

Wherever King went in Chicago, Rockwell shadowed him, reaping enor-mous publicity for days on end. For many Americans, highlights of Rockwell's harangues telecast on the evening news provided their first actual exposure to him. They heard him attack the "nigger scum" invading the good, clean, white neighborhoods of Chicago—and they heard the wild cheers of several thousand Chicagoans. Rockwell's arrest on charges of disorderly conduct, and another arrest ten days later for marching without a permit, garnered him even more publicity.

Rockwell seemed to accomplish in Chicago what no other racist leader of his generation had even attempted. To Rockwell, and to many of his follow-ers, he seemed to be on the brink of mobilizing the white majority that would make him a major political force in the United States.[23] One pro-ANP racist leader called Rockwell's performance in Chicago the "apex moment" of the 1960s.[24] But that victory proved illusory. Chicago's white ethnic population embraced his slogan and, in the momentary flush of battle, even embraced

Rockwell, but when King left Chicago and the passion of the moment passed, those who had marched and jeered along with Rockwell now rejected him, embarrassed in much the same way that a righteous man awaking from a drunken stupor in the bed of a painted harlot is embarrassed.

Rockwell didn't appreciate how shallow his victory in Chicago really was and became more determined than ever to pursue his "White Power" strategy to the fullest. In late 1966 he decided to change the name of his party, abandoning the swastika and all other Nazi trappings. When he consulted his most trusted adviser, Bruno Ludtke, on this anticipated move, Ludtke agreed with the logic of discarding symbols both men had come to understand would always be alien in America, an impediment to the attainment of political power. "'White Power' is a much more appropriate fighting symbol for our times and particularly [for] you in America," Ludtke wrote. "Hitler would most heartily approve."[25] On 1 January 1967, by edict of the commander, the name of the American Nazi party was officially changed to the National Socialist White People's party. Rockwell told top party leaders that "the time had come to change the party's image . . . to an American White People's movement" and announced the publication of a new mass-circulation newspaper, *White Power*.[26] He also began work on the final draft of his new book, *White Power*, to be published in early 1967.

Rockwell's legacy to future racists and the significance of his "White Power" phase was in creating a theoretical and strategic framework that enabled American racists to broaden their appeal to working- and middle-class ethnic white Americans who were reluctant to affiliate with Nordic-Germanic neo-Nazi movements or with organizations like the Ku Klux Klan that were steeped in the nativist-Protestant tradition. Under the "White Power" banner, Catholics, Italians, Poles, Greeks, Armenians, Turks, Spaniards, Russians—anyone who was not visibly "black" or a Jew—could find a place in Rockwell's "master race." Rockwell changed the definition of "white people" from select ethnic strains with a narrow range of religious beliefs to any American who was not born a Jew and did not have the outward physical characteristics of an African American. Other racist leaders were certainly moving in that direction by the mid-1960s, but Rockwell forced his definition on the racist right by the drama of his actions and gave his conception a rallying cry and a slogan that endured.

According to Robert Smith, secretary of the Nationalist Party of Canada, Rockwell's work formed "an ideological base" for "White Nationalists" internationally. Smith wrote in 1991 that Rockwell's book was held to be a classic in racist circles. It "explain[s] racial politics and reality from a modern-day layman's viewpoint," says Smith.[27] *White Power* directly shaped the philosophy of a later generation of more sophisticated racists like David Duke and even after thirty years was "considered the Bible of hardened racists and anti-Semites."[28] "[It] is still my best seller," Edward R. Fields, a prolific publisher of racist books, said in 1991. "The Skinheads are crazy for it. . . . It's kind of a bible of the Skinhead movement. It's a very powerful book, the most powerful thing I've ever read in my life."[29] Without a doubt, the force of Rockwell's imagery in *White Power* and the inclusiveness of his definition of "white people" have extended his influence to new generations of racists. He gathered to him those Hitler would have rejected, permitting them—and their children—to hate as "white people." In doing so, he changed the face of racism in America.

10 | HOLOCAUST DENIAL

I don't believe for one minute that any 6,000,000 Jews were exterminated by Hitler. It never happened. The photographs you've seen passed off as pictures of dead Jews are frauds, pure and simple.
—George Lincoln Rockwell, 1966

Adolf Hitler's vision of a National Socialist world order did not die with him in Berlin in April 1945. Those who survived him and those who followed him kept his vision alive among small bands of supporters in East and West Germany and throughout the world. True believers understood that military defeat was not necessarily permanent. They based their worldview on age-old instincts—totalitarianism and anti-Semitism—and believed that they could, in time, rehabilitate, repackage, and resurrect that worldview as a political force. The horror of the Holocaust impeded that resurrection.

Nothing in humankind's recent memory equaled the barbarity of Hitler's minions as they methodically implemented his "Final Solution." As the story of the death camps unfolded in the months after the war ended, and the enormity of the Nazis' crimes against humanity became apparent to the world, revulsion enveloped the Nazi regime. Photographs and films seared the world's collective memory with images of mounds of emaciated corpses, the deadened eyes in the skeletal faces of camp survivors, piles of eyeglasses, shoes, and human hair. Haunting celluloid images of the Jews of Europe, captured on film as they arrived at the death camps, testified to the genocide. Scenes so horrific that they defied comprehension condemned the Nazis and discredited their beliefs and symbols. The Holocaust laid bare before the world the consequence of state-sanctioned anti-Semitism and damned political systems built on hatred of Jews. The Holocaust linked nazism and fascism with the slaughter of innocents. For those who created the Third Reich, and for those who mourned its passing, the Holocaust condemned their political passions with the record of their deeds.

The Holocaust scholar Deborah Lipstadt correctly identifies the historic memory of the Holocaust as the single greatest impediment to a resurrection of nazism in the postwar world. Hitler's heirs understood that before his crusade could be resumed, "this blot must be removed." They would have to alter the historic memory and absolve nazism of Hitler's sins in order to "reintroduce it as a viable political system."[1] They would have to deny the very existence of the Holocaust and turn the condemnation of the world away from them and toward the Jews. To do so, postwar Nazis had to recast the Holocaust as a Jewish invention and evidence of Jewish perfidy.

George Lincoln Rockwell, the first postwar American neo-Nazi leader to appreciate the strategic necessity of Holocaust denial, incorporated it as a regular component of his propaganda program. Although Willis Carto, a Rockwell contemporary and ally, is generally regarded as the progenitor of American Holocaust denial, Rockwell preceded Carto in recognizing its value as a propaganda tool and may have actually influenced Carto in that direction, although the latter contention is speculative in the absence of documentation.[2] Clearly verifiable, however, is Rockwell's pivotal role in utilizing the media to disseminate Holocaust denial propaganda among anti-Semites and the general public. Rockwell's popularization of Holocaust denial propaganda, through crude parody and the manipulation of mass-circulation magazines—notably *Playboy*—far exceeded Carto's efforts.

Before World War II—and, more significant, before the Holocaust—anti-Semitism was deep and widespread in the United States.[3] In the decade before the outbreak of World War II, American pro-Nazi and pro-fascist organizations proliferated. These groups, which promoted anti-Semitism as a core doctrine, attracted numbers of followers that would be unmatched by neo-Nazi organizations in postwar America. Dozens of groups—most prominently Charles E. Coughlin and Roy Zachary's Christian Front, Fritz Kuhn's German-American Bund, and William Dudley Pelley's Silver Shirt Legion—commanded hundreds of thousands of followers in prewar America.[4] These organizations appealed to an anti-Semitic strain in U.S. culture that "was widespread and accepted in an age that had yet to experience the Holocaust."[5] Rockwell and other postwar anti-Semites regarded the prewar membership of fascist and anti-Semitic organizations as a realistic gauge of their potential strength. They believed that the Holocaust—or, more accurately, the historic memory of the Holocaust—vitiated the realization of that potential.

The Holocaust waged "war against both Jewish life and memory."[6] Although the Allied victory thwarted the Nazi war against Jewish life, if postwar Nazis could alter, revise, and recast the historic memory of the Holocaust, then the war against Jewish memory could continue—and its continuation would, Hitler's heirs believed, set the stage for an inevitable return of their war against the Jews. In one sense, the very enormity of the Holocaust played into their hands, because any historical representation of it strained credibility.[7] By the mid-1960s, those who wanted to rewrite Holocaust history found it easier to do so as time distanced humanity from the events themselves and as natural death silenced the survivors.

Two decades after the Holocaust, Rockwell promoted a distortion of historic memory designed to remove the stigma of the Holocaust from nazism, leading, he hoped, to nazism's rehabilitation as a political ideology. The significance of Holocaust denial as a strategic tool of the contemporary anti-Semitic right is well understood and documented, as is Willis Carto's role as the founder of the pseudohistorical Institute for Historical Review and its publication, the *Journal of Historical Review*. Less well understood is Rockwell's role in Holocaust denial, which predated and initially exceeded Carto's.

Willis Carto, born in 1926 in Fort Wayne, Indiana, joined a variety of right-wing groups and causes in the early 1950s, launched *Right* magazine in 1955, and expanded his influence with the founding of The Liberty Lobby in 1957. Rockwell and Carto enjoyed a close working relationship and intimate friendship from the mid-1950s until a breach in late 1964 over Rockwell's attack on Carto's mentor, Francis Parker Yockey. Rockwell wrote articles for *Right*, and the two men cooperated even after Rockwell veered into overt nazism in 1958–59.[8]

Although Carto—by nature a cautious and circumspect man—never openly embraced the swastika and took care to distance himself from Rockwell in public, their views were virtually indistinguishable, particularly pertaining to Jews. Rockwell, the older, more flamboyant showman, often awed and overwhelmed the quiet, bookish Carto. He distributed copies of Carto's *Right* until the magazine ceased publication in late 1960, and in return Carto published articles by Rockwell and favorable articles about Rockwell's American Nazi party. Both men seemed genuinely to like and respect each other, as is evident in their private correspondence. In one letter, Rockwell acknowledged receipt of a quantity of magazines from Carto and promised to distribute them "where they will bear fruit" while avoiding an open endorsement "lest it hurt more than it helps." In the same letter, Rockwell acknowledged Carto's reciprocal assistance to the ANP, which would help their recruitment efforts. Rockwell assured Carto that his assistance "entitles you . . . to ring-side,—or maybe I should say 'Gas-Chamber-side,' seats in 1972! [when the ANP takes power]"[9]

Carto's first venture into Holocaust denial, the publication of David Hoggan's *Myth of the Six Million* by his Noontide Press in 1969, followed five years of public Holocaust denial activities by Rockwell. Carto's founding of the Institute for Historical Review and the publication of the *Journal of Histori-*

cal Review—his major vehicles of Holocaust denial propaganda—did not oc-
cur until 1978–79. Rockwell's first documented public Holocaust denial activity occurred in 1964, in a speech at the University of Hawaii—five years
before Carto's publication of *The Myth of the Six Million*—and continued
unabated until his death in 1967.[10] By the time of his death—and two years
before Willis Carto entered the Holocaust denial movement in a meaningful
way—Rockwell had established himself as a vocal, public, veteran denial advocate. By 1967, Rockwell had familiarized the anti-Semitic right with standard Holocaust denial arguments and popularized the concept through his
speeches to college audiences and interviews in the mainstream press. Holocaust denial became a standard feature of Rockwell's public presentations after
1964. Again and again, to gatherings of anti-Semites and before college audiences throughout the country, he depicted the Holocaust as a "monstrous and
profitable fraud" and asserted that most of its six million victims "later died
happily and richly in the Bronx, New York."[11]

Bruno Ludtke, Rockwell's German mentor, introduced him to the concept
and instructed him on the elements and usefulness of Holocaust denial beginning in 1961. In November of that year, Ludtke brought the writings of
Harry Elmer Barnes—in Deborah Lipstadt's view, "one of the seminal figures
in the history of North American Holocaust denial"—and Charles C. Tansill,
whose 1952 *Back Door to War* was a classic work of pro-Nazi historic revision-
ism, to Rockwell's attention.[12] Throughout 1962, Ludtke shaped Rockwell's
thinking on the Holocaust, sharing with him the most significant early literature from anti-Semitic deniers in Europe and America and honing the arguments that would form the core of Rockwell's propaganda on the subject in
the mid-1960s. Through Freda Utley's arguments in *The High Cost of Ven-
geance,* Ludtke refined Rockwell's response to the historical incomparability
of the Holocaust by likening Nazi extermination of the Jews to Allied bomb-
ings of civilian targets in World War II. The argument that U.S. and Allied
atrocities against German civilians matched in brutality any acts committed
by the Nazis against the Jews became a fulcrum of Holocaust denial. Utley
advanced that argument and found her way to American anti-Semites through
Rockwell via Ludtke.[13]

In two January 1963 letters to Rockwell, Ludtke provided extensive instruction on the pseudofacts disputing the Holocaust that were emanating from
European Nazis. He briefed Rockwell on arguments developed by German
Nazis who were promoting the argument that those killings of Jews that really did happen were actually caused and directed by Zionist Jews to discredit
the Hitler regime. Furthermore, Ludtke argued, Jewish groups in Israel orchestrated the systematic inflation of the numbers of Holocaust victims to

increase reparation payments from the German government. These "facts," according to Ludtke, became well known within German government circles but remained unpublicized because of political pressure from powerful Jews in the United States and West Germany.[14]

Ludtke convinced Rockwell that Jewish-dominated Allied interrogators either fabricated confessions of Nazi prisoners or obtained them through torture. He wrote to Rockwell that British and American soldiers tortured hundreds of SS officers to obtain false confessions because they could not obtain evidence of nonexistent Nazi crimes in any other way.[15] During Adolf Eichmann's 1961 war crimes trial in Israel, Ludtke interpreted Eichmann's "admissions" as indisputable evidence of physical torture by the Israelis. He also argued against the very existence of the Holocaust, pointing to supposed numerical discrepancies in census data for pre- and postwar European Jewry and the purported lack of physical evidence of gas chambers in Germany— arguments that had just surfaced in the early writings of Paul Rassinier in Europe and Harry Elmer Barnes in the United States.[16]

In 1961 or early 1962, Ludtke came into possession of a draft of a Holocaust denial text by a young Harvard-trained historian, David Leslie Hoggan. A few early Holocaust revisionists knew of the American's work; in fact, Barnes probably drew on Hoggan's 1955 doctoral dissertation on the origins of World War II, in which he absolved Hitler and Germany of virtually all blame for initiating the war. During the late 1950s, Hoggan's work became more and more overtly anti-Semitic. His scholarship, always of marginal quality, deteriorated into bitter polemic. When Hoggan's unpublished manuscript on the Holocaust came to his attention in 1962, Ludtke suspected that Hoggan might be a Jewish agent because his claims of Jewish culpability strained even Ludtke's eagerness to believe in the fraudulence of the Holocaust. Once Ludtke determined that Hoggan was sincere, however, he brought his work to Rockwell's attention. It is possible, although not confirmable by extant documents, that Rockwell introduced Carto to Hoggan's work.[17] Carto's Noontide Press eventually published Hoggan's draft manuscript in 1969 as *The Myth of the Six Million*.

By late summer 1962, Ludtke had compiled a list of Germans who abetted the alleged Allied-Jewish conspiracy by publicizing Hitler's anti-Jewish actions and advised Rockwell that their soon-to-be realized Nazi regime should hang these "traitors" even before dealing with any Jew. Ludtke drummed into Rockwell that "there are things that cannot be said here and today," specifically "things" relating to Nazi wartime treatment of Jews. Ludtke believed that these matters must be kept hidden and secret.[18] Neither Rockwell nor Ludtke seemed to appreciate the logical inconsistency of denying Holocaust atrocities while simultaneously conspiring to conceal evidence of Hitler's "Final Solution."

Rockwell, an apt pupil, became a prime early agent for the transmittal of Holocaust denial propaganda throughout the anti-Semitic right. In 1963 he raised the issue of fabricated German war guilt with Conde McGinley, a major publisher and writer within the American anti-Semitic right. That same year, in a letter to Denis Pirie, Colin Jordan's chief publicist and pamphleteer, Rockwell explained Holocaust denial "facts"—in terms virtually identical to those used by Ludtke to explain the "facts" to him—and encouraged Pirie to make Holocaust denial issues an integral part of Jordan's propaganda efforts in Great Britain.[19] For the remainder of his career, Rockwell advocated Holocaust denial in the United States and among all chapters of the World Union of National Socialists. He saw, as Ludtke hoped he would, the strategic value of Holocaust denial for the rehabilitation of nazism and twisted the historical memory of the Holocaust to conform to the comfortable stereotypes about Jews accepted by his followers. In 1966, Rockwell wrote to Bernard E. Horgan, the leader of the Nazi movement in Ireland and of WUNS-Ireland, that the Holocaust was nothing more than a big lie perpetrated by a race of big liars.[20]

Throughout 1966 and 1967, Ludtke bolstered Rockwell's commitment to Holocaust denial. He provided Rockwell with the latest perspective on historical interpretation of the Holocaust, with new "facts" supposedly documenting Jewish fabrication of the Holocaust, and with current interpretations of old "facts" as they emerged around the world. He collected articles on Holocaust denial from international newspapers and provided translations and digests of those articles for Rockwell's use. He reported to Rockwell on the success of Holocaust denial propaganda efforts in Europe, including the fate of teachers who disseminated Holocaust denial theories in German schools.[21] Ludtke also bolstered Holocaust denial as a prime tenet of revived National Socialism among Rockwell lieutenants in the United States and Europe and took charge of WUNS's Holocaust denial portfolio.[22]

The West German government cracked down on Holocaust denial in 1965 and 1966 and arrested Ludtke and two of his chief German disciples, schoolteachers named Dietrich Schuler and Alfred Endrigkeit. Schuler, whom Ludtke warmly referred to as "my comrade," wrote a widely circulated essay in which he denounced the "supposed murder of the 6 million Yids" as one of the greatest "lies of world history."[23] Denying the historical validity of the Holocaust violated West German law, and Schuler not only lost his teaching position but served seven months in prison. As mentioned earlier, Ludtke himself spent months in prison for his activities. His refusal to recant or to curtail his activities elevated him to martyr status and increased his standing with Rockwell.[24]

Ludtke combed Nazi literature for documentation Rockwell could use in spreading Holocaust denial propaganda. In late 1965 he uncovered an article published in 1954 in *Der Weg,* a German-language Argentinean monthly. "The Lie of the Six Millions," whose author published under the pseudonym "Guide Heimann," contained all the "facts" and arguments that came to mark Holocaust denial in the late twentieth century, including supposed Zionist control of Allied interrogation of German war prisoners, inflation of morbidity data for the purpose of increasing reparations, fabrication of confessions, eliciting confessions by torture, and manipulating prewar census data to create the illusion of genocide. The author asserted that his data proved "clearly that there never was any planning of or factual genocid[e]" and that there "never were any gas chambers, gassing-vehicles, or any similar things in any concentration camp inside or outside of Germany. ALL publications or statements to the contrary are FORGERIES." The article concluded: "The final result is: The Jewish people has [*sic*] gained, by the smallest human sacrifice, the by far biggest increase in power, and thus made themselves to [be] the virtual victor of the second World War."[25] Ludtke's meticulous translation of the article provided Rockwell with data, concepts, and phraseology that accelerated his Holocaust denial activities in 1966. In an enthusiastic letter in which he thanked Ludtke for the translation, Rockwell informed Ludtke that the ANP would put out a special publication for mass distribution identifying the Holocaust as a Jewish lie.[26]

In 1965, Rockwell published a widely circulated piece of Holocaust denial propaganda that has remained popular within anti-Semitic groups ever since. *The Diary of Ann Fink*—which William F. Buckley Jr. called an "excrescence"—attempted to discredit *The Diary of Anne Frank* through ridicule and black humor.[27] Printed in a comic book format, with the illustrations drawn by Rockwell and John Patler, the piece featured photographs of emaciated prisoners and dead bodies from the Nazi death camps in grotesque poses amid "comic" illustrations. Under each photograph was a "humorous" caption, written by Rockwell.

Rockwell's greatest success in bringing Holocaust denial to broad public notice occurred in April 1966 in an interview with Alex Haley for *Playboy* magazine. Rockwell detailed many of the major beliefs of the Holocaust denial dogma in vivid and inflammatory language and through this popular medium brought Holocaust denial "facts" and arguments to the attention of millions of Americans and *Playboy* readers worldwide. "I emphatically deny," he said, "that there is any valid proof that innocent Jews were systematically murdered by the Nazis." He argued that photographs presented at war crimes trials were really pictures of German civilians killed during Allied air raids on Dresden who were "passed off" as dead Jews. He repeated the statistics contained in Ludtke's translation of "The Lie of the Six Millions." He recited the deniers' mantra: there were no gas chambers, no extermination, no atrocities. The significance of the *Playboy* interview to Holocaust denial, in addition to its publication three years prior to Hoggan's book *The Myth of the Six Million*, is the scope of its dissemination—to more than 3.6 million *Playboy* readers. By comparison, Carto's *Journal of Historical Review*, the major vehicle for post-Rockwell Holocaust denial articles, has seldom exceeded a circulation of 2,500 since its first year of publication.[28]

One of the most dramatic claims Rockwell made in the *Playboy* interview was that he had proven, in early 1958, that the Jewish-controlled popular press willingly promoted Holocaust fraud. His "proof" took the form of an article he wrote under the pseudonym "Lew Cor"—"Roc-Wel" spelled backward—for the March 1958 issue of *Sir!* a popular men's magazine. In that article, "When the Nazis Tried Human Vivisection," Rockwell offered a soft-porn version of sexual sadism, complete with illustrations, regarding Nazi medical experiments on naked Jewish women. He admitted that he had fabricated everything in the article, yet the Jewish publishers of *Sir!* printed it verbatim in order to discredit Nazis. In an issue of the *Rockwell Report* published the year before the *Playboy* interview, Rockwell refers to the "Lew Cor" hoax as "one of the most smashing proofs of the enormous arrogance of the Jews with their lies about the six million supposedly gassed Jews and the 'evil' Nazis." He confided to his readers—and repeated in the *Playboy* interview—that the "Lew Cor" article provided a "laboratory test of the big Jew lie about the six million poor, innocent gassed Jews." He explained: "I used to be a free-lance magazine writer. So I sat down and wrote the most horrendous LIES about how the Nazis tortured and experimented on sweet, innocent Jew girls. . . . The Jews printed these awful LIES about the Nazis."[29]

In fact, Rockwell's later description version of the "Lew Cor" article conveniently rewrote the history of the event. No evidence whatsoever exists that prior to 1965 Rockwell regarded his 1958 article as anything other than a sadistic fantasy that he peddled for much-needed cash. Whether Rockwell resurrected the "Lew Cor" article in 1965 as a tactical device or simply reacted creatively to threats to expose his authorship of the article when he emerged as America's premier Holocaust denier cannot be determined from extant documents. Regardless of the circumstances surrounding his 1965 use of the "Lew Cor" article, it is highly probable that Rockwell's sole motivation for authorship in 1958 was the check for seventy-five dollars he received from the publishers of *Sir!*

The endurance of the myths Rockwell fostered and popularized in the early 1960s speaks to his influence on the racist right, which recognized him as the father of American Holocaust denial. For the anti-Semitic right, the Holocaust became a "hoax, one concocted by Jewish and Zionist organizations in order to win undeserved sympathy for Jews in general and Israel more particularly." Rockwell's propaganda became the anti-Semitic right's canon.[30]

Rockwell's assault on the historical memory of the Holocaust served resurgent nazism. He understood that by reshaping history to his own liking, he could eliminate the power of the Holocaust over National Socialism, for as "history overtakes memory, the latter is conquered and eradicated."[31] He also understood that the rehabilitation of Nazism as a prelude to the establishment of a National Socialist world order rested on the success of this effort. When reporters asked Rockwell about the Holocaust, he told them that Hitler didn't do what the Jews claimed, but privately he assured Bruno Ludtke that they would soon "rectify that mistake" and make "honest liars" out of the Jews.[32] For Rockwell and Ludtke, as for Hitler, the ideal National Socialist world order was unquestionably *Judenfrei.*

11

CHRISTIAN IDENTITY

The same power which gets filthy niggers to quit dope, screwing, liquor, gambling and crime, and become abstemious, clean and devout Muslims is available to US.
—George Lincoln Rockwell, 1965

Rockwell had rejected his Methodist upbringing and abandoned Christianity as a young man. When asked about his personal beliefs, he described himself as an agnostic. Still, he recognized the power religious belief held over people in all social classes and sought to harness that power for his own purposes. He frequently discussed the strategic value of a Christian-based front for American nazism with his most trusted advisers. He argued that a Christian veneer would lend theological justification to anti-Semitism and legitimize and broaden the American Nazi party's appeal among Christian fundamentalists. Rockwell seized on a small, aberrant, Christian spin-off sect—Christian Identity—as the channel for this effort. Several of his most loyal followers became Christian Identity ministers, and their congregations embraced "the worldly goals of National Socialism." Christian Identity theology and racist, anti-Semitic theory eventually intertwined so completely—a process Rockwell initiated and encouraged—that Christian Identity became "the accepted religion of not only most Klansmen and Nazis but of most all White Nationalists."[1]

Christian Identity is a twentieth-century American variation of nineteenth-century British Israelism, with several important differences. British Israelism was philo-Semitic and benign; Christian Identity is anti-Semitic and pernicious.[2] British Israelism, sometimes known as Anglo-Israelism, centers on the belief "that the British are lineal descendants of the 'ten lost tribes' of Israel." This notion is found in British religious history as far back as the seventeenth century. John Wilson, a nineteenth-century British millennialist, coalesced the fragmented elements of British Israelism into a religious movement. Joseph Wild, a Congregationalist minister in Brooklyn, New York, popularized Anglo-American Israelism, a variant of British Israelism, in the United States during the last quarter of the nineteenth century. For the next fifty years, the American version of British Israelism remained a quaint and harmless obsession among a limited number of marginal congregations.[3]

During the 1920s, Anglo-Israelism attracted American white supremacists and anti-Semites as a comfortable religious haven for their social beliefs. They reasoned that if the Anglo-American—the "white man," in the parlance of the time—was the true Israelite, and if the white race was God's "Chosen People," then a White Christian Republic in America logically would satisfy God's plan for humankind. In the hands of rabid anti-Semites like Henry Ford's protégé William Cameron and Howard Rand, Anglo-American Israelism metamorphosed into a cult of hatred and a refuge for practitioners of racist and anti-Semitic fringe politics. During the Great Depression of the 1930s, Gerald Winrod, the "Jayhawk Nazi," and Wesley Swift shaped the first Anglo-American Israelite churches that were recognizably "Christian Identity" as bastions of religious and racial purity.[4]

Swift emerged in the 1940s as the dominant Christian Identity figure in the United States. He shaped Identity doctrines of racial purity and created congregations throughout the nation, with particular success in California and the southeastern states. The son of a fundamentalist Methodist minister, the protégé of Gerald L. K. Smith, and a former California Ku Klux Klan organizer, Swift proselytized relentlessly and built Christian Identity into a small but viable fringe sect.

In the 1950s he recruited Richard Girnt Butler, a onetime member of William Dudley Pelley's pro-Nazi Silver Shirt Legion. Butler proved to be Swift's most important convert. He described meeting Swift as "the total turning point" in his life. For Butler, "the light turned on. [Swift] had the answers I was trying to find."[5] Butler, a former Lockheed aerospace engineer, lived comfortably on royalties from a device he invented to change aircraft tires.[6] After meeting Swift, Butler devoted his life to his Christian Identity ministry. Until Swift's death in 1970, Butler served as his chief aide and defender, his most ardent minister, and his heir apparent. His turn to Identity religion did not entail the abandonment of Nazi politics; rather, he saw the two as inseparable. Butler's Nazi and Identity beliefs formed a compatible core for a worldview that merged theology and ideology and redirected Swift's emphasis on racial purity to out-and-out race hatred.[7] Within a framework of virulent anti-Semitism, Christian Identity holds that contemporary Jews are not the Biblical Israelites but impostors and frauds, the literal spawn of Satan, devils incarnate among God's children. In Identity doctrine, Anglo-Saxons, or "Aryans," are the true Israelites, engaged in an apocalyptic struggle with the Satanic Jews and their lackeys, the dark people of the earth, the pre-Adamite "Mud People."

In this eschatological theology, Aryan triumph is prophesied after a violent "time of tribulation."[8]

Butler introduced Rockwell to Christian Identity in the early 1960s.[9] Rockwell's ties to seminal Christian Identity figures are numerous and well documented. Oren Fenton Potito, Conrad "Connie" Lynch, and Gordon Winrod (the son of Gerald Winrod) were part of the close-knit cadre of right-wing racists who, along with Rockwell, helped launch the National States Rights party in 1958. All three men toiled with Rockwell as high-level campaign workers for John G. Crommelin's Alabama political campaigns from 1958 to 1962 (Potito served as Crommelin's campaign manager in the admiral's 1962 race for the U.S. Senate against Lister Hill); all three became Christian Identity ministers under Swift through Butler. Swift sanctioned the use of Christian Identity facilities and personnel for NSRP organization and membership drives as well as for Crommelin's campaigns. The NSRP served as a meeting and breeding ground for emergent American Nazis in 1958, and Crommelin's campaigns, where they "cut their teeth" as practicing politicians, forged alliances and friendships among political Nazis—Rockwell, Matt Koehl, James K. Warner—and Identity ministers—Swift, Butler, Winrod, Potito, and Lynch.[10] The "'cross-pollination' that abounds on the racist right" allowed both groups to appreciate the strategic value of cooperation toward common ends.[11]

Even before he met Butler, Rockwell entertained the idea of a Christian front for his Nazi politics. In the fall of 1957, Rockwell discussed a "proposed religious organization based upon the world view of Adolf Hitler" with Emory Burke, a racist and anti-Semitic ally. He showed Burke detailed drawings of movement leaders in military-style clerical attire, depicting the various "orders" of his proposed "religious" brotherhood. According to Burke, Rockwell discussed the feasibility of starting such an organization at that time. Burke, who remained a Rockwell adviser and friend until Rockwell's death, believed he was quite serious. Rockwell brought the matter up "constantly" and "discussed [it] for hours" during his visits with Burke in Atlanta.[12] Fast-moving events after 1957 sidetracked Rockwell's idea: the 1958 Atlanta synagogue bombing and the maelstrom surrounding Rockwell's linkage with that event (Emory Burke was a suspect but was not arrested for lack of evidence), the founding of the ANP in 1958–59, and the formation of the World Union of National Socialists in 1962. But the potential of a Nazi-controlled religious front continued to intrigue Rockwell. In 1962 the concept blossomed once more within the fertile exchange of ideas between Rockwell and his German mentor, Bruno Ludtke.

In the spring of 1962, Ludtke translated Rockwell's autobiography, *This Time the World,* for distribution in West Germany. He recommended that Rockwell soften the book's anti-Christian rhetoric and suggested the tactical value of religion to the resurrection of nazism. He created for Rockwell the imagery of a mountain, with only those at the top of the mountain—Ludtke and Rockwell—able to see and comprehend the totality of the mountain. Their followers, Ludtke continued, saw only pieces, not the whole. Ludtke urged Rockwell to think of their movement within that imagery. From the top of the mountain, Rockwell could proclaim dogma with the authority of one who sees the whole, could speak with the divine clarity of one who sees farther and clearer than his disciples. Rockwell's message would carry the sanction of ultimate authority. Speak with the voice of God, Ludtke urged.[13] Rockwell responded enthusiastically. Ludtke's letters unleashed Rockwell's long-dormant dreams of a Nazi-based religion. He revealed to Ludtke his plans for the creation of a church he called the Christian Naturalist Church. This church—which Rockwell would create, control, and manipulate from behind the scenes—would advocate a "Positive Christianity" with Adolf Hitler as a spiritual role model and a portrayal of an Aryan Jesus "who took a whip to the Kikes." Ludtke encouraged Rockwell to implement his plan, predicting that "millions of boobs" would swell its ranks and sweep them to power.[14]

Ludtke and Rockwell agreed that the "Christian" designation had mass appeal and should be retained for that purpose, but their religion was in no manner Christian, was in no way part of a belief system they derided as "just as Jewish as Bolshevism." Ludtke rejected a religion based on the teachings of Jesus Christ, which held hope for those he considered weak and degenerate and unable to defend themselves. Instead, Ludtke wrote to Rockwell, National Socialism, the creation of Adolf Hitler, could emerge as the new religion of the masses within a Rockwell-crafted pseudo-Christian exterior. This religion, under the guise of a nominally Christian sect, would allow Rockwell to impose his will—and Hitler's worldview—with "the authority of God." Ludtke made sure Rockwell clearly understood his message. He emphasized that Rockwell could harness the force of religious passion as the St. Paul of their new religion.

Never losing sight of the purpose of the discourse as strategy and not theology, Ludtke reminded Rockwell that Paul created Christianity as a world religion from the limited life of a radical, itinerant Jewish rabbi with fewer than a hundred followers at the time of his death. Like Paul, who made Christianity a mass-movement—thereby insulating it from the effects of persecution—Rockwell could make National Socialism a mass movement under the guise of Christianity. And, Ludtke reminded Rockwell, it's not easy to destroy a mass movement fired by religious passion.[15]

Rockwell assured Ludtke that his Christian front was purely tactical and that Hitler's inspired doctrine was his only religion. Rockwell also insisted that "the peanut brains" of most Americans made obfuscation prudent. He reminded Ludtke that Hitler—"the Master"—taught that a good leader makes the masses of followers see all their enemies as one. Using the rhetoric and form of Christianity, Rockwell believed, made that task easier. Ironically, Rockwell, the leader, could assume the mantle of Christianity to slay the Jewish enemy with the full understanding that true Christians, followers of Jesus Christ, were dangerous enemies of National Socialism as well.

To implement that strategy, Rockwell proposed organizing a church under the exterior countenance of Christianity. The name for the church, as originally proposed—the Christian Naturalist Church—was designed to make the masquerade less repugnant to the masses. At its essence, Rockwell argued, the object was to organize the masses for political gain, and the means he used was irrelevant. What could be a better fate for the Jews, Rockwell gloated, than to have thousands of "priests" and "monks" one day cast off their habits and robes to reveal the Nazi insignia beneath.[16]

The 1963 Rockwell-Ludtke transatlantic correspondence refined both the concept and the strategy of a Christian front for Rockwell's Nazis. Following Rockwell's assurance that the Christian aspect of the venture was Christian in name only, Ludtke judged the Christian Naturalist Church to be a potentially useful tool. He never wavered from his conviction that "religious passion" led by godlike leadership could mobilize the masses to the Nazi cause. His and Rockwell's task, Ludtke wrote, was to mobilize and direct that passion.[17] He reasoned that once Americans equated racial purity with obedience to God's law and saw racial treason as a great sin, he and Rockwell could manipulate the people's "religious fury" to seize political power.[18]

The third person in the WUNS triumvirate, Colin Jordan, did not share Ludtke's enthusiasm for Rockwell's religious strategy. Ludtke interceded with Jordan on Rockwell's behalf. He patiently explained the strategic value of a Christian cloak while assuring the anti-Christian Jordan that he shared his aversion to Christianity, which both Ludtke and Jordan regarded as weak, feminine, and Jewish at its core. But Jordan never seemed to appreciate Rockwell's distinction between the strategic value of a Christian front and the Christian philosophy, which he abhorred. He didn't have Rockwell's or Ludtke's moral flexibility. Rockwell himself sensed the depth of Jordan's dissatisfaction with the Christian front strategy and wrote to reassure him that he too rejected Christianity but saw the pseudo-Christian initiative as useful in their political struggle. He explained that there was propaganda value to be gained by placing the Nazis on the side of the Christian majority on issues like prayer in schools and the display of Christian symbols on public property. The Nazis could best exploit these issues through a Christian front, Rockwell argued.[19]

Jordan remained unconvinced and repeatedly bristled when Rockwell raised the issue of exploiting a Christian front as a recruitment or propaganda strategy. Jordan conceded that there might be short-term value in Rockwell's Christian front, but he also argued that National Socialism was so fundamentally opposed to the "Christian *Weltanschauung*," that even oblique support undermined their long-term objective of changing the entire value system on which Christianity rests. Jordan remained a good soldier and refrained from publicly disputing his commander on this issue, but he never accepted nor fully reconciled himself to Rockwell's point of view.[20] Despite Jordan's reluctance, Rockwell continued to use religious imagery—depicting himself as a Christ-like martyr to the avaricious Jews—and continued to encourage WUNS chapters, especially in Catholic nations, to harness the power of religious passion for the Nazis' political ends. And the predictably faithful Ludtke continued to bolster and defend Rockwell's efforts in this arena.[21]

Energized by Ludtke, Rockwell courted Wesley Swift. There is no direct evidence of Butler's role in bringing Swift and Rockwell together, but his involvement was likely pivotal, given his close relationship with both men. On the night of 10 June 1964, at a secret location known only to a few top officials of Rockwell's ANP and Swift's Christian Identity Church, the two men met to discuss "a merger for the purpose of exchanging and compiling intelligence information . . . and to devise a command order." No minutes are extant from that meeting, but a close working relationship between Swift and Rockwell followed, which facilitated complementary propaganda and recruitment efforts. Nazis who needed religious sustenance found a welcome home in Swift's Christian Identity Church, and Identity Christians found an outlet for their political passions in the American Nazi party.[22]

Rockwell also channeled one of his most-trusted ANP officers, Ralph Perry Forbes, directly into an Identity ministry. Forbes, born in 1940, held a fanatical devotion to Rockwell. His uncompromising loyalty, combined with his unbridled hatred for Jews and blacks and a mystical belief in signs and prophecies, made him the perfect prototype Nazi–Christian Identity minister. Forbes held the rank of captain in the ANP and was the party's youngest division commander when Rockwell tapped him for the important new assignment.[23] In Forbes, Rockwell had an allegiant zealot who would cloak National Socialist political doctrines with a pseudo-Christian theology and promote his new faith and his old master with equal fervor. In August 1965, Rockwell laid his plan before Forbes. Faith is a "powerful weapon," he wrote. "Our side desperately needs such a faith, and I believe you may be the man sent by Destiny to provide exactly that. . . . I think you can do it, Ralph!" Rockwell's intention is unmistakable. In the same letter to Forbes, Rockwell wrote: "I cannot do it, because I must organize and maintain a POLITICAL movement.

But I can provide a political outlet for religious converts you can win." He suggested California, where Forbes headed the ANP's Western Division, as "the ideal place to start." Citing the work done by Swift and William Potter Gale as proof that a race-based anti-Semitic "Christian" appeal held the potential for mass appeal, Rockwell instructed Forbes: "You can gather in a nucleus and form a Church, which will seize all the little outfits trending this way already." Rockwell suggested that Forbes recruit William V. Fowler, a militant follower of Swift, as a useful connection to Swift's organization and a potential leader in their new church.[24]

Rockwell appreciated the opposition that many Nazis, including Colin Jordan, had to even a strategic deference to Christianity, which they regarded as anathema to National Socialism. He was prepared to deal with the ideological purists while Forbes, in effect, merged the party's southern California operation with a new Christian Identity congregation. "There will be large numbers of pissed off people in the movement," Rockwell warned Forbes, "but I will hold all that together." He planted ideas in Forbes's mind on how to portray Hitler as a Christian redeemer by illustrating the "many, many parallels" in the lives of Hitler and Jesus Christ. Rockwell's gift for discerning just the right button to push to motivate a dedicated follower worked well with Forbes. "I am betting we will one day learn," Rockwell suggested, "that the Second Coming has already taken place,—and, just as predicted in the Bible, the World Knew Him not the SECOND time, either." He told Forbes to "come up with the New Doctrine of the Second Coming."[25] We must appreciate the irony of Rockwell, an agnostic, using biblical allusions to promote Hitler, an anti-Semitic Odinist, as spiritual heir to Jesus of Nazareth, a radical Jewish rabbi.

Rockwell also effectively manipulated Forbes's well-known obsession with mystical symbols and prophetic signs. He used etymology to suggest hidden connections between Christ and the Nazi movement. "I have often noticed the amazing similarity between the name of the birthplace of the great Prophet and leader of Christianity, which is NAZareth," Rockwell wrote to Forbes, and "have long felt strongly that there is more here than meets the eye in THAT word." In case Forbes missed his meaning, Rockwell explained: "Change just ONE letter, and it becomes NAZIreth! Surely the Almighty is telling us something!"[26]

Forbes followed Rockwell's directive, became a Christian Identity minister, proselytized for the party and the church throughout southern California, and built up a sizable flock, which he continued to shepherd long after Rockwell's death. The distinction between political propaganda and religious revelation, if it ever existed in Forbes's mind, has long since blurred. Forbes has enshrined Rockwell in the Christian Identity pantheon of deities. He marks each anniversary of Rockwell's death as a religious observance, referring to Rockwell as "God's latter day apostle to America and all the lost sheep, the nations of *true* Israel."[27]

Swift and Rockwell continued their working relationship until Rockwell's death in 1967. By the time Swift died in 1970, Rockwell's ally and Swift's protégé, Richard G. Butler, had shaped the Christian Identity movement into a seamless synthesis of Nazi philosophy and Identity theology. A current Nazi activist, R. E. Cooper, recognizes Swift as the founder of Nazi-based Christian Identity but identifies Butler as the man who "directly reached the vast majority of contemporary activists."[28] Through Forbes, Swift, and, most important, Butler, Rockwell redirected Christian Identity to create a safe haven for American Nazis and their ideological descendants.[29]

After Rockwell's death, Identity Christians and Nazis, often one and the same, revered his memory as the architect of the Identity-Nazi fusion that carried the message of racial purity and anti-Semitism to new audiences of potential recruits. Matt Koehl, Rockwell's political successor, reflected how completely Rockwell's representation of nazism as reborn Christianity had permeated the movement. Writing after Rockwell's death, Koehl portrayed Rockwell's role as "analogous to that of [St. Paul,] the great apostle of the [Christian] Church." Koehl wrote: "If Adolf Hitler stands as the author of National Socialism, then Commander Rockwell is certainly the St. Paul of the new Aryan Creed."[30]

Although he did not live to see the transition fully accomplished, Rockwell set in motion a fertile union between the political Nazis and the anti-Semites of Christian Identity. That union produced a hybrid ideology that allowed a new generation of anti-Semites to call down the wrath of God on the "Satanic Jews." Under cover of a Christian sanction, anti-Semites enjoyed a religious validation of their prejudices. Good and evil were easy to identify, their separation divinely ordained. Religion provided a psychological shield for anti-Semites and white supremacists so that their hatreds were no longer an arbitrary impulse but a "religious condemnation." Striking out against their race enemies, the Jews and the blacks, became a "redemptive act."[31]

As a key element of his long-term strategy for the acquisition of power, Rockwell's Christian Identity efforts did not bear fruit in his lifetime. But his spiritual heirs cling to the belief that it will yet prove to be the catalyst for a mass movement based on Rockwell's anti-Semitic and racist worldview. "When the time comes that the broad masses of White people want to be both Christians and racists," Cooper predicts, "Identity Christianity will become the religion of our people."[32]

12

SETTLING FOR NOTORIETY

[T]hings are coming rapidly to a head. Either I will soon have the world by the tail, or I will be wiped out.
—George Lincoln Rockwell, 1966

Rockwell reached his zenith between 1964 and 1966. The American Nazi party engaged in hundreds of street actions and stunts that kept his name in the headlines; party membership, although never significant, reached its high-water mark; and Rockwell achieved the notoriety that he believed was the necessary first step in mobilizing public support. Yet these years also fixed his place on the farthest margin of political influence. Most observers realized that Rockwell would not reach his goal of political power by 1972. Few believed that he would ever wield legal power—at any level— in the United States. Despite his bluster and increasingly desperate public agitation, he remained an annoyance, a curiosity, a public obscenity. He was notorious but essentially powerless.

According to Rockwell, the ANP's stagnation could be blamed on the incompetence of his subordinates. He vented his frustration to Bruno Ludtke, complaining bitterly about the poor quality of ANP recruits. Few of them, he wrote, really understood National Socialism as a political philosophy. At the root of the problem, of course, was the pervasive influence of the Jews and a litany of Jewish-instigated social conditions—immigration policy, poverty, poor education—that retarded the intellectual development of the white masses. Rockwell also blamed American culture itself for the ANP's failure to flourish, complaining that in America there "simply is no good 'soil'—no good 'earth'" in which National Socialis[m] could take root and prosper.[1] Unthinkable to him were the more obvious reasons for the ANP's failure: the sheer repulsiveness of its assumptions and his own shortcomings as a political leader.

Matt Koehl, one of Rockwell's few intimates who met his expectations for efficiency and dedication, often complained to his commander about the lack of discipline in the ANP. Rockwell sympathized with Koehl but tried to get his deputy to accept the limitations confronting them. "I do not believe any machine can do more than the parts which compose it are designed to do," he wrote. "The 'parts' of our 'machine' are . . . PEOPLE, . . . not little squares on an organizational chart. Unless the people who are placed in these organizational boxes . . . are made of good quality stuff . . . the machine will falter and sputter, as ours does." He concluded: "I have not been able to find the human material who CAN do what I know needs to be done."[2]

Characteristically, Rockwell refused to accept defeat and tried new approaches to recruitment. He launched a front organization—the United White Christian Majority—in an attempt to broaden the ANP's appeal and tried to revive an ANP youth auxiliary—the White Youth Corps—to bring new blood into the party. Neither effort succeeded. Only two ANP chapters, in Texas and southern California, grew appreciably between 1964 and 1966.[3]

Rockwell's 1964–65 recruitment efforts brought to the party a man who would become a major influence on Rockwell's thinking for the remainder of his career. William Luther Pierce had a Ph.D. degree in physics from the University of Colorado and was the best-educated member of Rockwell's entourage, quickly assuming the role of house intellectual. An assistant professor of physics at Oregon State University, Pierce joined the John Birch Society in 1962 but resigned the following year because he deemed the Birchites "too passive" for his temperament. Before meeting Rockwell, Pierce sharpened his racist and anti-Semitic beliefs on the writings of Madison Grant, Lothrop Stoddard, and Francis Parker Yockey. As Rockwell's trusted adviser, Pierce promoted Nordic superiority and his belief that the natural leadership of the party must come from men of "pure Germanic stock." He enthusiastically agreed with Rockwell's international vision and helped shape the resurgent National Socialist ideology. He created and edited *National Socialist World,* a WUNS publication, as the primary tool for the international dissemination of that ideology.[4] Although Pierce didn't actively participate in ANP street actions, he was the party's most aggressive advocate of physical confrontation. He believed that instigating a National Socialist revolution required acts of strategic violence. More than any other member of Rockwell's inner circle, Pierce advocated violence as a political strategy.[5]

Never doubting the inevitability of Rockwell's political triumph, Pierce instructed Rockwell in the use of power in a National Socialist America. He concentrated on the natural conclusions to which their shared beliefs would inevitably lead, including the unilateral destruction of Communist China, presumably by an unprovoked nuclear first strike. Pierce warned Rockwell that such plans should be kept secret for the time being since most Americans would probably be horrified by them. With time, however, Pierce believed that

Americans could be conditioned to accept such plans once the ANP fully controlled the media and the apparatus of government. He hinted darkly at "other problems" that would require "ultimate solutions"—a code phrase for the genocide of the Holocaust—which Pierce prudently avoided specifying in writing.[6] He energized Rockwell and the ANP and was partly responsible for Rockwell's last major publicity triumph, the Chicago "White Power" marches during the summer of 1966. Still, his best efforts could not reverse the party's fortunes or rescue Rockwell from the political periphery where public judgment had cast him.

By 1966 Rockwell's estrangement from his family was complete and irreversible. He hardly spoke to his brother, Bobby, whose family and business suffered greatly from the backlash associated with the Rockwell name. His cousins, with whom he had been exceptionally close in childhood and adolescence, drew away from him as his public behavior grew more and more outrageous. His boyhood friends Stan Tupper and Eben Lewis and Brown classmates Bob Grabb and Vic Hillery were shocked and mystified by the turn their friend's life had taken. At first they tried to reason with him; several came to suspect mental illness; eventually, all shunned him. Doc Rockwell tried, from time to time, to convince his son to mute his anti-Semitic ravings and abandon politics, but their contacts grew infrequent and invariably ended in bitter, recriminative arguments. Rockwell rarely saw his first wife, Judith Aultman, or their children; their limited communication centered on the child support payments he routinely neglected to send.

Worst of all, Rockwell's beloved second wife, Thora, kept herself and their children completely isolated from him. Years later, Rockwell referred to the "unspeakable hell" he suffered when Thora left him.[7] He eventually stopped writing to her, but only after years of returned letters. He had come to accept that the one great love of his life would forever remain outside his reach, locked in the protective embrace of her family in Iceland. Only his mother, the patient and enigmatic Claire, and his sister, Priscilla, maintained contact with him.

Claire Schade Rockwell never wavered in her devotion to her son. They corresponded faithfully throughout his life and saw each other whenever possible. His letters to her were different, in a fundamental way, from his letters to any other person. To whatever extent Rockwell could suppress his posturing, to whatever degree he could separate himself from the role he played for the world, he did so before his mother. She expressed concern for his health and his mental well-being, although there is no evidence that she shared the belief, held by many of Rockwell's relatives and friends, that his behavior suggested a mental or emotional aberration. Her concern centered on his peace of mind and his ability to withstand the continual assaults by his enemies.

Rockwell reassured her that he was at peace with himself, "clean inside," unafraid, proud of his work. She believed that her son's hatred for his enemies disturbed his inner peace, and she sent him books on meditation and positive thinking, urging him to abandon the emotional death grip his hate engendered. But Rockwell replied that hate could be as cleansing to the soul as love.[8]

Barbara von Goetz, described by the columnist Jack Anderson as "a mystery woman, a tall fading blonde," was Rockwell's secretary and mistress from 1961 until his death.[9] She loved Rockwell, provided him with the emotional sustenance denied by the break with his family, and tried to buffer him from the ravages of his turbulent life. She fought tenaciously for precious moments away from the maelstrom within the American Nazi party. She created time for them to go camping and hiking in the forests and mountains of rural Virginia and understood that such escapes provided the only chance for him to briefly shed the obsession that drove him onward. Von Goetz also recognized the meaningful role his mother played in Rockwell's life and, like a dutiful almost-daughter, nurtured the relationship by writing frequently to Claire. She mostly wrote warm and chatty letters about camping trips and days sailing on Chesapeake Bay,[10] providing depictions of Rockwell's life that hinted at normalcy. She offered vignettes that Claire Schade Rockwell treasured, such as the description of an idyllic afternoon in California's Sierra Nevada mountains. She described hiking to the top of a mountain peak and gushed over Rockwell's physical endurance despite the fact that he was fourteen years her senior. She congratulated Claire for producing "a Superman."[11]

When possible, von Goetz shared, in minute detail, the triumphs Rockwell enjoyed. One such occasion occurred during a particularly successful western trip, when she and Rockwell spent time with Westbrook Pegler. Pegler and his wife insisted that Rockwell and von Goetz leave their hotel and stay instead at the Peglers' Tucson ranch, where Rockwell and von Goetz were feted as visiting dignitaries and given lavish, but separate, accommodations, von Goetz in a suite of rooms and Rockwell in the guest house. Von Goetz also eagerly shared news of Rockwell's infrequent reunions with his children, such as the time, after leaving the Peglers' ranch, that Rockwell and von Goetz visited his eldest daughter by Judith Aultman. Bonnie Rockwell, an eighteen-year-old college student, lived in Utah and had converted to Mormonism. She abided by her mother's wishes and had little contact with her father or his family. But, according to von Goetz, she welcomed her father's visit and greeted him enthusiastically. Although Rockwell offered to meet his daughter in front of a hotel to avoid embarrassing her, von Goetz wrote that Bonnie wouldn't hear of it and took him to her dormitory, where she introduced him to her friends. Later that night, Rockwell introduced Bonnie to several admiring ANP members in Spanish Fork, Utah, who, von Goetz claimed, were prominent Mormons.[12]

Von Goetz also shared with Claire news of Rockwell's occasional contacts with his father. Claire maintained no relationship with her former husband, but she knew how important Doc's approval was to their son and how devastating his criticism had been. On one camping trip through New England, Rockwell, von Goetz, and an ANP comrade, Frank Niles, made a point of diverting toward the Maine seacoast to see Doc. The meeting was a disaster. As von Goetz described it, Doc visited them in their camper and berated his son for his political activities.[13] Shortly afterward, Rockwell himself wrote to his mother about the encounter in Maine and corroborated von Goetz's account of the meeting.[14] Reconciliation no longer seemed possible. Doc Rockwell was "heartsick" over the course his son's life had taken and, after that last encounter on the desolate coast of Maine, simply refused to talk to him, or of him, anymore.[15]

Although she avoided open identification with her son's political activities, Claire Schade Rockwell was the most sympathetic of all Rockwell family members toward his beliefs. Von Goetz faithfully sent her tape recordings of Rockwell's speeches, all of which graphically addressed his racist and anti-Semitic views. Nowhere in the lengthy correspondence between the two women does Claire express shock or disapproval at her son's vitriolic attacks on blacks and Jews. She was kept up to date on the American Nazi party's fortunes, with von Goetz reassuring her, probably falsely, that Rockwell had financial reserves even after the disastrous IRS seizure of ANP assets. Claire regularly sent her son money for personal medical and living expenses, and she may also have made periodic contributions to the party, although documentation supporting that assertion is suggestive but by no means definitive. After a raid on party headquarters by unspecified law enforcement authorities in 1966, von Goetz wrote to Claire and assured her that her name was not among those in the files that had been seized and that Claire's "property" was secure.[16] It is unclear precisely what "files" and what "property" von Goetz was referring to, but she and Rockwell, accustomed to frequent raids by law enforcement agencies and suspicious of spies within the ANP, kept lists of contributors—the party's most precious asset—segregated from administrative files and hidden from all party officers.

Claire may have best revealed her sympathy for her son's worldview in a poignant letter to him in which she attempted to bolster his flagging spirits. "For a long time I, too, have felt that the people do not deserve you," she wrote. "You will be old and bent before the yellow masses will be in sufficient misery to creep from under the bed to unite in full force." She would have preferred Rockwell out of politics for his own sake—for his physical well-being, his material comfort, and his mental tranquillity—but she gave no indication that she disapproved of his views or disagreed with his philosophy or with the

ANP program. "I want you to know," she continued, "that [I] think you have done and are doing a super human job and we are proud of you. In whatever direction your decision leads you, we are ready to stand by you." Her profession of support meant a great deal to Rockwell, and he responded with effusive expressions of gratitude and admiration for her courage.[17]

Financial crises, which had plagued Rockwell since the formation of the ANP, climaxed in early 1966 when the IRS seized the party's possessions and property, including party headquarters in Arlington, Virginia, and held a public auction on 18 February to satisfy a lien for delinquent taxes.[18] As financial pressures mounted—and as any realistic expectation of seizing political power grew more and more remote—Rockwell increasingly turned to the psychically gratifying and financially lucrative college lecture circuit.

As early as 1962, Rockwell viewed appearances before college audiences as an important component of his public strategy. They afforded him access to young, malleable political activists and a public platform conducive to media attention. The returns on this strategy for recruitment purposes were dismal—virtually all students in his audiences regarded him with derision and scorn—but paid handsome dividends in Rockwell's most coveted commodity, publicity. His first attempt, at Pennsylvania's Bucknell University, garnered him a bonanza of publicity that exceeded his most optimistic expectations. The controversy surrounding his invitation by the Bucknell Student Forum, and the invitation's subsequent withdrawal after intense pressure from local American Legion, VFW, and DAR chapters, kept his name on the front page of the region's daily newspaper for the better part of a month.[19] Although he never actually spoke at Bucknell, the furor raised by even the possibility of his appearance convinced him that college campuses nationwide were promising territory for a rich harvest of publicity and for the recruits and contributions that he hoped would inevitably follow.

Rockwell followed his Bucknell triumph with an even more rewarding foray into the nation's media capital, New York City. In April, he was invited to address the Student Forum at Hunter College, in the Bronx. At the last minute—possibly tipped off about an impending arrest on an old warrant if he entered New York City—Rockwell sent a surrogate, an ANP captain named Seth David Ryan, who addressed an audience of about five hundred students while "over a thousand pickets protested outside the college hall." Solomon Andhil Fineberg's quarantine (see chapter 5), which had in the past effectively limited Rockwell's access to the New York media, ruptured in the rush to cover the events at Hunter College. Later that spring, an outraged student further aided Rockwell's cause by charging the platform during a Rockwell speech at San Diego State College and striking the ANP leader on the side of the face.[20]

As a result, Rockwell garnered nationwide publicity and the sympathy of free-speech advocates.

From the fall of 1962 through 1964, Rockwell accelerated his campus efforts and drew large crowds, which in turn fed media attention.[21] At every stop, most students laughed, jeered, and ridiculed Rockwell, but they turned out in impressive numbers to see him. He spoke before three thousand students at the University of Colorado and more than two thousand at the University of Kansas. At both venues, auditorium capacities limited the size of the crowd, and many students were turned away.[22] Rockwell set off a near-riot at the University of Washington when almost two thousand couldn't get in to hear him speak after fire marshals closed the doors of the packed auditorium. Media attention at one campus increased the crowd at the next, and as Rockwell's public profile rose, even his surrogates drew impressive crowds.[23]

By 1965, although the number of appearances remained high (in fact, they steadily increased until his death in 1967), media coverage of Rockwell's appearances, and of what he had to say, significantly diminished in both frequency and prominence. It's impossible to determine whether the change resulted from Fineberg's ability to reinstitute the quarantine that had earlier proved so effective or whether the media simply lost interest in Rockwell once the novelty wore off. He was becoming old news, but he refused to abandon the college lecture circuit or switch to a new strategy. Instead, he focused on the money he was earning on colleges campuses, sometimes as much as $200 per appearance.

Having tasted commercial success, Rockwell proposed a business partnership to William L. Pierce to exploit the notoriety their activities had brought them. What he had in mind was an "Extremist Speakers Bureau," and he offered Pierce a 20 percent commission on all bookings, with Pierce being put in charge of speaker procurement—the "lower and crud[d]ier" the better. Rockwell characterized the list of potential speakers as "a menu of 'forbidden fruit'" and promised to produce a "jim dandy" brochure that would be irresistible to college students.[24]

The "Extremist Speakers Bureau" never materialized, but Rockwell's career as a campus curiosity blossomed. For the first time in his adult life, he was generating a steady income. His bookings rose and so did his gross income. By 1966, his fee escalated to $300 per appearance plus expenses; by 1967, to $350 plus expenses. Rockwell's engagements included Ivy League schools—in particular, Harvard, Brown, Columbia—and consumed most of his time and attention beginning in mid-1965.[25]

During the last eight months of his life—January to August 1967—Rockwell's bookings and earnings escalated to point where he was supporting the ANP almost entirely from his speaking fees. By January he had more invitations from colleges than available dates; by March he often scheduled two campus speeches a day. Rockwell reported to Matt Koehl: "I'm gathering in more than $2,000 in the next week or so speaking, and the trend is UP!" He promised Koehl that he would soon have raised enough money to get the administrative and clerical help Koehl had repeatedly requested. He also confided to his friend and comrade, the retired marine corps general Pedro A. del Valle, that in one week he spoke at seven colleges, taking in almost $1,500.[26]

Rockwell made a respectable amount of money during the last months of his life but gained few converts. The columnist Max Lerner attended one of Rockwell's campus performances in late 1966 and wrote: "I wondered what we were all doing there, and how insane a people could get in a democracy, to have the flower of their youth listening to plans for mass murder, and treating [Rockwell] as if he represented some substantial body of rational if wrong-headed opinion."[27]

Rockwell had become a spectacle, a parody of himself. He used just the right words and epithets and postures to inflame and outrage. If he could not convert, he felt satisfied to shock and entertain. He held center stage and reveled in the spotlight. In those last months of his life he didn't seem to notice, or care, that the brass ring of political power had moved beyond his grasp. The attention and the financial rewards of notoriety now fed the demons that drove him.

13

BETRAYAL AND DEATH

*I worshipped Rockwell and I loved him dearly. There seemed to
be practically nothing I would not do for him. To me, he was
everything. I loved him like a father and he loved me like his son.*
—John Patler, 1972

When a lone gunman put a bullet into George Lincoln
Rockwell as he backed his car out of a parking space in front of a laundromat
in a strip mall in Arlington, Virginia, on 25 August 1967, the American Nazi
party effectively came to an end. The Commonwealth of Virginia arrested,
tried, and convicted John Patler, a twenty-nine-year-old disaffected former
ANP officer for Rockwell's murder. Neither event proved conclusive. Rockwell's influence in death dwarfed any power he wielded in life; and Patler's
conviction ended none of the speculation within the radical right of who killed
George Lincoln Rockwell.

Several theories emerged soon after Rockwell's death, among his admirers and followers, as to the identity and motive of their commander's assassin.
One camp held that some Jewish-based organization—the Anti-Defamation
League figured prominently in this scenario—orchestrated Rockwell's assassination because he alone, among prominent anti-Semites, had the potential
to acquire political power.[1] Karl Allen, a high-ranking ANP officer and devoted
Rockwell loyalist, organized a John Patler Defense Fund in the months following the murder. He initially accepted the conclusion of the police that Patler
was Rockwell's killer, but he soon came to see the markings of a Jewish conspiracy in the affair—if not in the murder itself, then certainly in the arrest of
Patler. Allen wrote to Pedro A. del Valle of his belief that Patler was innocent
and that Rockwell's assassination was the centerpiece of an elaborate Jewish
plot to rid the world of Rockwell while at the same time discrediting his legacy
by blaming his death on one of his own disciples.[2]

Although the notion of ADL involvement in Rockwell's assassination appealed—and continues to appeal—to Rockwell partisans, not one scintilla of
real evidence exists to support it. Since Rockwell had ceased to be an actual

threat to the Jewish community by 1967, his murder served no purpose. To the contrary, as a visible and vocal symbol of anti-Semitic extremism, Rockwell had value as a beacon around which the Jewish community could be mobilized. Through Rockwell, the ADL could sustain the emotional engagement of its constituency. His stunts and public pronouncements helped keep the Jewish community vigilant and committed in support of the ADL's program against more dangerous, but less visible, threats to American Jewry. As a practical matter, by 1967 the ADL had no reason to desire Rockwell's death and some reason to tolerate his activities in a contained environment. Despite the attraction of the Jewish-ADL conspiracy theory, most of Rockwell's followers accepted the state's conclusion that John Patler had killed Rockwell.

John Patsalos (he changed his name to Patler in 1960) was born in New York City on 6 January 1938. He grew up in a violent and anti-Semitic household dominated by his father, Christ Patsalos, a Greek-born immigrant who possessed a vicious temper and mixed his ritualistic religious fervor with heavy doses of anti-Semitism. Christ Patsalos married a young, New York-born woman of Greek descent, Athena Mavroglan, when he was in his early forties; his bride was barely twenty. The union produced two sons, John and George (born in 1939). In 1943, Christ Patsalos shot and killed his wife in the kitchen of their New York City apartment. He believed that she was flirting with other men behind his back. Christ Patsalos went to prison; his sons, ages five and four, were placed in the custody of their maternal grandmother. A day did not pass, Patler later recalled, that his grandmother did not weep over the death of her daughter. Through her tears, the old woman repeated the account of Athena's death and burned the guilt of their father's deed into the boys' minds. "He was to us the personification of all evil," Patler later wrote, "and we were his sons!"[3]

Christ Patsalos served less than ten years in prison for the murder of his wife. His mother-in-law died within a short time after his release on parole, and he claimed custody of his sons. Soon after moving back with his father, whom he feared and hated, John Patler initiated a series of petty crimes and destructive antisocial acts that kept him in trouble with the police throughout his teenage years. When he violated probation for auto theft, New York's Juvenile Court remanded him to the Morrisania Hospital Mental Hygiene Clinic as a chronic truant and for his failure to "adjust satisfactorily" to society.[4] During a series of evaluative interviews, the psychiatric caseworker described young Patler as "tense and sullen" and recorded Patler's frequent anti-Semitic comments to the hospital's Jewish staff. One Morrisania psychiatrist made special note of "the hatred expressed" by Patler and quoted him as boasting, "I go to Church every Sunday morning and fight the Jews." That same psychiatrist concluded that Patler's "impaired judgment, his rigidity, his very immature emotionality, his narcissism, his irrelevant suspiciousness, his be-lief in his righteousness—with probable repressed homosexuality, lead the examiner to the tentative diagnosis of *paranoia.*" In 1956, when Patler was eighteen years old, a psychiatrist entered this notation on his Morrisania file: "This patient may become dangerous—he appears as a potential murderer." Patler was observed extensively and received court-mandated outpatient treat-ment, but by early 1957 the same psychiatrist recognized a deterioration in his mental state. "The patient is delusional," the psychiatrist wrote, "and the diagnosis of paranoia is confirmed." He reemphasized his earlier notation that Patler demonstrated violent tendencies and could one day commit murder.[5]

After 1957, Patler slipped through the cracks of the city's mental health system. Early in the year he stopped keeping his outpatient appointments at Morrisania, but the hospital lacked the manpower to pursue the matter and merely recorded the missed appointments in his file. In late fall 1957, his psy-chiatric caseworker wrote in his file: "No Further Service. Case Closed." The system did not quite know what to do with him. Identified as "a potential murderer," he was deemed "not a suitable candidate for psychotherapy" on an outpatient basis and was recommended for "in-patient [psycho-therapy] at Bellevue [a state mental hospital]." Incongruously, the psychiatrist who made those notations also prompted the closure of Patler's file by concluding that "[Patler] is now being seen weekly by private psychiatrist and [his] probation officer feels he is making satisfactory adjustment in the community."[6]

By 1956–57, Patler was exhibiting well-formed anti-Semitic attitudes, in-cluding an expressed belief that the United States was controlled by Jews and that "Hitler was right" in attempting to liquidate the Jews of Europe.[7] His anti-Semitism mirrored his father's oft-expressed beliefs as well as those of DeWest Hooker, a notorious New York hatemonger. Hooker founded the Nationalist Youth League specifically to mobilize young men from the city's streets for an anticipated Nazi resurgence. Suave, urbane, free to pursue his political ob-session using his inherited wealth, Hooker drew young Patler into his perverse circle with an almost erotic seduction. "Hooker was my idol," Patler later wrote, "and I became his follower." In Hooker, Patler found the first of two great surrogate fathers.[8]

Patler's participation in the NYL embroiled him in further criminal activi-ties, which resulted in an arrest for criminal libel. Facing revocation of his probation and prosecution as an adult, he accepted the court's alternative and joined the U.S. Marine Corps. While he was in basic training at Camp Lejeune, North Carolina, his father died. Liberated from the physical ties to a man he despised, Patler would soon be condemned to a more pervasive form of psy-chological bondage in an endless search for a new father figure.

In 1960, while stationed at Quantico, Virginia, John Patler renewed his friendship with George Lincoln Rockwell, whom he'd met two years earlier through DeWest Hooker. Patler joined the ANP and quickly rose through the ranks to become the party's youngest staff officer. Rockwell liked Patler's courage and enthusiasm, and he was flattered by Patler's slavish devotion to him. Like Rockwell, Patler was a talented cartoonist and graphic artist, which would prove useful to the ANP. In addition, his marine corps uniform brought the American Nazi party a measure of respectability at rallies—until his involvement in the ANP forced the marines to release him on a general discharge. Once free, Patler devoted all of his time and energy to Rockwell and the party. He shed his hated surname and adopted the Anglo-Saxon-sounding "Patler." With Rockwell's blessing, he took a submissive German-American bride, Erika von Gundlach, and quickly produced two strapping quasi-Aryan future warriors for Rockwell's National Socialist world order. At Rockwell's direction, Patler moved his family from Virginia to New York City to organize an ANP chapter there. Within two years of the move, Patler's marriage had deteriorated. He gave Erika a divorce, along with custody of their sons, and returned to Rockwell's Virginia headquarters.[9]

Back in Virginia, Patler's life revolved around Rockwell. He followed him everywhere, serving as his aide-de-camp, chauffeur, bodyguard, and gofer. One journalist observed that Patler "loved Rockwell passionately, drawn to him by an irrational loyalty."[10] From early 1963, when he returned to Virginia, until mid-1966, when his relationship with Rockwell abruptly turned, Patler allowed his life to center on Rockwell's needs. Indeed, Rockwell's dominant personality consumed John Patler's identity.

In 1964, Patler met Alice Ervin, the daughter of an Arlington television repairman. Alice was nineteen years old, Patler twenty-six. A seductive beauty with expressive eyes and long, honey-blonde hair, Alice conveyed sensuousness with a look, a gesture, a smile. Those who knew her at that time describe her as a "fragile beauty" who had an unsettling effect on men, especially older men, and as the kind of woman who displayed her sensuality with a guileless candor. She was aroused by uniforms and didn't hide her "erotic attraction" to John Patler.[11] The two were married in 1966, by which time she had already given birth to their first son and would soon give birth to their second. From that time on Patler was a different man, more self-confident and more assertive. A renewed sense of self-esteem emboldened him. For the first time since Rockwell drew Patler into his orbit in 1960, Patler conceived of an identity apart from Rockwell. He asserted his independence by breaking with Rockwell and resigning from the ANP. He took his new wife and their infant sons—the oldest was not yet two, the younger only two months— to New York City. Still propelled by his Nazi beliefs, Patler and Dan Burros, his closest friend and another Rockwell defector, created a practical clone of Rockwell's American Nazi party. "It was a difficult thing for me," Patler confessed, "because I still loved him, although I was no longer a blind follower."[12]

As he had during his earlier separation from Rockwell, Patler soon grew restless, incapable of functioning for long apart from the father figure who validated him. In mid-1966, not long after moving to New York, he returned to Virginia with his family. Rockwell welcomed him as a father welcomes a prodigal son and restored his place in the ANP hierarchy. But there was still a void within him and nothing, not even Rockwell's firm hand, seemed able to guide John Patler toward whatever it was he sought. He bickered with his ANP comrades, imagined plots against him within the party, and alternated between attacks on Rockwell and plaintive tears for forgiveness. A frustrated Rockwell wrote: "My reasoning with you, my most strenuous efforts to rehabilitate you, my downright brotherly feeling of real love for you, my best efforts to please you, my efforts to discipline you—NOTHING helps. You react to all of these precisely the way a spoiled kid would react to all of them." Patler responded angrily to Rockwell's reprimand and returned the letter with all the fault-finding passages crossed out and cryptic phrases added in the margins. Within two days, however, he sent another letter begging Rockwell's forgiveness.[13]

Patler's letters reveal an anguish and turmoil within him that alternated, often uncontrollably, between self-loathing and hateful recrimination against all forms and representations of authority. Rockwell had come to embody authority for John Patler, and Patler swung wildly between a pitiful yearning for Rockwell's approval and a menacing rebellion against his control. He blamed Rockwell for his disastrous first marriage and for forcing him to abandon his ethnic identity to conform to Rockwell's Aryan ideal. "Self-hate and self-shame" led to "a name change and a marriage to a woman who was the ideal 'Nordic' type," Patler wrote. "All my life I've been 'running away' from myself. This whole ugly way of deceiving myself has just about 'castrated' me, spiritually." He concluded plaintively: "The hurt and the pain has brought me to tears many, many times."[14]

From late 1966 through early 1967, Patler drifted in and out of the ANP, alternating between unconditional devotion to Rockwell and a brooding, solitary hostility. As the summer of 1967 reached its midpoint, his mood swings grew wider and more pronounced. His periods of isolation became total and more extended, his reconciliations with Rockwell more passionate. In his last known letter to Rockwell, Patler used terms of endearment most often reserved for lovers. "I feel much better after talking to you," he wrote. "I want sooo badly to get back into the spirit of things and push for you all the way. I don't think there are two people on earth who think and feel the same as we do. . . . You are a very important part of my life. I need you as much as you need me. Without you there is no future."[15]

When Arlington police arrested John Patler moments after Rockwell's assassination, he was alone, on foot, and less than two miles from the murder scene. The evidence used to convict him was entirely circumstantial and less than compelling.[16] In seeking to establish a motive for the killing, Arlington police claimed Patler acted out of anger, that he was seeking revenge against Rockwell for expelling him from the ANP in March 1967. Although Patler and Rockwell had repeatedly fought and reconciled, the altercation in March bore the markings of a final break. Instead of disciplining Patler himself, Rockwell delegated Matt Koehl, whom Patler hated, to deliver the expulsion order. Koehl added to Patler's humiliation by instructing ANP stormtroopers to examine Patler's room and personal possessions to ensure that Patler would not abscond with party property.[17] Patler spent the spring of 1967 seething over the treatment he had received from Rockwell via Koehl. In letters to a sympathetic comrade, he attacked the ANP as a "cult of personality built by Rockwell" and vowed to "write an expose on his vile habits." But by midsummer Patler was once again begging Rockwell's forgiveness.[18]

Another possible motive for the killing was Patler's alleged anger at Rockwell's unwillingness to protect him from those in the party—notably, Matt Koehl and William L. Pierce—who derided him as a "swarthy, greasy, Greek."[19] Factional dissension within the ANP over dominance by Germanic-Nordic racial types certainly existed—and Koehl, supported by Pierce, certainly agitated against those he considered genetically inferior—but Rockwell favored Patler's position and at the time of his death was moving the ANP toward a broader, pan-white inclusiveness. Tension within the party on this issue existed between Rockwell and Koehl, *not* between Rockwell and Patler.

A third possible motive never surfaced at Patler's trial. Patler discovered that Rockwell and Alice Patler were having an affair. Some believe that this discovery—and the attendant anguish of betrayal—drove Patler to kill Rockwell.[20] But this explanation doesn't stand up to scrutiny, because shortly after Patler learned that the man he idolized and the woman he loved were engaged in a torrid sexual liaison, he wrote a letter to Rockwell sanctioning the relationship. "If Alice wants to make it with you," Patler wrote in a final gesture of total submission, "I wouldn't object. That is the truth."[21]

What remains by way of explanation is the irrational and the unprovable. A variety of events had crippled Patler's mental processes and his capacity for rational thought long before he met Rockwell, and their tumultuous relationship offered no opportunities for Patler to heal. The events of 1966–67 depict Patler as a man precipitously close to the margins of irrationality, and in that mental state, no action can be discounted, no matter how implausible. For his part, Patler steadfastly maintains that he did not kill Rockwell.[22]

Many key Rockwell intimates—including Robert Surrey, Floyd Fleming, George Ware, Frank Smith, and Barbara von Goetz—believed that a high-level conspiracy within the American Nazi party executed a successful coup by eliminating Rockwell and elevating him to martyr status while seizing control of his party. The target of their speculation was Rockwell's chief deputy and successor, Matt Koehl. None believed that Koehl himself pulled the trigger, since such overt action would have been totally out of character for the brooding, reclusive ANP administrator. But they believed that Koehl, with the complicity of William L. Pierce and a weapons expert named Robert Allison Lloyd, orchestrated the killing.[23]

The night before his assassination, Rockwell had an acrimonious showdown with Koehl, Pierce, and Lloyd at ANP headquarters over the direction of the party. According to an eyewitness, an enraged Rockwell locked the three men out of their offices and confided to a stormtrooper on duty that the trio would be expelled from the party by week's end.[24] The break between Rockwell and Koehl's faction hung on two issues: Rockwell's recent emphasis on the lucrative college lecture circuit at the expense of pursuing the party's revolutionary goals; and Rockwell's abandonment of Hitler's standards of Germanic-Nordic racial purity in favor of a broader-based pan-white movement. By January 1967, Rockwell had decided to "de-Nazify" the ANP and change its emphasis from Nazi resurgence to "White Power." To accelerate this process, he changed the name from the American Nazi party to the National Socialist White People's party and replaced the swastika with a stylized American eagle. Neither change sat well with Koehl, who was unable to abandon his fanatical attachment to both the swastika and the notion of Germanic racial purity.[25]

Barbara von Goetz, Rockwell's mistress and the closest person to him at the time of his death, initially accepted the police charge against Patler. Koehl needed her to hold the party together and made a concerted effort to win her loyalty. In December 1967, four months after Rockwell's death, von Goetz seemed resigned to accepting Koehl as Rockwell's successor and the movement's new leader. She confided to Rockwell's mother that Koehl had many shortcomings and virtually none of Rockwell's strengths but was, for the time being, the best man the party had. Less than six weeks later, she sensed that she was being distanced from Koehl and his clique. She complained to Claire Schade Rockwell that Koehl and his closest advisers were intentionally excluding her from major party decisions. Fearing for her safety, she moved out of party headquarters and begged Rockwell's mother to keep her home address secret. By the spring of 1968, von Goetz believed unequivocally that Koehl had arranged Rockwell's murder in order to seize control of the ANP. She confided that conclusion to Rockwell's mother, saying that she hesitated to give voice to her suspicions until they were confirmed to her satisfaction. She claimed that longtime Rockwell loyalists Floyd Fleming and George Ware believed, as she now did, that Koehl, Pierce, and Lloyd had conspired to assassinate Rockwell and then framed Patler, whom they disliked intensely. Barbara von Goetz officially resigned from the party on 20 March 1968.[26]

Francis Joseph "Frank" Smith, Rockwell's personal bodyguard, mourned his fallen leader and couldn't shake the memory of a confidence Rockwell shared with him less than two months before his death. Smith, a burly Boston street tough, had served seven years in a Massachusetts prison for a dynamite bombing and attempted murder. He worshiped Rockwell, who in turn valued Smith's fearlessness, his street savvy, and his unswerving loyalty. Rockwell dubbed Smith the "Holy Father" because of the scars he bore on his neck and chest from a gang shootout in his youth. In June 1967, after two men fired shots at Rockwell from a passing car as he emerged from party headquarters, Rockwell told Smith he thought he recognized one of the men, adding, "I suspect treachery from someone very close to me." Smith pressed Rockwell for the identity of the traitor, but Rockwell refused, replying, "Frank, I don't dare mention my suspicions because if I am wrong, it could do irreparable harm to the party."[27]

Distrustful of the police—and fulfilling a pledge he made to Rockwell in the event of his death by assassination—Smith conducted his own investigation. It led him to conclude that Koehl, Pierce, and Lloyd had masterminded the assassination. Smith identified Christopher Vidnjevich, a violent and unstable ANP officer from the party's Chicago headquarters, as Rockwell's killer. Vidnjevich, a fanatical racial purist and devoted Nazi, shared Koehl's anger at Rockwell's abandonment of Nazi racial dogma and symbolism. Smith's investigation and subsequent accusations culminated in a gunfight between Smith and Vidnjevich in rural Maine. Both men survived. Smith declined to pursue his allegations through conventional channels.[28]

In the aftermath of his brother's death, Bobby Rockwell initiated legal action to claim the body for a private family burial in New England. Matt Koehl, who wanted to turn the funeral into an ANP publicity extravaganza, had infuriated Bobby with his abortive attempt to have Rockwell buried at Arlington National Cemetery in full Nazi regalia. Bobby characterized the party's handling of Rockwell's remains as a "disgusting exhibition" by "nitwits." Koehl countered by threatening to surround Claire Schade Rockwell's home, in a Jewish section of Brooklyn, New York, with uniformed stormtroopers in a display of "mourning." When Bobby realized that Koehl intended to carry out his threat and embroil the family in a party spectacle, he capitulated. On his elderly mother's behalf, he announced to the press: "The family no longer wishes to contest the claim of Matt Koehl regarding the party's right to make funeral arrangements for George Lincoln Rockwell." He added that "it was unlikely any member of the family would attend the services."[29]

After being turned away at Arlington National Cemetery, Koehl mounted a second, publicity-driven assault on Culpeper National Cemetery in Virginia. He claimed that Rockwell, as a navy veteran of two wars, merited a military burial in a national cemetery. The authorities agreed but would not permit the burial—as Koehl well knew—with Rockwell dressed in a Nazi uniform inside a coffin draped with a Nazi flag. Koehl led a uniformed ANP contingent bearing Rockwell's coffin to the gates of Culpeper National Cemetery, where a squad of American soldiers, under the command of U.S. Army Provost Marshal Carl C. Turner, turned them away. When the press lost interest in the fiasco, Koehl had Rockwell's body cremated.[30]

Another death in the Rockwell family, that of his five-month-old daughter by Barbara von Goetz—just one week before his own—went almost unnoticed. In the late winter of 1967, von Goetz left Arlington for an extended visit with Frank and Claudia Smith in Ellsworth Falls, Maine. Unknown to Rockwell, von Goetz was pregnant with his child and needed time away to sort things out. She knew that Hatemonger Hill was the wrong environment in which to raise a child, yet she desperately wanted this baby, for her own sake and for Rockwell's. Early in their relationship she bore another Rockwell daughter, but that baby had died in infancy and Rockwell had grieved mightily.[31] Now, five years later and pregnant with another Rockwell baby, von Goetz feared opening old wounds if this infant also suffered the same respiratory defect that took the life of their first child. She decided to have the baby in secret and only share it with Rockwell if it was born healthy and strong.

Von Goetz trusted the Smiths, devoted friends to both her and Rockwell, to keep her secret. She lived with them in rural Maine while the baby came to term. Admitted to the hospital under the name Florence Mary Getz, von Goetz delivered an apparently healthy baby girl at 2:46 P.M. on 1 March 1967. The birth certificate listed Francis J. Smith and Florence Mary Getz as the infant's parents. The baby was named Gretchen Virginia Smith. The only person von Goetz confided in about the birth, beside the Smiths, was Claire Schade Rockwell. Ten days after Gretchen's birth, von Goetz wrote to Rockwell's mother, revealing her whereabouts and the baby's true paternity and enclosing a copy of the birth certificate. She also sent along papers detailing the birth and instructions about protecting Gretchen if something happened to either of her parents. When Gretchen was one month old, von Goetz arranged for a local Maine housewife to care for her and returned to Arlington to be with Rockwell. She decided to wait a while longer, to make sure their daughter would live, before telling Rockwell about Gretchen.[32]

When von Goetz finally confided in Rockwell, later that spring, he was ecstatic and insisted that she bring the baby to Arlington. For a couple of months their life together approached normalcy. Rockwell adored Gretchen and spent every possible moment doting on her. But in late July, Gretchen began having trouble breathing, just as their first daughter had. Gretchen's respiratory system was in full collapse, and the doctors informed von Goetz and Rockwell that her condition was terminal. They said that she suffered from a rare condition, Werdung-Hoffman syndrome, resulting from recessive genes in both parents. It was the same disease that had killed their first child. Von Goetz wrote to Rockwell's mother, describing the infant's worsening paralysis and increasing respiratory distress. She sadly recalled a recent camping trip, before the diagnosis, and Rockwell's joy at having a family again after being alone for so long. Now, she reported, Rockwell was inconsolable.[33]

On several nights Gretchen—choking, gasping for air, unable to cry—had to be rushed to the hospital. Each time the doctors revived her, but she grew steadily weaker. By 4 August her condition was such that she could not leave the hospital and was put on a respirator. An anguished von Goetz, describing the medical efforts to keep Gretchen alive, which only prolonged her suffering, told Claire Rockwell that she longed for the simple mercy of death for her daughter. In that same letter, von Goetz expressed concern about Rockwell's health, describing him as drawn and extremely fatigued. At her insistence, he had a complete physical, which revealed a prediabetic condition. A distraught Von Goetz insisted that she would see that he followed the doctor's instructions as she clung even closer to him in her grief.[34] Gretchen died on Friday, 18 August 1967. Her mother wrote to Claire Rockwell of the baby's last moments and of laying her to rest.[35] Her father wept uncontrollably beside her grave.

CONCLUSION:
ROCKWELL'S LEGACY OF HATE

We are the very same Movement which arose in 1919, which was crushed in 1945, which was resurrected under the inspired leadership of Lincoln Rockwell, and which has persisted in a continuous, unbroken line up to this day.
—Matt Koehl, 1994

George Lincoln Rockwell never commanded more than a few hundred loyalists and never rose above the status of a curiosity to most Americans. Yet his influence on the racist right in American politics is lasting and profound. He shattered the barriers of Nazi Nordic elitism and Ku Klux Klan nativism and opened racist politics in America—through his pan-white construction of "White Power"—to all who were not visibly African or born Jewish. He popularized the insidious anti-Semitic propaganda tool of Holocaust denial within the racist right and introduced its precepts to the American public. And he created a safe haven for American Nazis in the Christian Identity movement, which has allowed his racist and anti-Semitic beliefs to smolder within a spurious theology until some future time when external events might call them forth to ignite another destructive conflagration.

Within the racist right, Rockwell holds a place of honor and homage. Virtually all contemporary racist leaders recognize his role in carrying Americanized National Socialism and anti-Semitism to the brink of the twenty-first century. They specifically recognize his pivotal role in rescuing Nazi icons in the dismal days following Hitler's defeat in World War II, crediting him with a heroic, "phoenix-like act in picking the fallen torch of National Socialism up out of the ashes of 1945." According to the contemporary racist right, by rescuing the core beliefs of German National Socialism, Rockwell preserved its essence and "gave the modern racial cause its orientational focus and established the tenor of its discourse."[1]

Rockwell assembled a nucleus of true believers and held them together during the critical postwar era. According to William L. Pierce, a former Rockwell follower and leading contemporary National Socialist theorist, in the 1960s Rockwell "gave Hitler's doctrine currency. He gave thousands of people the conviction that National Socialism was indeed the wave of the future, and he gave a few the courage to begin working for a National Socialist world." James Mason believes that no subsequent leader of the racist right had Rockwell's flair for capturing the public's attention or his potential to expand the influence of the movement. Mason asserts: "In the comparatively short time Rockwell was running things he made a much bigger splash than have any of his followers." He goes on to argue that Rockwell's strategy for seizing power "could have worked had he lived to see it through." For Mason, "the youngest card-carrying member of George Lincoln Rockwell's American Nazi Party" and a leader of the contemporary racist right, Rockwell's influence will be felt for generations through the adherents—including himself—that Rockwell attracted to the movement. Rockwell was, in Mason's view, "the bridge over which so many . . . have crossed."[2]

Internationally, Rockwell's stature and continuing influence within the National Socialist resurgence movement is even greater than in the United States. Manfred Roeder—an unreconstructed "old" Nazi who saw "the Third Reich and its glory" and a leading figure in Germany's contemporary Nazi movement—recognizes Rockwell as a pivotal figure in mobilizing the faithful survivors of Hitler's defeat. A Nazi resurgence in Germany is particularly troublesome to T. W. Adorno, a leading scholar of fascism and totalitarianism. Adorno believes that the inability of Germans to accept and mourn the recent past can lead to the reemergence of anti-Semitism as a social force. Adorno also argues that "the continued existence of National Socialism within democracy [is] potentially more threatening than the continued existence of fascist tendencies against democracy."[3] Rockwell's hand is clearly evident in the modern conditions in reunited Germany that trouble Adorno.

Colin Jordan, a Rockwell intimate and currently the revered elder statesman among British National Socialists, evaluates Rockwell's legacy from a pan-European perspective. He maintains that Rockwell's leadership had a "galvanising effect" among the Nazi remnant in Europe of the early 1960s. "With the power of his exuberant and commanding personality, and his flair for publicity which went hand in hand with his gift for simplified expression," Jordan says, "Lincoln Rockwell made alive something hitherto considered dead and gone."[4]

Had he lived, it is unlikely that Rockwell would have achieved electoral success within the American political system. His public actions fixed an image in the electorate's mind early in his career that was incompatible with fundamental and deeply held American values. His supporters, however, believe that Rockwell's actions to de-Nazify his party, which he took in the months prior to his death, would have enabled him, eventually, to redefine himself within the right wing of the American political mainstream. From that redefinition, they believe, Rockwell would have emerged as the leader of a George Wallace–like third party with his racial and anti-Semitic views "respectable-ized" for mass consumption.[5] His ability to have accomplished such a transformation is extremely doubtful, but David Duke—a Rockwell disciple as a young man—demonstrated the feasibility of such a transition within one political generation. Duke, a member of the American Nazi party as well as the Ku Klux Klan, consciously "cleaned" his image by shedding the symbols of the ANP and the Klan and moderating his rhetoric. He replaced his stormtrooper uniform with a three-piece suit and entered electoral politics in Louisiana as a "conservative" Republican. In the 1980s and 1990s, Duke stunned the pundits by capturing a seat in the Louisiana legislature, making a respectable run for governor, and nearly winning election to the U.S. Senate. David Duke embodied the new National Socialist, the mainstream neo-Nazi, that Rockwell envisioned for the future.

During his own career, Rockwell influenced the parameters of the political dialogue in the United States. His explicit racism, raw anti-Semitism, and public charges of pervasive Jewish influence in American economic and political life allowed those who shared his fundamental views but rejected his crudity to appear moderate by comparison. In his classic essay on what he termed "the paranoid style in American politics," Richard Hofstadter argues that a pattern exists in American history in which events are framed within the context of a titanic struggle between the forces of good and evil. The villains in that struggle change from generation to generation—the Illuminati, Papists, Freemasons, Jews—but all are, in their time, described as being part of a conspiracy of unimaginable power and influence.[6] In his time, Rockwell embodied Hofstadter's "paranoid style" at the farthest fringe of American politics. As such, he extended the boundary of the political spectrum, making his contemporaries on the radical right who also subscribed to a conspiratorial worldview—notably Robert Welch, H. L. Hunt, Russell Maguire, and Willis Carto—seem tame by comparison. By redefining the fringe, Rockwell opened the mainstream of American public discourse to more circumspect expressions of his own worldview.

Rockwell's mental state is fertile ground for speculation. His charisma and self-confident bearing seduced most observers. One admirer described him as "smooth, intelligent and likable," noting that he "had been a naval aviator and such men are not lightweights." But the closer one got to Rockwell, the less stable he appeared. Within the ANP barracks, he held himself aloof from his stormtroopers, confided in only a handful of intimates, and socialized with no one. To many in the barracks, he seemed incapable of dealing with people one on one and most often hid behind "his posture as the Commander."[7]

Rockwell's relatives describe him as a narcissistic man who obsessed with the limelight, determined "to be recognized," far more concerned with "recognition, adoration, notoriety" than with the consequences of his actions. These traits, evident throughout his life, intensified as Rockwell aged. Those who interacted with him during the last three or four years of his life observed behavior that indicated emotional or mental instability. One witness describes him as "a profoundly disturbed man. . . . who had a lot of really peculiar tics and a blustery, compensating masculinity." While he perceived Rockwell to be "quite intelligent," this observer remembers him as a "very troubled man." Rockwell's boyhood friend Stanley R. Tupper recalls Rockwell visiting him in Washington—Tupper was a U.S. congressman from Maine—in 1967, having made the appointment under an assumed name. Tupper, who abhorred and rejected all that Rockwell stood for, was shocked and saddened by the "marked change in [Rockwell's] personality" from the "good-natured, funny, talented" young man he knew growing up in Boothbay Harbor. "I have to wonder," Tupper recalls, "if he was entirely sane."[8]

In 1964, William F. Buckley Jr.—who consistently rejected Rockwell's politics and forcefully denounced his anti-Semitism—tried to get Rockwell to seek psychiatric counseling. In an unpublicized gesture of compassion, Buckley arranged for a friend, a Catholic priest and an experienced counselor, to meet with Rockwell, in May of that year. The priest reported to Buckley that Rockwell "is oddly personable, in a heavy, rude [way], and not incapable of winning over single people of the same stripe. But that is the end of it. He is gross (I read his book on the way home), fanatical, and urges criminally insane suggestions. . . . on the surface, he doesn't have any scruples about the morals of the nazi movement." He described Rockwell's mind as "a disaster area," his thought process as "corrupted by snap verbal comparisons," and concluded that Rockwell "lusts for demagogic success." He saw Rockwell's "desire to go on talking" as the "only sign of hope."[9] Rockwell didn't keep his promise to meet again with the priest.

Only after Rockwell's death did Buckley write of his brief meeting with the man Buckley referred to as "Father Jude." According to Buckley, Rockwell "was given, from time to time, to writing me obscene communications." One letter struck Buckley as "what the psychologists classify as a 'cry for help,' that cry which is so often made by those in despair." In a humanitarian gesture, Buckley brought Rockwell together with "a young priest, an old friend of mine, brilliantly learned and persuasive." The meeting showed "that even Rockwell had the glimmering of a conscience, and sometimes that conscience stirred like a three-month fetus, and that he might . . . one day have turned on himself with the fury with which he assaulted others . . . and thus might, just might, have won redemption." But "Father Jude never heard again from Rockwell."[10]

The extent of Rockwell's reach is unknowable. To simply say that he failed is to dangerously underestimate the ultimate course of the struggle. The failure of anti-Semitic and racist political ideology in twentieth-century America has been ascribed to "the unusual strength of liberal values" in the United States. But that triumph should not be taken as evidence of an "immutable ideological commitment on the part of Americans." Rather, it is the result of relentless vigilance and heroic effort in battle after battle against "opponents whose values were decidedly illiberal." The outcome of that struggle "was, by no means, preordained."[11] And the victory against "true believers" of Rockwell's persuasion can hardly be considered final. The historian Eugene Genovese's insight into the resilience of the true believer's cause resonates a warning against complacency by those who see in Rockwell's failure the conquest of those who share his obsession. "When the ramparts of heaven do not yield to human assault, and the latest version of the Cause lies in ashes, the refrain returns: we failed for this reason or that, and we were betrayed from within. Next time we will be thorough and leave nothing to chance. Whatever went wrong," Genovese warns, "the Cause will remain a shining beacon to future generations."[12]

Rockwell's legacy remains in those who carry on his work. For them, his words and deeds reach beyond those people he touched and inspire new generations of racists and anti-Semites. In the final analysis, his contribution to American politics was as his generation's embodiment of "the ageless impulse of men and women eaten by the disease of hatred to find a political expression or rationalization for their malady."[13] That is why his movement did not end with his death. Rockwell's movement was essentially nothing more—nor less—than his conception of that "ageless impulse." He seized upon it, shaped it, changed it, and gave it new form, but its soul was ancient. Leashing George Lincoln Rockwell did not leash the beast forever. Each generation must confront that demon anew.

NOTES

Introduction

1. Leonard Dinnerstein, *Antisemitism in America* (New York: Oxford University Press, 1994), 164; Morris Fine and Milton Himmelfarb, eds., *American Jewish Year Book 1963*, vol. 64, (Philadelphia: Jewish Publication Society of America, 1963), 138; George Lincoln Rockwell, *Legal, Psychological and Political Warfare* (pamphlet) (1965; rpt., Reedy, W.Va.: White Power Publications, 1977), 3; Dan Burros, *American Nazi Party Official Stormtrooper's Manual* (pamphlet) (Arlington, Va.: American Nazi Party, 1961), 4; George Lincoln Rockwell, "*Playboy* Interview: George Lincoln Rockwell," by Alex Haley, *Playboy,* April 1966, 82; U.S. Department of Justice, Federal Bureau of Investigation, FBI File #9-39854: George Lincoln Rockwell, Monograph, "American Nazi Party," June 1965, 17–30, quote on 18.

2. See Peter H. Merkl, "A New Lease on Life for the Radical Right?" in Peter H. Merkl and Leonard Weinberg, eds., *Encounters with the Contemporary Radical Right* (Boulder, Colo.: Westview Press, 1993), 204–27, esp. 205.

3. Umberto Eco, "Ur-Fascism," *New York Review of Books,* 22 June 1995, 12–15, quote on 14.

4. Ibid. To understand the relationship between leader and followers in a charismatic movement, see Eric Hoffer's classic book *The True Believer* (New York: Harper & Bros., 1951).

Chapter 1: The Family

1. The specifics of Rockwell's early life are drawn from the following sources, except where otherwise noted: George Lincoln Rockwell, *This Time the World,* 3d ed. (Liverpool, W.Va.: White Power Publications, 1979); William L. Pierce, *Lincoln Rockwell: A National Socialist Life* (pamphlet) (Arlington, Va.: NS Publications, 1969); James

Mason, *George Lincoln Rockwell: A Sketch of His Life and Career* (pamphlet) (Chillicothe, Ohio: Universal Order, n.d.); "Rockwell," *Facts,* September 1960, 161–66; P. Claire (Priscilla) Rockwell, interviewed by author, 17 August 1991; Peter Smyth, interviewed by author, 24 July 1991; Nancy Smyth Stefani, interviewed by author, 6 June 1991.

2. Rockwell, *This Time the World,* 7, 13; *Vaudeville News,* 10 September 1920, 4; Jack Mabley, "Nazi Boss' Dad Was Big in Vaudeville," *American* [?], 8 September 1966, and "George L. Rockwell Is Dead at 88; Comedian, Writer and Cartoonist," [unidentified newspaper], 2 March 1978, both clippings in the private collection of P. Claire Rockwell.

3. George Burns, the only intimate of Doc Rockwell who was still living at the time of this writing, chose to distance himself, in retrospect, from the Rockwells. Through his publicist, he wrote to the author: "It is true that Mr. Burns had met Mr. [Doc] Rockwell at one time, might even have been on the same bill, but he did not know him personally." Jack Langdon to author, 16 July 1991. Most of the sources previously cited contradict Mr. Burns's memory.

4. Arline Schade's name is spelled alternately "Arline" and "Arlene" in family documents and letters. Often, the same writer will use each spelling at different times. To avoid confusion, "Arline" will be used throughout this work.

5. Rockwell, *This Time the World,* 17.

6. Ibid., 18.

7. George Lincoln Rockwell (hereafter "GLR") to Claire Schade Rockwell, 9 September 1958, private collection of P. Claire Rockwell.

8. GLR to Claire Schade Rockwell, 18 October 1966, private collection of P. Claire Rockwell.

9. GLR to Claire Schade Rockwell, n.d. [1952], private collection of P. Claire Rockwell.

10. GLR to Claire Schade Rockwell, 23 July 1961, private collection of P. Claire Rockwell.

11. GLR to Eben Lewis, 3 August 1963, Special Collections, Bentley Historical Library, University of Michigan.

12. Harry Golden to GLR, 23 October 1961, "Media, Rockwell 58–62" folder, box 138, Blaustein Library, American Jewish Committee, New York (hereafter AJC). See also Harry Golden, *Only in America* (1958; rpt., New York: Permabooks, 1959), 47–50.

13. GLR to Harry Golden, 30 October 1961, "Media, Rockwell 58–62" folder, box 138, Blaustein Library, AJC.

Chapter 2: The Artist and the Warrior

1. The specifics of Rockwell's life from 1931 to 1953 are drawn from the following sources, except where otherwise noted: Rockwell, *This Time the World;* Pierce, *Lincoln Rockwell;* Mason, *George Lincoln Rockwell;* P. Claire Rockwell, Peter Smyth, and Nancy Smyth Stefani interviews; Eben Lewis, interviewed by author, 7 August 1995;

Harvey M. Spear, interviewed by author, 18 August 1995; FBI File #9-39854, "American Nazi Party."

2. Rockwell, *This Time the World,* 21.

3. Ibid.

4. Ibid., 30.

5. Victor J. Hillery to author, 17 September 1995. Hillery, one of Rockwell's two closest friends at Brown, emphasizes that "as an undergraduate at Brown, Rockwell was not a young anti-Semitic Nazi" and that "his later espousal of anti-Semitism and Nazism came after he sustained a complete change of personality that resulted from mental illness. I was a partial witness to this change which both frightened and saddened me." Hillery stresses that any accurate characterization of Rockwell must take into account "two different personalities: the very friendly and likable young man and the transformed individual who frightened not only his old friends but the whole country." Virtually all who knew Rockwell prior to World War II concur, to a greater or lesser degree, with Hillery's impression of Rockwell. The time frame of Rockwell's transformation—and of intimations of mental illness—varies, but the reality of a profound personality change in Rockwell's early adulthood is unmistakable.

6. Brooks Adams, *The Law of Civilization and Decay: An Essay on History* (New York: Alfred A. Knopf, 1951); Gustave Le Bon, *The Crowd: A Study of the Popular Mind,* 5th ed. (New York: Viking Press, 1966).

7. Rockwell, *This Time the World,* 42.

8. Ibid., 43.

9. *Providence* (R.I.) *Sunday Journal,* 25 April 1943, clipping in the private collection of P. Claire Rockwell.

10. Smyth interview.

11. *Evening Bulletin* (Providence, R.I.), 8 April 1948, and *Press Herald* (Portland, Maine), 5 April 1948, both clippings in the private collection of P. Claire Rockwell.

Chapter 3: The Coming Out

1. Smyth interview.

2. Stefani interview.

3. GLR to Claire Schade Rockwell, n.d. [1952], private collection of P. Claire Rockwell. Rockwell again turned to alcohol when his second marriage, to Thora Hallgrimsson, was breaking apart in late 1958 and 1959. Rockwell interview. See also James K. Warner, *Swastika Smearbund* (pamphlet) (Wilkes-Barre, Pa.: American Nationalist Bookstore, 1961), 6–7, located in "Media-Rockwell, 61" folder, box 138, Blaustein Library, AJC; and FBI File #9-39854, "Confidential Report," 5 November 1959.

4. Rockwell, *This Time the World,* 80–85, 93–94.

5. Ibid., 94–96; Stefani interview; FBI File #9-39854, "American Nazi Party."

6. Rockwell, *This Time the World,* 95.

7. Ibid.; Stefani interview; Mason, *George Lincoln Rockwell.*

8. Letter of Agreement between GLR and Thomas H. Burrowes, 12 November 1955

(Burrowes specialized in new product marketing); John E. Holden to GLR, 28 August 1957 (Holden was director of marketing of the Hubley Manufacturing Co., a large toy maker); Richard J. Cutler (*American Mercury*) to GLR, 2 November 1956; Robert L. Johnson Jr. (*Saturday Evening Post*) to GLR, 5 April 1957; Douglas S. Kennedy (*True: The Man's Magazine*) to GLR, 5 April 1957; Martin I. Cooley (Devin-Adair Co., Publishers) to GLR, 8 April 1957, all in the private collection of James Mason.

9. GLR to Robert Tripp Ross, Assistant Secretary of Defense, 9 January 1956, private collection of James Mason; Rockwell, *This Time the World*, 99–107; Pierce, *Lincoln Rockwell*, 13; Mason, *George Lincoln Rockwell*, n.p.

10. GLR to William F. Buckley Jr., 8 August 1956 and 5 December 1956; William F. Buckley Jr. to GLR, 12 December 1956 and 26 December 1956, both in the William F. Buckley Jr. Papers, Sterling Memorial Library, Yale University.

11. GLR to Dan Smoot, 21 March 1956; GLR to Edward Strohecker, 14 May 1956, both in the private collection of James Mason.

12. Bonnie Rockwell to GLR, n.d. [August 1957?], private collection of P. Claire Rockwell; H. F. Hallgrimsson to GLR, 14 August 1957, and Buell A. Patterson to GLR, 8 April 1957, both in the private collection of James Mason.

13. John George and Laird Wilcox, *Nazis, Communists, Klansmen, and Others on the Fringe: Political Extremism in America* (Buffalo, N.Y.: Prometheus Books, 1992), 251–65.

14. FBI File #9-39854, "American Nazi Party"; GLR to Congressman Wint Smith, 4 June 1956, private collection of James Mason; Rockwell, *This Time the World*, 108–16.

15. FBI File #9-39854, "American Nazi Party"; Rockwell, *This Time the World*, 123–33.

16. F. Garner Ranney (archivist, Episcopal Diocese of Maryland) to author, 27 July 1995; Very Rev. John N. Peabody, *Cathedral of the Incarnation: A History* (Baltimore: N.p., 1976). See also the Rev. H. N. Arrowsmith's obituary, *Maryland Churchman*, November 1955, 4; and *Stowe's Clerical Directory* (1953): 10.

17. Rockwell Deposition Extracts, "Rockwell 60–62, Followers & Supporters" folder, box 138, Blaustein Library, AJC; H. Keith Thompson to author, 20 July 1993; FBI File #9-39854, "American Nazi Party."

18. Rockwell Deposition Extracts, 3. The Arrowsmith physical description is from H. Keith Thompson to author, 20 July 1993. Stephenson's role is described in FBI File #9-39854, "American Nazi Party."

19. Rockwell Deposition Extracts; FBI File #9-39854, "American Nazi Party"; Rockwell, *This Time the World*, 154–73; Pierce, *Lincoln Rockwell*, 16–17.

20. Melissa Fay Greene, *The Temple Bombing* (New York: Fawcett Columbine, 1996), 219–24.

21. Ibid., 33–39.

22. California Department of Justice, Office of Attorney General Thomas J. Lynch, *Para-Military Organizations in California: A Report to the California State Senate Judiciary Committee* (12 April 1965), NSRP-7; *Independent*, August 1962, clippings in the private collection of H. Keith Thompson (*The Independent* was a right-wing

periodical published by Lyle Stuart, a racist); George and Wilcox, *Nazis, Communists, Klansmen,* 382–89; FBI File #9-39854, SAC, Richmond[, Va.,] to Director, FBI, memorandum, 10 March 1959.

23. Throughout his life Rockwell consistently denied involvement in the bombing, and I have found no evidence to dispute that denial. Such an act of overt terrorism would have been uncharacteristic of him. He agitated and cajoled, assaulted with horrible words and grotesque gestures, but he never physically attacked the targets of his hate. See Warner, *Swastika Smearbund.*

24. Rockwell, Smyth, and Stefani interviews.

25. Robert K. Rockwell to GLR and Thora Rockwell, 20 October 1958, private collection of James Mason; see also Smyth interview. Robert Rockwell's definition of paranoia is from J. F. Brown, *Psychodynamic of Abnormal Behavior* (New York: McGraw-Hill, 1940).

26. GLR to Robert K. Rockwell, 24 October 1958, private collection of James Mason.

27. GLR to Claire Schade Rockwell, 8 December 1958, private collection of P. Claire Rockwell.

28. Rockwell and Smyth interviews; Rockwell, *This Time the World,* 174–84.

29. Rockwell, *This Time the World,* 177.

30. William F. Buckley Jr. to GLR, 23 December 1958, William F. Buckley Jr. Papers, Sterling Memorial Library, Yale University. See also GLR to William F. Buckley Jr., 6 December 1958, ibid.

31. See GLR to William F. Buckley Jr., 29 December 1958, 13 August 1961, 3 July 1962, 17 October 1962, 9 September 1963, 20 September 1963, 29 November 1963, 10 December 1963, 6 May 1964, 15 January 1965, and 24 November 1965, ibid.

32. Warner, *Swastika Smearbund,* 6–7, 13.

33. GLR to Claire Schade Rockwell, 16 December 1959, 26 December 1959, and 31 December 1959, private collection of P. Claire Rockwell.

Chapter 4: The ANP's Members, Followers, Funding

1. FBI File #9-39854, "American Nazi Party," 64–68; Rockwell, *This Time the World,* 239–62; Pierce, *Lincoln Rockwell,* 24–25.

2. FBI File #9-39854, "American Nazi Party," 17.

3. James Mason, *Siege: The Collected Writings of James Mason,* ed. Michael M. Jenkins (Denver: Storm Books, 1992), 90.

4. "U.S. Nazi Leader Shot Dead," *Manchester Guardian* (Eng.), 26 August 1967, 1.

5. [William Loeb], "'Der Fuehrer' Is Rebuffed," *Manchester* (N.H.) *Union Leader,* 31 January 1964, 13.

6. Alex Haley, preface to Rockwell, *"Playboy* Interview," 72.

7. Ernest Volkman, *A Legacy of Hate: Anti-Semitism in America* (New York: Franklin Watts, 1982), 119–20.

8. David H. Bennett, *The Party of Fear: From Nativist Movements to the New Right in American History* (Chapel Hill: University of North Carolina Press, 1988), 325.

9. *Para-Military Organizations in California,* ANP-8, 19–20.

10. Summary of deposition contained in a letter from AJC staffer Roy H. Millenson to AJC officer Edwin J. Lucas, 12 February 1960, box 138, "Misc. Corresp.," AJC.

11. [Isaac Frank], Jewish Community Council of Greater Washington to Member Organizations, memorandum, 27 July 1960, box 138, "Misc. Corresp.," AJC.

12. Robert J. Greene to Solomon Andhil Fineberg, 4 January 1961, box 138, "Misc. Corresp.," AJC.

13. American Jewish Committee, *Bigot Seeking Buildup: The 'News' Techniques of George Lincoln Rockwell* (pamphlet) (New York: American Jewish Committee, May 1962), 9.

14. "George L. Rockwell, U.S. Nazi," *Facts,* October 1963, 271, 280.

15. Warner, *Swastika Smearbund,* 16; Hal Kaiser, interviewed by author, 15 October 1991.

16. R. E. Cooper, interviewed by author, 24 April 1991.

17. Alan M. Schwartz, ed. *Hate Groups in America: A Record of Bigotry and Violence* (New York: Anti-Defamation League of B'nai B'rith, 1988), 24, 27.

18. Tony Ulasewicz, *The President's Private Eye* (Westport, Conn.: MACSAM Publishing Co., 1990), 139–40.

19. Roy H. Millenson to Edwin J. Lucas, 12 February 1960, box 138, "Misc. Corresp.," AJC.

20. Sylvia Edelman to Isaac Frank, 11 July 1960, box 138, "Misc. Corresp.," AJC.

21. [Isaac Frank], Jewish Community Council of Greater Washington to Member Organizations, memorandum, 27 July 1960, AJC.

22. Robert J. Greene to Solomon Andhil Fineberg, 4 January 1961, box 138, "Misc. Corresp.," AJC.

23. "George L. Rockwell, U.S. Nazi," 272.

24. GLR, fund-raising letter, n.d. [Winter 1960], William F. Buckley Jr. Papers, Sterling Memorial Library, Yale University.

25. [George Lincoln Rockwell], "Tax Problems Now Solved!" *National Socialist Bulletin,* September 1961, 10.

26. Lee Larson to author, 30 November 1990.

27. GLR to Bruno Ludtke, 25 December 1963, 18 July 1964, 23 February 1966, and 2 April 1966, all in the private collection of James Mason.

28. GLR to Ron Gostick, 25 March 1964; GLR to John Hamilton, 7 April 1964; and GLR to Ned Touchstone, 25 September 1966, all in the private collection of James Mason.

29. GLR to Major [Matt] Koehl, 1 August 1966, Criminal Archives, Office of the Clerk, Circuit Court of Arlington County, Commonwealth of Virginia, File C-5575, Defense Exhibit K.

30. Edward R. Fields, interviewed by author, 7 August 1991.

31. GLR to IRS District Director, 17 February 1964, private collection of James Mason.

32. GLR to R. J. Stakem, Chief, IRS Exempt Organizations Branch, 27 March 1965, private collection of James Mason.

33. GLR to Robert K. Rockwell, 24 October 1958, private collection of James Mason.

34. FBI File #9-39854, SAC, WFO [Special Agent in Charge, Washington Field Office] to Director, FBI, memorandum, 10 July 1959.

35. "Rockwell," 164.

36. Max Amann [Robert Surrey], "Memorandum to 'Admirers and Supporters of the late George Lincoln Rockwell,' June 1968," private collection of James Mason.

37. Jim Lehrer, "Dallas Nazis: Merchants of Fear, Hate," *Dallas Times-Herald*, 11 April 1965, 1, 19. DePugh is quoted in William W. Turner, *Power on the Right* (Berkeley, Calif.: Ramparts Press, 1971), 93–94. Clint Murchison, a wealthy Texas oil baron and generous sponsor of far-right-wing political and social causes, seemed to have held racist and anti-Semitic sentiments. He was a patron and close friend of FBI Director J. Edgar Hoover and a major contributor to Republican candidates in the 1950s and 1960s. Hoover biographer Anthony Summers also claims that Murchison "was a primary source of money for the American Nazi Party and its leader, Lincoln Rockwell." Summers probably relied on the DePugh statement—which was consistent with the belief of many of Rockwell's contemporaries on the racist right—that Murchison was a Rockwell backer, but I have not been able to document any contributions to Rockwell from Murchison. If Murchison did make untraceable contributions to Rockwell, they were not large enough or frequent enough to raise Rockwell's cash flow beyond a bare subsistence level. See Anthony Summers, *Official and Confidential: The Secret Life of J. Edgar Hoover* (New York: Pocket Books, 1993), 205–6.

38. Ulasewicz, *President's Private Eye,* 137.

39. Roy H. Millenson to Edwin J. Lucas, 12 February 1960, box 138, "Misc. Corresp.," AJC.

40. Warner, *Swastika Smearbund,* 8.

41. "George L. Rockwell, U.S. Nazi," 271.

Chapter 5: Agitating for Power

1. FBI File #9-39854, "American Nazi Party," 18.

2. GLR, audiotape, address to supporters, Dallas, Texas, 1964.

3. Ibid.

4. FBI File #9-39854, "American Nazi Party," 61; Richard Barrett to author, 26 June 1991. Barrett is the head of a Mississippi-based segregationist organization, the Nationalist Movement. He contends that the swastika is "abhorrent" to most American rightists.

5. GLR, audiotape, address at the University of North Dakota, November 1965.

6. GLR, audiotape, address to supporters, Dallas, Texas, 1964; GLR, audiotape, address to supporters, location unknown, 1965. In the latter tape, Rockwell makes the unsubstantiated claim that "the Washington [D.C.] cops are with us lock, stock, and barrel. They'd join [the ANP] if they could get away with it." While the District Police force was notoriously racist in the early to mid-1960s, there is no credible evidence of mass support for Rockwell and the ANP within that department.

7. GLR, audiotape, address to supporters, location unknown, 1965.

8. Morris Fine and Milton Himmelfarb, eds., *American Jewish Year Book 1960,* vol.

61 (Philadelphia: Jewish Publication Society of America, 1960), 46; GLR, "Letter to the Editor," unpublished but sent to the *Washington Post* and the *Dallas Times-Herald,* 22 March 1960, Michigan Historical Collections, Bentley Historical Library, University of Michigan; Rockwell, *This Time the World,* 3.

9. Wagner is quoted in Samuel Walker, *Hate Speech: The History of an American Controversy* (Lincoln: University of Nebraska Press, 1994), 104. See also Morris Fine and Milton Himmelfarb, eds., *American Jewish Year Book 1961,* vol. 62 (Philadelphia: Jewish Publication Society of America, 1961), 108.

10. GLR to Claire Schade Rockwell, 7 July 1960, private collection of P. Claire Rockwell.

11. GLR letter to supporters, n.d. [1960], Michigan Historical Collections, Bentley Historical Library, University of Michigan.

12. "Statement of Commander George Lincoln Rockwell, United States Naval Reserve, Presented at a Hearing before a Board of Officers of the Navy Department," 1 February 1960, Washington, D.C., and GLR, Certificate of Honorable Discharge, 5 February 1960, Michigan Historical Collections, Bentley Historical Library, University of Michigan; Fine and Himmelfarb, *American Jewish Year Book 1961,* 108.

13. GLR to Gerald L. K. Smith, 16 April 1960 and 14 June 1963, Gerald L. K. Smith Papers, Michigan Historical Collections, Bentley Historical Library, University of Michigan; GLR to Edward R. Fields, 7 February 1964, private collection of James Mason; GLR to Ned Dupes, 3 October 1964, GLR to Mrs. E. L. Bishop, 3 October 1964, GLR to Matt Murphy, 3 January 1965, Matt H. Murphy Jr. to Edward R. Fields, 6 August 1965, J. B. Stoner to Matt H. Murphy Jr., 13 August 1965, Settlement Agreement, State of Virginia, County of Arlington, GLR and Edward R. Fields, [15?] September 1965, Edward R. Fields to GLR, 27 September 1965, Settlement Decree, *George Lincoln Rockwell v. Dr. Edward R. Fields, et al.,* Civil Action #64-570, Office of the Clerk, Northern District of Alabama, 1 October 1965, Affidavit of Edward R. Fields, Notarized Richmond County, Georgia, 13 October 1965, all in the private collection of R. E. Cooper.

14. [Edward R. Fields], "Proof Rockwell Cooperates with Drew Pearson and ADL," *Thunderbolt,* August 1962, 6; Warner, *Swastika Smearbund,* 7. Warner, the ANP's national secretary from 1959 until his resignation on 28 October 1960, verified Fields's charges and added that the publicity Pearson provided was so important to Rockwell that "without Pearson, Rockwell would have very few members."

15. Warner, *Swastika Smearbund,* 8–14.

16. Morris Fine and Milton Himmelfarb, eds., *American Jewish Year Book 1962,* vol. 63 (Philadelphia: Jewish Publication Society of America, 1962), 200–202; Burros, *Official Stormtrooper's Manual.*

17. GLR to "Family" [Claire Schade Rockwell, P. Claire Rockwell, Robert K. Rockwell], 19 February 1961, private collection of P. Claire Rockwell.

18. GLR to Claire Schade Rockwell, 23 July 1961, private collection of P. Claire Rockwell.

19. Fine and Himmelfarb, *American Jewish Year Book 1963,* 138–39.

20. GLR, audiotape, speech at Lynchburg, Va., City Armory, 20 August 1963.

21. GLR to Captain Herlihy, Washington, D.C., Metropolitan Police Department, 9 July 1963, Michigan Historical Collection, Bentley Historical Library, University of Michigan. See also GLR to Robert Murray, Chief of Police, Washington, D.C., Metropolitan Police Department, 8 August 1963; T. Sutton Jett, Regional Director, National Park Service, to GLR, 15 August 1963; GLR to T. Sutton Jett, 15 August 1963, all in ibid.

22. GLR to [Congressman John L. McMillan] Chairman, House District Committee, 17 July 1963; GLR to Congressman Watkins M. Abbott, 17 July 1963; Congressman John L. McMillan to GLR, 19 July 1963; GLR to Senator Warren Magnuson, 1 August 1963; Congressman Charles E. Bennett to GLR, 21 August 1963; Congressman Joe D. Waggoner Jr. to GLR, 22 August 1963; GLR to Congressman Charles E. Bennett, 24 August 1963; GLR to Congressman Joe D. Waggoner Jr., 24 August 1963, all in the private collection of James Mason.

23. GLR to George Singleman, 3 August 1963, ibid.

24. GLR to George C. Wallace, 12 August 1963, and GLR to Ross Barnett, 12 August 1963, Michigan Historical Collections, Bentley Historical Library, University of Michigan.

Chapter 6: Quarantine

1. George Lincoln Rockwell, "Nazism: The White Man's Ultimate Weapon," *RIGHT,* May 1960, 6.

2. Glen Jeansonne, "Combating Anti-Semitism: The Case of Gerald L. K. Smith," in *Anti-Semitism in American History,* ed. David A. Gerber (Urbana: University of Illinois Press, 1986), 158–59.

3. Solomon Andhil Fineberg, *Appraising the Quarantine Treatment* (New York: [American Jewish Committee,] Community Relations Service, 1949), 3.

4. Solomon Andhil Fineberg to American Jewish Committee Chapter Officers, memorandum, 17 April 1947, AJC.

5. Solomon Andhil Fineberg, *Punishment without Crime: What You Can Do about Prejudice* (Doubleday & Co., 1949), 133–34.

6. Ibid.

7. Glen Jeansonne, *Gerald L. K. Smith: Minister of Hate* (New Haven, Conn.: Yale University Press, 1988), 207–8, 216–17.

8. "A Master at Stirring Hate," *St. Petersburg* (Fla.) *Times,* 27 August 1967, 7A.

9. Fred C. Shapiro, "The Last Word (We Hope) On George Lincoln Rockwell," *Esquire,* February 1967, 103.

10. Ibid., 101.

11. George Lincoln Rockwell, *Who's a "Hate-Monger"?* (pamphlet) (Arlington, Va.: World Union of Free Enterprise National Socialists, 1958).

12. Isaiah Terman to [AJC] Area Directors and Executive Assistants, memorandum, 22 October 1958, AJC.

13. Pierce, *Lincoln Rockwell,* 20–21.

14. Rockwell quoted in Leland V. Bell, *In Hitler's Shadow: The Anatomy of American Nazism* (Port Washington, N.Y.: Kennikat Press, 1973), 116.

15. Solomon Fineberg to Mr. Riegelman, 7 April 1947, AJC.

16. Harold Wolozin to Solomon Fineberg, 5 November 1958, AJC. Fineberg asked Wolozin to contact Stern. See Solomon Fineberg to John Slawson, 14 November 1958, AJC. The quarantine was never monolithic; the *Sun* always printed any Rockwell or ANP activities that were truly newsworthy, and Rockwell received a great deal of coverage in the paper throughout his career, according to Herman J. Obermayer, another *Sun* editor and associate of Phil Stern during the Rockwell era. Herman J. Obermayer, interviewed by author, 15 August 1995. On several occasions Rockwell expressed gratitude to the *Sun* for impartial coverage. See GLR to Herman J. Obermayer, 30 July 1963, and GLR to [Herman J. Obermayer], Editor, *Northern Virginia Sun,* 18 December 1965, in the private collection of Herman J. Obermayer.

17. GLR to Editor, *Washington Post,* 22 March 1960, (unpublished), Michigan Historical Collections, Bentley Historical Library, University of Michigan.

18. GLR fund-raising letter to financial supporters, n.d. [1960], ibid.

19. John Slawson to the AJC Executive Board, memorandum, 11 July 1960, AJC.

20. David McReynolds, "Kill the Bigots!" *Village Voice,* 3 June 1960, 5.

21. John Slawson to the AJC Executive Board, memorandum, 11 July 1960, AJC.

22. Shapiro, "Last Word," 139.

23. Ibid., 104.

24. Tony Ulasewicz, interviewed by author, 20 July 1991. Ulasewicz made several visits to ANP headquarters in 1960 as the NYPD officer in charge of monitoring hate group activities in New York City.

25. Ibid.

26. Ulasewicz, *President's Private Eye,* 142.

27. George Lincoln Rockwell, *In Hoc Signo Vinces,* 3d ed. (pamphlet) (Arlington, Va.: World Union of National Socialists, 1971), 20–21.

28. Mrs. Richard Orgell, "George Lincoln Rockwell: American Nazi," *Spot News,* December 1960, 1, 5.

29. Warner, *Swastika Smearbund,* 13.

30. [George Lincoln Rockwell], "Proof of the Pudding—from the Jews!" (flyer) (Arlington, Va.: [American Nazi Party], n.d. [1961]).

31. GLR to Claire Schade Rockwell, 19 February 1961, private collection of P. Claire Rockwell.

32. George Lincoln Rockwell, "Office of the Commander," *National Socialist Bulletin,* September 1961, 3, William F. Buckley Jr. Papers, Sterling Memorial Library, Yale University.

33. Solomon Andhil Fineberg to Roy Millenson, 21 August 1961, AJC.

34. Robert J. Greene to George Kellman, 6 October 1961, AJC.

35. [George Lincoln Rockwell], "The American Nazi Party Is Not Subversive!" *National Socialist Bulletin,* September 1961, 2, 10, William F. Buckley Jr. Papers, Sterling Memorial Library, Yale University.

36. See "Death of a 'Storm Trooper,'" *New York Times,* 27 August 1967, 4E; Shapiro, "Last Word," 105. Also substantiating Rockwell's attitude toward governmental investigations is a letter written by Barbara von Goetz: "The Attorney General of New Hampshire is investigating us tomorrow—which is JUST what Lincoln wants." Barbara von Goetz to Claire Schade Rockwell, 5 February [1964], private collection of P. Claire Rockwell.

37. Solomon Andhil Fineberg to Kenneth B. Keating, 21 August 1961, AJC.

38. Documentation on the debate over this issue—including internal AJC memoranda and correspondence between AJC leaders and U.S. Attorney General Robert F. Kennedy, New York State Attorney General Louis J. Lefkowitz, U.S. Senator Kenneth B. Keating, and U.S. Representative Seymour Halpern of New York—is available in the Special Collections of AJC.

39. See Frederick A. Schreiber to George Kellman, 5 March 1962, AJC. Schreiber, a leader of the American Jewish Committee's Los Angeles chapter, details the quarantine efforts, including persuading television station KTTV to cancel a scheduled interview with Rockwell and conversations with Norman Chandler of the *Los Angeles Times* as well as other southern California media leaders.

40. Solomon Andhil Fineberg to Jules Cohen, 9 August 1962, AJC.

41. Solomon Andhil Fineberg to John Slawson, 17 September 1962, AJC.

42. Carol Fineberg to Walter Zand, 25 March 1963, AJC.

43. For examples of the sizable crowds and significant publicity Rockwell drew in connection with his college lectures, see "ADL Asks C.U. [Colorado University] to Explain Rockwell Appearance before 3000," *Intermountain Jewish News,* 17 May 1963, 1; and "2,500 Jam Union to Hear Nazi," *University Daily Kansan* (University of Kansas), 21 February 1964, 1. Dr. Fineberg continued trying to minimize the number of appearances by Rockwell on American college campuses, using the same approach to college officials and student leaders that he used with newspaper editors. Although difficult to quantify, his efforts probably succeeded to some degree. In any event, Rockwell spoke often enough and made enough money from these appearances to keep Fineberg occupied with this activity. While I believe Fineberg tolerated this marginal level of success, preferring to see Rockwell engaged in this arena rather than forced to renewed his battle in the streets, I found no specific writings of Fineberg that confirm my belief. For a typical example of Fineberg's approach to Rockwell's college sponsors, see Solomon Andhil Fineberg to Laird Wilcox, 21 January 1964, Wilcox Collection, Spencer Research Library, University of Kansas, Lawrence.

44. "How to Handle Rockwell," *ADL Bulletin,* April 1967, 6.

45. Solomon Andhil Fineberg to Boris Smolar, 31 March 1960, AJC.

46. Milton Friedman, "Rockwell Pickets: 'Berlin in Early 30s,'" *Examiner* (Brooklyn, N.Y.), 21 March 1960, 1.

47. Quoted by U.S. Representative Pucinski on the floor of Congress. See U.S. House of Representatives, Representative Pucinski of Illinois, Extension of Remarks (1 September 1960), *Cong. Rec.,* 86th Cong., 2d sess., A6792.

48. J. I. Fishbein, "How To Handle Crack-Pots," *Sentinel* (Chicago), 1 December 1960, 7.

49. See J. I. Fishbein, "Don't Be Frightened by a Bogey-Man," *Sentinel* (Chicago), 23 March 1961, 5. In this proquarantine editorial, Fishbein cites similar sentiments expressed in other important Jewish newspapers, specifically the *Brookline* (Mass.) *Jewish Times,* the *Boston Jewish Advocate,* and the *Jewish News of Newark.* Fineberg also maintained regular personal contact with Fishbein, continually reassuring him of the correctness of their alliance on quarantine. For example, see Solomon Andhil Fineberg to J. I. Fishbein, 9 October 1961, AJC.

50. Solomon Andhil Fineberg to Eleazer S. Goldstein, 28 September 1960, AJC.

51. See, for example, Solomon Andhil Fineberg to Milton K. Sussman, 22 September 1961, AJC. Sussman, the editor of the *Jewish Criterion,* published his editorial "More Than Quarantine Is Needed" on 23 June 1961.

52. Solomon Andhil Fineberg to John Slawson and other top AJC staff officers, 6 April 1962, AJC.

53. Manfred George to Solomon Andhil Fineberg, 5 April 1962, AJC.

54. [Manfred George], "Fallen Sie nicht auf Rockwell herein" ["Don't Fall for Rockwell"], *Aufbau,* 6 April 1962.

55. Louis Lempel to Ed Lukas et al., 20 April 1962, AJC.

56. Robert J. Greene to John Slawson, 12 August 1960, AJC.

57. Solomon Andhil Fineberg to Robert J. Greene, 30 August 1960, AJC.

58. Solomon Andhil Fineberg to Alan D. Kandel, 15 September 1960, AJC.

59. Edwin J. Lukas to Robert J. Greene, 29 August 1960, AJC.

60. David G. Bress to [AJC, Washington, D.C.] Chapter Members, memorandum, 21 September 1960, AJC.

61. Solomon Andhil Fineberg to Joseph F. Barr, 15 September 1960, AJC.

62. Solomon Andhil Fineberg to Joseph F. Barr, 2 November 1960, AJC.

63. Robert J. Greene to Solomon Andhil Fineberg, 4 January 1961, AJC.

64. See Samuel Katz to Solomon Andhil Fineberg, 31 January 1961, AJC.

65. Walter E. Klein to Jewish Community Council of Metropolitan Detroit, memorandum, 13 February 1961, AJC.

66. Robert J. Greene, "A Summary Report on the Washington Aspects of the Rockwell Phenomenon," prepared for the American Jewish Committee Annual Meeting, 29 April 1960, AJC.

67. See Samuel Katz to Solomon Andhil Fineberg, 27 February 1961; Samuel L. Scheiner to Joseph Barr, Ed Lukas, and Phil Jacobson, 25 May 1961; and George Kellman to Ed Lukas, 29 June 1961, all in AJC.

68. The major organizations of Nazi concentration camp survivors were the Jewish Nazi Victims Organization of America, the United Jewish Survivors of Nazi Persecution, and the Labor Zionist Farbund, which was by far the most militant and least cooperative with quarantine. By mid-1962 all were, in principle, in agreement with quarantine, although the Labor Zionist Farbund, like the Jewish War Veterans, consistently had difficulty restraining individual members. See Solomon Andhil Fineberg to Henry Wimpfheimer, 12 April 1962, and Louis Lempel to David Danzig and Edwin J. Lucas, 17 April 1962, AJC.

69. *White Man on the March!* (Arlington, Va.: American Nazi Party, n.d. [1960]), flyer, Michigan Historical Collections, Bentley Historical Library, University of Michigan.

70. Robert J. Greene to George Kellman, 3 March 1961, AJC.

71. George Lincoln Rockwell, "Jew Ostriches Beating Nazis to Death with Fat Bottoms!" *Rockwell Report,* 1 July 1962, 2–3, 4.

72. GLR to Bruno Ludtke, 20 January 1964, private collection of James Mason. Quarantine was a regular topic of discussion in the Rockwell-Ludtke correspondence.

73. GLR to Major [Matt] Koehl, 1 August 1966, Criminal Archives, Office of the Clerk, Circuit Court of Arlington County, Commonwealth of Virginia, File C-5575, Defense Exhibit K.

74. Quoted in Byron Klapper, "Nazi's Ambitions Told to KU Crowd," *Topeka* (Kans.) *Daily Capitol,* 21 February 1964, 2.

75. George Lincoln Rockwell, "Jews Expose Themselves as Terrorists at Colorado University," *Rockwell Report,* 1 June 1963, 5.

76. Ben H. Bagdikian, "The Gentle Suppression," *Columbia Journalism Review* 4 (Spring 1965): 17. To put the Rockwell quarantine issue in the free speech/hate speech historical and legal context, see Walker, *Hate Speech.* Also useful in this regard is Lee C. Bollinger, *The Tolerant Society* (New York: Oxford University Press, 1986); Nat Hentoff, *Free Speech for Me—but Not for Thee* (New York: Harper Collins, 1992); and Philip B. Kurland, ed., *Free Speech and Association: The Supreme Court and the First Amendment,* 8th ed. (Chicago: University of Chicago Press, 1975).

77. Bagdikian, "Gentle Suppression," 16.

78. Ibid., 17.

79. Ibid.

80. Ibid., 17–18. For a useful contemporary analysis of the issues Bagdikian raised in 1965, see Laura Lederer and Richard Delgado, eds., *The Price We Pay: The Case against Racist Speech, Hate Propaganda, and Pornography* (New York: Hill & Wang, 1995). These essays explore the relationship between the First Amendment and socially destructive speech and nonverbal communications.

81. Bagdikian, "Gentle Suppression," 18.

82. Ibid.

83. Solomon Andhil Fineberg, *Deflating the Professional Bigot* (New York: American Jewish Committee, 1960), 9.

84. See notes from the Multi-Agency Strategy Session, 8–10 January 1961, AJC.

Chapter 7: The Scorned

1. GLR to Bruno Ludtke, 5 February 1965, private collection of James Mason. For a representative presentation of Rockwell's view of the scope and magnitude of the "Jewish conspiracy," refer to GLR, audiotape, address at the University of North Dakota, November 1965. For a typical Rockwell qualification of his genocidal intentions, refer to GLR, audiotape, appearance on "The Michael Jackson Show," 9 May 1965, KNX-LA Radio. Rockwell's depictions of Jews as masterminding the infiltration and undermining of Aryan society are graphically portrayed in *Fable of the Ducks and the Hens* (pamphlet) (Chillicothe, Ohio: Universal Order, n.d. [ca. 1958]).

2. Rockwell's view of the Jews as "satanic" and "subhuman" was not unique to him. This characterization was the result of progressively more virulent anti-Semitism in

Western culture. See Joel Carmichael, *The Satanizing of the Jews: Origin and Development of Mystical Anti-Semitism* (New York: Fromm International Publishing Corp., 1992); William Nicholls, *Christian Antisemitism: A History of Hate* (Northvale, N.J.: Jason Aronson, 1993); Gavin I. Langmuir, *Toward a Definition of Anti-Semitism* (Berkeley: University of California Press, 1990); Dinnerstein, *Antisemitism in America;* and Frederic Cople Jaher, *A Scapegoat in the New Wilderness: The Origins and Rise of Anti-Semitism in America* (Cambridge, Mass.: Harvard University Press, 1994).

3. From Crommelin's 1962 campaign for the U.S. Senate in the Alabama Democratic primary, quoted in Fine and Himmelfarb, *American Jewish Year Book 1963,* 137. See also Greene, *Temple Bombing,* 163. While working in the 1958 Crommelin gubernatorial campaign in Alabama, Rockwell met several associates—Matt Koehl, James K. Warner, and Emory Burke—who would figure prominently in the early years of his American Nazi party. Koehl and Burke were followers and friends for the remainder of Rockwell's life. Rockwell's passion for racist military figures is not limited to Crommelin. See Rockwell's extensive correspondence with retired Marine Corps General Pedro A. del Valle, a notorious racist-fascist admirer of Spain's Generalissimo Francisco Franco, Pedro A. del Valle Papers, Special Collections, University Library, University of Oregon.

4. GLR, audiotape, appearance on "The Michael Jackson Show," 9 May 1965, KNX-LA Radio. For elaboration of Rockwell's views on the "blood contamination" and Jewish-led racial agitation positions, see also GLR, audiotape, debate with Tony Todaro, director, NAACP Hawaii Chapter, n.d. [ca. 1964], KTRG-TV-Honolulu, Don Cater, moderator.

5. GLR, audiotape, address at the University of North Dakota, November 1965. See also GLR, sound recording, "Commander George Lincoln Rockwell Speech at Brown University, 1966" (Arlington, Va.: G. L. Rockwell Party, n.d.).

6. Burros, *Official Stormtrooper's Manual,* 4.

7. GLR, audiotape, debate with Tony Todaro, director, NAACP Hawaii Chapter, n.d. [ca. 1964], KTRG-TV-Honolulu, Don Cater, moderator. See also FBI File #9-39854, "American Nazi Party," 18.

8. Quoted in Mason, *Siege,* 136.

9. GLR to Bruno Ludtke, 5 April 1963, private collection of James Mason.

10. Mason, *Siege,* 37; GLR to Eben Lewis, 3 August 1963, Michigan Historical Collections, Bentley Historical Library, University of Michigan.

11. [GLR], ANP newsletter, n.d. [*Rockwell Report,* ca. 1966], private collection of James Mason; George Lincoln Rockwell, *White Power,* 3d ed. (Reedy, W.Va.: Liberty Bell Publications, 1983), passim, esp. 259–92.

12. Rockwell, *Legal, Psychological and Political Warfare,* 3.

13. [GLR], ANP newsletter, n.d. [*Rockwell Report,* ca. 1966], private collection of James Mason.

14. GLR to Congressman John L. McMillan, Chairman, House District Committee, 30 October 1963, ibid. See also GLR to John L. McMillan, 8 November 1963 and 1 December 1963; John L. McMillan to GLR, 3 December 1963; and James T. Clark,

Clerk, House Committee on the District of Columbia, to GLR, 12 November 1963, all in ibid.

15. Morris Fine and Milton Himmelfarb, eds., *American Jewish Year Book 1967*, vol. 68 (Philadelphia: Jewish Publication Society of America, 1967), 73; Mason, *Siege,* 10; Henry Hampton and Steve Fayer, *Voices of Freedom: An Oral History of the Civil Rights Movement from the 1950s through the 1980s* (New York: Bantam Books, 1990), 298–319; Stephen Oates, *Let the Trumpet Sound: The Life of Martin Luther King, Jr.* (New York: NAL, 1982), 411–16.

16. GLR, audiotape, speech at Lynchburg, Va., City Armory, 20 August 1963; GLR, audiotape, debate with Tony Todaro, director, NAACP Hawaii Chapter, n.d. [ca. 1964], KTRG-TV-Honolulu, Don Cater, moderator; GLR, audiotape, appearance on "The Michael Jackson Show," 9 May 1965, KNX-LA Radio. Rockwell's use of "Martin Luther Coon" on the air so enraged Jackson that he threatened to terminate the show unless Rockwell stopped using that term. Rockwell complied and the show went on. The popular talk show received a record number of calls during Rockwell's appearance.

17. This episode and Clark's reaction are described in Taylor Branch, *Parting the Waters: America in the King Years, 1954–1963* (New York: Simon & Schuster, 1988), 653–55.

18. Ibid.; FBI File #9-39854, "American Nazi Party," 45; *Para-Military Organizations in California,* ANP-9–10; Fine and Himmelfarb, *American Jewish Year Book 1963,* 140.

19. Oates, *Let the Trumpet Sound,* 329–35; Ralph David Abernathy, *And the Walls Came Tumbling Down: An Autobiography* (New York: Harper Perennial, 1990), 313–15.

20. Abernathy, *And the Walls,* 314.

21. Reported in *Para-Military Organizations in California,* ANP-10–11.

22. FBI File #9-39854, "American Nazi Party," 40.

23. GLR to Ralph Ginsburg, 9 February 1964, private collection of James Mason. Rockwell's hatred of homosexuals is evident throughout his writings and speeches. See, for example, numerous references in *This Time the World* and GLR, audiotape, appearance on "The Michael Jackson Show," 9 May 1965, KNX-LA Radio.

24. Dotson Rader, "The Deadly Friendship: George Lincoln Rockwell and John Patler," *New Republic* 157 (23 September 1967): 13–15. See also Rockwell, "*Playboy* Interview," 82. Rockwell's intention to eventually exterminate homosexuals was common knowledge among ANP stormtroopers. Lee Larson to author, 24 June 1993.

25. Rockwell, "*Playboy* Interview," 82.

26. FBI File #9-39854, "American Nazi Party," 34. Regarding Rockwell's concern about infiltration of the party by homosexuals, see Rader, "Deadly Friendship," 14.

27. FBI File #9-39854, "American Nazi Party," 34.

28. American Jewish Committee Trend Analysis Division, "Profile of An 'Acting Fuehrer': Matthias (Matt) Koehl, Jr.," 7 September 1967, box 138, AJC. See also George and Wilcox, *Nazis, Communists, Klansmen,* 352–54, 382–89.

29. R. E. [Rickey] Cooper, interviewed by author, 24 April and 13 August 1991. Cooper contends that he detected a "genetic defect in Koehl, something queer in his

background" and suspects that Koehl is both a homosexual and a Jew; R. E. Cooper to author, 17 April 1991; R. E. Cooper to William Pierce, 28 March 1982, private collection of R. E. Cooper. In this letter to former top ANP official Pierce, Cooper gives details of the alleged 1951 incident involving Koehl, Mullins, and Fleckstein. Details of the same incident are repeated in James Mason to [John] Jewell, 22 January 1982, private collection of James Mason. Mason, like Cooper, is a former Koehl aide (1968–76). James Mason, interviewed by author, 22 August 1991. Mason believes Koehl was "probably" a homosexual but has no direct evidence. See James Mason, "Facts in Regard to the Matt Koehl Question" (flyer), 15 March 1976, ibid.; flyer promoting allegations of Koehl's homosexuality, unattributed, n.d. [ca. 1976], private collection of R. E. Cooper.

30. H. H. [Herbert Hillary] Booker II to R. E. Cooper, 7 January 1982, ibid. According to Cooper, who maintained a friendship and correspondence with him, Booker was Rockwell's third cousin. R. E. Cooper to author, 22 May 1991. Lee Larson, an ANP probationary stormtrooper (1964–66), claims that ANP stormtrooper Daniel P. Skelley legally changed his name to "Herbert Hillary Booker." Lee Larson to author, 30 November 1990.

31. GLR to supporters, n.d., private collection of James Mason; Rockwell, "*Playboy* Interview," 82; GLR to Ralph Ginsburg, 29 January 1964, private collection of James Mason; H. Keith Thompson to author, 12 July 1993; GLR to Claire Schade Rockwell, 18 October 1966, private collection of P. Claire Rockwell.

32. GLR quoted in Mason, *Siege,* 297. Bruno Ludtke suggested the Nietzsche quote to Rockwell as consistent with their view of gender roles. Bruno Ludtke to Colin Jordan, 28 June 1965, private collection of James Mason; GLR, audiotape, address at the University of North Dakota, November 1965.

33. Warner, *Swastika Smearbund,* 8. For an analysis of women's role in the ANP, see FBI File #9-39854, "American Nazi Party," 36.

34. Rockwell, *Legal, Psychological and Political Warfare,* 18; Burros, *Official Stormtrooper's Manual,* 8; Rockwell, *In Hoc Signo Vinces,*

Chapter 8: The World Union of National Socialists

1. "WUNS Reorganized," *NS* [National Socialist] *Bulletin* 330 (Fourth Quarter 1992): 1–3. Manfred Roeder, a German attorney and publisher of *Teutonic Unity,* a Nazi revival newsletter, confirms Rockwell's status as an influential postwar agent of Nazi revival in Europe. Manfred Roeder to author, 29 July 1991.

2. Pierce, *Lincoln Rockwell,* 24.

3. Bill G. Cody, WUNS International Secretary, to Bruno Ludtke, 21 June 1962, private collection of James Mason. In his speeches and writings Rockwell never acknowledged the postwar division of Germany into East and West. This was consistent with his belief that Germany's defeat and division was temporary and that a united Germany, under a restored Nazi regime, would inevitably reemerge as a world power.

4. FBI File #9-39854, J. Walter Yeagley, Acting Assistant Attorney General, Internal Security Division, to Director, FBI, memorandum, 31 October 1958; Rockwell

Deposition Extracts. In the Deposition Extracts, Rockwell claims that Harold Noel Arrowsmith Jr. arranged a meeting between Rockwell and the "head of Nasser's secret service" in late July 1958. There is no independent verification of this alleged meeting and no evidence of any further contact between Rockwell and officials of Nasser's government, although Tony Ulasewicz, the former New York City police detective mentioned earlier, told the author that Rockwell visited the United Nations frequently in the late 1950s and early 1960s and that he believed Rockwell received a "substantial income" from "Arab sources at the UN." Ulasewicz interview. This claim cannot be verified from existing documents. U.S. State Department Memorandum, 30 January 1959, Case Control #9200099, released 24 April 1992, reports on Rockwell visits to the Embassy of the United Arab Republic on 28/29 January 1959. According to State Department sources, Rockwell's overtures were rebuffed by Embassy Minister Amin M. Mouftah. FBI File #9-39854, SAC, WFO [Special Agent in Charge, Washington Field Office] to Director, FBI, memorandum, 12 February 1959, details information from the newspaper columnist Drew Pearson regarding contact between Nasser and Rockwell. FBI File #9-39854, memorandum to file, contains the text of a letter from Rockwell to Nasser offering cooperation against Israel, 17 February 1959. See also GLR to Ambassador of the Dominican Republic to the United States, 8 July 1959, and GLR to Salazar, Premier of Portugal, 4 September 1963, private collection of James Mason.

5. "Savitri Devi: A Souvenir," *NS* [National Socialist] *Bulletin* 330 (Fourth Quarter 1992): 7. Devi's main works of Aryan mysticism and National Socialist philosophy are *Gold in the Furnace* (1949), *Defiance* (1951), *Pilgrimage* (1953), and *The Lightning and the Sun* (1956). Savitri Devi died in France on 23 October 1982 at the age of seventy-seven.

6. Bruno Ludtke to Colin Jordan, 2 August 1965, and Bruno Ludtke to Bill G. Cody, International Secretary of WUNS, 13 June 1962, private collection of James Mason.

7. Bruno Ludtke to GLR, 11 January 1962, ibid.

8. Bruno Ludtke to GLR, 7 July 1965, ibid.

9. Bruno Ludtke to GLR, 29 June 1964, ibid. In this letter Ludtke defers to his precarious legal position by admonishing Rockwell: "you should never announce me to anyone as 'commander of the German unit.'" See also Bruno Ludtke to GLR, 19 February 1966; Bruno Ludtke to Colin Jordan, 28 June 1965; Bruno Ludtke to Matt Koehl, 16 January 1966, all in ibid.

10. Bruno Ludtke to GLR, n.d. [ca. September 1964], ibid.

11. Bruno Ludtke to GLR, n.d. [ca. October 1964], ibid. In May 1964, Ludtke also drafted for Rockwell a detailed constitution of the coming worldwide National Socialist government. Given the state of the movement at that time, this draft was probably more for Rockwell's psychological benefit than for any practical purpose. See Bruno Ludtke to GLR, "Ideas and Suggestions for the final constitution and organization of WUNS," memorandum, n.d. [May 1964], ibid.

12. GLR to Bruno Ludtke, 19 September 1964, ibid.

13. Bruno Ludtke to GLR, 5 May 1962, ibid.

14. Bruno Ludtke to GLR, 30 May 1962, ibid. See also Bruno Ludtke to GLR, 4 February 1962, and Bruno Ludtke to Bill G. Cody, 13 June 1962, ibid.

15. Bruno Ludtke to Colin Jordan, 5 May 1964 and 2 August 1965, ibid.

16. Bruno Ludtke to GLR, 29 June 1964, ibid. See also Martin Webster to Frank W. Rotella, 13 February 1964, ibid. Webster was one of Colin Jordan's top aides; Rotella was an American correspondent not affiliated with Rockwell.

17. Fine and Himmelfarb, *American Jewish Year Book 1963*, 139; FBI File #9-39854, A. Rosen to Mr. Belmont, memorandum, 24 August 1962, reports on Rockwell's trip to England and his activities at Cotswold. See also Pierce, *Lincoln Rockwell*, 24; FBI File #9-39854, "American Nazi Party."

18. Rockwell's domination of the Cotswold Conference is best seen in the close parallel between the Cotswold Agreements, the operating document that emerged from the conference, and the earlier "Program of the World Union of Free Enterprise National Socialists," which Rockwell drafted before Cotswold or any association with Colin Jordan and other European Nazi leaders. The Cotswold Agreements are clearly derived from Rockwell's document and embody Rockwell's vision of worldwide National Socialism. See "Program of the World Union of Free Enterprise National Socialists," William F. Buckley Jr. Papers, Sterling Memorial Library, Yale University. See also American Nazi Party, *National Socialist Bulletin* 4 (November [1960]), in which Rockwell announces the organization of the WUFENS, predecessor to WUNS, and describes the structure and goals of WUFENS. The structure and goals of WUNS, as agreed to at the 1962 Cotswold Conference, mirror Rockwell's earlier vision in virtually every respect.

19. "First Working Draught of the Cotswold Agreements," "Rockwell 60–62, Followers & Supporters" folder, box 138, AJC.

20. Fine and Himmelfarb, *American Jewish Year Book 1963*, 139; FBI File #9-39854, "American Nazi Party," June 1965; GLR to Bruno Ludtke, 26 September 1962, and Bruno Ludtke to GLR, n.d. [ca. May 1965], private collection of James Mason. For a concise description of the Cotswold Conference and subsequent law enforcement actions against Rockwell and Colin Jordan, see the intelligence summary in *Para-Military Organizations in California*, ANP-5–ANP-7.

21. GLR to Colin Jordan, 20 January 1963, private collection of James Mason. See also Bertha Beecham Jordan to GLR, 22 December 1962, ibid. From this and other letters it is obvious that Bertha Jordan was not a neutral courier but an ardent National Socialist who fully supported her son's activities.

22. Colin Jordan to GLR, 18 August 1962; GLR to Bruno Ludtke, 25 December 1963; Bruno Ludtke to GLR, 4 November 1965, all in ibid. See also Erika Himmler [a.k.a. Barbara Warren], interview, *Spiegel* 39 (19 September 1966): 130, translated by Bruno Ludtke for Rockwell; Bruno Ludtke to GLR, 23 September 1966, both in ibid. Himmler/Warren was secretary of the ANP's Chicago chapter and the only female to hold a position of authority in the party.

23. For example, see Alan Welch to Colin Jordan, 12 June 1966, ibid.

24. GLR to Colin Jordan, 15 May 1966, and Colin Jordan to Yves Jeanne, 6 February 1964, ibid.

25. Bruno Ludtke to GLR, 10 March 1965, ibid.

26. Regarding Lebanon, see Antoine Jaouiche to Françoise Dior, 9 November 1964; Zaven Tachdjian to Françoise Dior, 18 November 1964; Françoise Dior to GLR, 8 December 1964, all in ibid. Regarding Japan, see American Nazi Party, *National Socialist Bulletin* 4 (November [1960]); GLR to Colin Jordan, 31 August 1963, private collection of James Mason.

27. Regarding Sweden, Goren Oredsson led a reasonably active WUNS chapter that was involved in extended legal disputes with the Swedish government over the distribution of anti-Semitic literature. See Colin Jordan to GLR, 26 May 1965; Friedrich Kuhfuss to Colin Jordan, 13 May 1965; Bruno Ludtke to GLR, 24 May 1965, private collection of James Mason. Regarding Denmark, Sven Salicath, leader of the Danish National Socialist Workers party, was an enthusiastic organizer of WUNS-Denmark and a devoted Rockwell disciple. See Colin Jordan to GLR, 23 September 1962, and Colin Jordan to GLR, 26 May 1965, ibid.

28. Colin Jordan to GLR, 25 August 1963, 27 August 1963, and 31 October 1964; GLR to Colin Jordan, 31 August 1964 and 20 November 1964; Colin Jordan to Ray K. Rudman, 19 August 1965, all in ibid.

29. [Franz] Pfeiffer to GLR, 6 December 1962; GLR to Colin Jordan, 3 September 1962 and 29 July 1963; GLR to Bruno Ludtke, 19 September 1964; Bruno Ludtke to GLR, 20 July 1965, all in ibid.

30. Bruno Ludtke to GLR, 14 September 1964; Colin Jordan to GLR, 4 February 1965; GLR to Colin Jordan, 20 February 1965, all in ibid.

31. Bruno Ludtke to Colin Jordan, n.d. [ca. July 1964] and 18 February 1967; GLR to Colin Jordan, 20 December 1964 and 1 January 1965; Bruno Ludtke to GLR, 10 March 1965 and 26 December 1966, all in ibid. See also GLR, audiotape, address at the University of North Dakota, November 1965.

32. GLR to Colin Jordan, 31 August 1963, 1 January 1966, 6 February 1966, and 15 May 1966; Colin Jordan to GLR, 27 August 1963, 20 January 1966, 19 April 1966, and 26 May 1966; Colin Jordan to Paul Martin [a.k.a. Arthur Smith], 19 August 1965; Colin Jordan to Howard Williams, 1 August 1966, all in ibid.

33. Fine and Himmelfarb, *American Jewish Year Book 1961*, 108–9; Fine and Himmelfarb, *American Jewish Year Book 1962*, 287.

34. Ludtke quoted in Colin Jordan to GLR, 16 June 1965, private collection of James Mason. See also Robert Smith to author, 28 June 1991. Smith is the national secretary of the Nationalist Party of Canada (the renamed Western Guard party) and chief aide to Don Andrews.

35. Bruno Ludtke to GLR, 7 July 1965; GLR to Colin Jordan, 15 May 1966 and 26 June 1966; GLR to John Beattie, 6 May 1967, all in the private collection of James Mason. For internal political purposes, Beattie always played down his connection to Rockwell, but their relationship was close, friendly, mutually supportive, and cooperative. In addition to the correspondence cited above, see John Garrity, "I Spied on the Nazis," *Maclean's Magazine*, 1 October 1966, quoted in Fine and Himmelfarb, *American Jewish Yearbook 1967*, 268. According to Fine and Himmelfarb, the Canadian

Jewish Congress confirmed the "general accuracy" of the Garrity article, in which he documents a meeting between Beattie and Rockwell and concludes that a strong and dependent link existed from Beattie to Rockwell. To research the article, Garrity, an investigative reporter, infiltrated Beattie's organization.

36. General Arpad Henney, a former member of the fascist Szalasi government living in exile in Canada, proposed organizing an "underground" chapter of WUNS in Hungary since that country's communist regime would not permit an openly National Socialist party. Rockwell refused to authorize an underground chapter under Henney (though he had no problem with an underground chapter in Germany under Ludtke). Since Henney was the only credible Hungarian fascist interested in identifying with a National Socialist revival, the Hungarian operation never advanced to any significant degree. See Matt Koehl to GLR, 14 July 1966, and GLR to Colin Jordan, 21 October 1966, private collection of James Mason. Giuseppe Torracca was the nominal leader of WUNS-Italy but apparently did little more than distribute flyers from time to time. See Colin Jordan to GLR, 25 August 1963, and Denis Pirie to GLR, 20 March 1964, ibid. G. A. Amaudruz, head of the Swiss-based New European Order, was regarded by Rockwell and Jordan as "their man" in Switzerland, although he seems to have played no overt role on behalf of WUNS in Europe.

37. GLR to Colin Jordan, 20 November 1964 and 15 May 1966; Colin Jordan to GLR, 9 March 1964, 20 August 1964, and 31 October 1964; Bernard E. Horgan to GLR, 26 March 1966; GLR to Bernard E. Horgan, 20 April 1966, all in ibid.

38. "Friedrich Kuhfuss" was the pseudonym used by an unidentified German Nazi. Colin Jordan to GLR, 29 July 1964 and 19 August [1965]; Friedrich Kuhfuss to Colin Jordan, 13 May 1965; Friedrich Kuhfuss to GLR, 30 May 1965, all in ibid.

39. Although this study does not attempt to quantify the numerical strength of WUNS chapters (as it does for the American Nazi party), the description of any WUNS chapter as "large and active" must be understood in relative terms. At no time during the period under examination did a WUNS-affiliated political party establish electoral significance in any country. WUNS supporters outside the United States, as with the ANP within the United States, are more accurately numbered in the hundreds than in the thousands. Their significance, as with Rockwell and the ANP in the United States, lies with the sustenance of a virulent and violent racist and anti-Semitic political impulse and antidemocratic political tradition rather than with any real potential to seize political power through legitimate means.

40. As an indication of Jordan's devotion and subservience to Rockwell, Jordan routinely featured taped messages from Rockwell as the highlight of NSM celebrations. In a gesture unheard of on the egomaniacal racist right, Jordan's own addresses to his followers, after 1962, were frequently little more than a prelude to the main event: a taped message from "the Commander." See, for example, Colin Jordan to GLR, 19 November 1963, ibid.

41. Bruno Ludtke to GLR, 5 May 1962, ibid.

42. Bertha Beecham Jordan to GLR, 22 December 1962; Colin Jordan to GLR, 27 August 1963, 3 August 1963, 27 July 1963, 29 July 1963, and 28 October [1963]; Bruno

Ludtke to Colin Jordan, n.d. [ca. December 1963], all in ibid. Before recruiting Normand, Rockwell and Jordan suffered a "false start" when they tried unsuccessfully to collaborate with Jean-Claude Monet, editor of *Le Viking* and head of the French Organization of the Swastika. See Colin Jordan to GLR, 25 August 1963, ibid.

43. Bruno Ludtke to GLR, n.d. [ca. 1965]; Colin Jordan to GLR, 19 August [1965] and 26 May 1966; Colin Jordan to Yves Jeanne, 1 August 1966, ibid. The circumstances of Yves Jeanne's assumption of command from Claude Normand are unclear from extant documents. One former ANP member I interviewed believed that Yves Jeanne was really Claude Normand/Claude Janne and that the "old fighter" himself led the abortive coup. Although not to be dismissed since *anything* is possible in the byzantine world of Nazi politics of this era, I found no corroboration for this theory.

44. Colin Jordan to GLR, 20 July [1963], 3 August 1963, and memorandum, n.d. [ca. August 1965], ibid.

45. Colin Jordan to GLR, 28 October [1963] and Colin Jordan to Rudiger van Sande, 29 July 1965, ibid.

46. Bruno Ludtke to GLR, 8 January 1965, ibid. Ludtke also urged Rockwell to consider Robert H. Ketels as an alternative if Rockwell was unwilling to pursue Degrelle.

47. Colin Jordan to GLR, memorandum, n.d. [ca. August 1965], and 16 August 1965; Colin Jordan to Rudiger van Sande, 29 July 1965; Bruno Ludtke to Colin Jordan, 29 October 1966; Bruno Ludtke to GLR, 17 April 1966, all in ibid.

48. Bruno Ludtke to GLR, [2?] September 1961, 9 November 1961, 4 February 1962, and 18 August 1962; GLR to Bruno Ludtke, 1 October 1961, all in ibid.

49. Among the most active disciples Ludtke enlisted were Wolfgang Kirchstein, Erich Lindner, Reinhold Ruppe, Werner Knoss, and Dietrich Schuler. GLR to Bruno Ludtke, 11 July 1964; Werner Knoss to GLR, n.d. [ca. March 1964]; GLR to Werner Knoss, 5 April 1964; Bruno Ludtke to GLR, 5 May 1964, 24 May 1964, and 31 July 1965; Bruno Ludtke to Colin Jordan, 2 August 1965 and 18 February 1967; Colin Jordan to GLR, 26 May 1966; Bruno Ludtke to William L. Pierce, 10 August 1966, all in ibid. See also "Are Europe's Jews in Danger?" *ADL Bulletin* 22 (September 1965): 1–2, 6. The West German government frequently complained to the U.S. government about the flood of pro-nazi and anti-Semitic literature entering West Germany from the United States. See FBI File #9-39854, "American Nazi Party." Rockwell was the source and Ludtke the distributor.

50. GLR to Colin Jordan, 21 October 1966, private collection of James Mason. See also Colin Jordan to GLR, 16 August 1965, ibid.

51. Heinrich Mangold to GLR, 19 June 1963, ibid.

Chapter 9: White Power

1. The quotes are verbatim from an audiotape of a 1964 address to supporters in Dallas, Texas, at which Rockwell confided his intention to run for governor of Virginia the following year. At that meeting he discussed his strategy and campaign themes. The illustrative "campaign appearance" described here is a composite drawn from several

such meetings throughout the campaign at which Rockwell repeated his theme, frequently using the precise words in the context described.

2. Rockwell described this anticipated unfolding of events on many occasions throughout his career. See FBI File #9-39854, "American Nazi Party," 15–16.

3. GLR to Bruno Ludtke, 20 January 1964, private collection of James Mason. A race for political office was clearly on Rockwell's mind even earlier. The summer before he wrote to Ludtke, he informed his boyhood friend Eben Lewis, "I believe I have serious possibilities of making political office [in Virginia]." GLR to Eben Lewis, 3 August 1963, ibid.

4. The text of Rockwell's campaign speech was drafted by his adviser William L. Pierce. See William L. Pierce to GLR, 9 August 1965, Michigan Historical Collections, Bentley Historical Library, University of Michigan. Rockwell ran a short, unsuccessful campaign for president in the 1964 New Hampshire Republican primary. That campaign, which centered on opposition to the Civil Rights Bill then before Congress, allowed Rockwell to refine the themes that emerged, more fully developed, in his race for governor of Virginia the following year. Stuart McKeever, a prominent attorney and New England publisher, believes that Rockwell received funding and encouragement in 1964 from mainstream right wingers, specifically a Mississippi-based anti–civil rights lobbying group, The Committee for Coordinating Fundamental Freedoms, which may have encouraged Rockwell's 1965 foray into electoral politics. Stuart McKeever, interviewed by author, 16 June 1991.

5. Rockwell detailed his strategy in "Confidential Report on the Campaign in Virginia," 2 June 1965, private collection of James Mason.

6. GLR to Eben Lewis, 3 August 1963, ibid.

7. GLR to Colin Jordan, 5 March 1965, ibid.

8. GLR to Colin Jordan, 17 July 1965, ibid.

9. GLR to Bruno Ludtke, 12 November 1965, ibid.; GLR, audiotape, address at the University of North Dakota, November 1965.

10. GLR, audiotape, lecture at Brown University, n.d. [Fall 1966].

11. Oates, *Let the Trumpet Sound,* 411–13; Hampton and Fayer, *Voices of Freedom,* 298–319.

12. GLR to Bruno Ludtke, 5 February 1965, private collection of James Mason. From the beginning, Rockwell's movement was directed at "white people" and the "white race," but his refinement of that concept, beyond what was traditionally understood by pre-Rockwell white supremacists, didn't come until late 1964 or early 1965. See Bill G. Cody to Bruno Ludtke, 21 June 1962, and *NS Report,* October/December 1989, 2, ibid. On Rockwell's origination of the slogan "White Power," see Sean C. Maguire to author, 3 September 1991. Maguire was an ANP stormtrooper in 1966.

13. The term "pan-white" was coined by Professor Michael Lind to describe the latest phase of American nativism and racism. It is my argument that Rockwell was the progenitor of that phase. See Michael Lind, "Power to the People," *New Republic* 185 (4 September 1995): 37–41.

14. GLR, audiotape, address to supporters, Dallas, Texas, 1964.

15. The pioneering work in this field is Ashley Montagu's *Man's Most Dangerous Myth: The Fallacy of Race* (1964). Also useful in understanding the complexity of race as a form of biological classification is Luigi Luca Cavalli-Sforza's *History and Geography of Human Genes* (1994). Winthrop Jordan's classic *White over Black: American Attitudes toward the Negro, 1550–1812* (1968), explores in detail the sociological construct of race and the process by which that construct has become embedded in American culture. Valuable companions to Jordan's work are Theodore W. Allen's *Invention of the White Race* (1994) and Audrey Smedley's *Race in North America: Origin and Evolution of a Worldview* (1993).

16. File C-5575, Commonwealth Exhibit #63, Criminal Archives, Circuit Court of Arlington County, Commonwealth of Virginia, "The Commander [GLR] to Captain [John] Patler, [29 June 1966]."

17. Frank C. Roberts, "George Lincoln Rockwell," in *Obituaries from the "Times,"* *1961–1970* (Reading, Eng.: Newspaper Archive Developments, 1975), 681.

18. Quoted in Oates, *Let the Trumpet Sound*, 411.

19. For a detailed analysis of militant dissatisfaction with mainstream civil rights activism in the 1960s, see Herbert H. Haines, *Black Radicals and the Civil Rights Mainstream, 1954–1970* (Knoxville: University of Tennessee Press, 1988). Also useful in this regard is Clayborne Carson, *In Struggle: SNCC and the Black Awakening of the 1960s* (Cambridge, Mass.: Harvard University Press, 1981); Raymond S. Franklin, "The Political Economy of Black Power," *Social Problems* 16 (Winter 1969): 286–301; Manning Marable, "Martin Luther King's Ambiguous Legacy," *WIN Magazine* 19 (15 April 1982): 15–19; August Meier, "On the Role of Martin Luther King," *New Politics* 4 (Winter 1965): 52–59; August Meier, "The Dilemmas of Negro Protest Strategy," *New South* 21 (Spring 1966): 1–18; Gene Roberts, "The Story of Snick: From 'Freedom Rides' to 'Black Power,'" *New York Times Magazine*, 25 September 1966, 27–29; Bayard Rustin, "'Black Power' and Coalition Politics," *Commentary* 42 (September 1966): 35–40; Hanes Walton Jr., "The Political Leadership of Martin Luther King, Jr.," *Quarterly Review of Higher Education among Negroes* 36 (July 1968): 163–71; Roy Wilkins, "Whither 'Black Power'?" *Crisis*, August/September 1966, 354; and Robert L. Zangrando, "From Civil Rights to Black Liberation: The Unsettled 1960s," *Current History* 62 (November 1969): 281–86, 299.

20. Quoted in Hampton and Fayer, *Voices of Freedom*, 313.

21. Quoted in Oates, *Let the Trumpet Sound*, 413.

22. Quoted in ibid., 413.

23. Fine and Himmelfarb, *American Jewish Year Book 1967*, 73; Mason interview.

24. Mason, *Siege*, 10.

25. Bruno Ludtke to GLR, 22 December 1966, private collection of James Mason.

26. *NSV* [Nationalist Socialist Vanguard] *Report*, (The Dalles, Wash.), October/December 1993, 2–3, series of newsletters in author's files; "Max Amann [Robert Surrey] to Admirers and Supporters of the late George Lincoln Rockwell," June 1968, private collection of James Mason.

27. Robert Smith to author, 28 June 1991.

28. Michael Zatarain, *David Duke: Evolution of a Klansman* (Gretna, La.: Pelican Publishing Co., 1990), 116.

29. Fields interview.

Chapter 10: Holocaust Denial

1. Deborah Lipstadt, *Denying the Holocaust: The Growing Assault on Truth and Memory* (New York: Plume/Penguin, 1994), 23. Lipstadt's work is the most comprehensive scholarly refutation of Holocaust denial available; see also "Deniers, Relativists, and Pseudo-Scholarship," *Dimensions* 6 (1991): 6, and "Holocaust Denial: An Overview," *Dimensions* 8.1 (1994): 3–7. Other works on Holocaust denial include: Kenneth S. Stern, *Holocaust Denial* (New York: American Jewish Committee, 1993); Pierre Vidal-Naquet, *Assassins of Memory: Essays on the Denial of the Holocaust*, trans. Jeffrey Mehlman (New York: Columbia University Press, 1992); Gill Seidel, *The Holocaust Denial: Antisemitism, Racism and the New Right* (Leeds, Eng.: Beyond the Pale Collective, 1986); Shelly Shapiro et al., eds., *Truth Prevails: Demolishing Holocaust Denial—The End of the "Leuchter Report"* (New York: Beate Klarsfeld Foundation, 1991); Dorothy Rabinowitz, *About the Holocaust: What We Know and How We Know It* (New York: American Jewish Committee, 1980); Serge Klarsfeld, *The Holocaust and the Neo-Nazi Mythomania* (New York: Beate Klarsfeld Foundation, 1978); and Lucy Dawidowicz, "Lies about the Holocaust," *Commentary,* 70 (December 1980): 31–40. One of the best refutations of Holocaust denial in the popular press is Paul Berman, "Gas Chamber Games," *Village Voice* 26 (10 June 1981): 1, 37.

2. Willis Carto acknowledges that Rockwell was "scornful of the holocaust" in his "speeches and writings" but claims that all of his files on the Rockwell era "have been destroyed by arson or theft." Willis A. Carto to author, 11 September 1995.

3. See Dinnerstein, *Antisemitism in America;* Jaher, *Scapegoat in the New Wilderness;* Linda Gordon Kuzmack, *The Hate Business: Anti-Semitism in America* (New York: Franklin Watts, 1993); David A. Gerber, ed., *Anti-Semitism in American History* (Urbana: University of Illinois Press, 1986); Seymour Martin Lipset, "Prejudice and Politics in the American Past and Present," in *Prejudice U.S.A.,* ed. Charles Y. Glock and Ellen Siegelman (New York: Frederick A. Praeger, Publishers, 1969); George Salomon, ed., *Jews in the Mind of America* (New York: Basic Books, 1966); and Volkman, *Legacy of Hate.*

4. See Susan Canedy, *America's Nazis—A Democratic Dilemma: A History of the German-American Bund* (Menlo Park, Calif.: Markgraf Publications Group, 1990), and Philip Jenkins, "Home-Grown Terror," *American Heritage* 46 (September 1995): 38–46. Also useful in appreciating the extent of prewar Nazi influence in the United States is John Roy Carlson [Avedis Derounian], *Under Cover: My Four Years with the Nazi Underground of America* (Philadelphia: Blakiston Co., 1943; rpt., New York: American Books–Stratford Press, 1943).

5. Jenkins, "Home-Grown Terror," 42.

6. Alan L. Berger, "The Holocaust, Second-Generation Witness, and the Voluntary Covenant in American Judaism," *Religion and American Culture* 5 (Winter 1995): 24.

7. See James E. Young, *Writing and Rewriting the Holocaust: Narrative and the Consequences of Interpretation* (Bloomington: Indiana University Press, 1988).

8. James Ridgeway, *Blood in the Face: The Ku Klux Klan, Aryan Nations, Nazi Skinheads, and the Rise of a New White Culture* (New York: Thunder's Mouth Press, 1991), 64; Frank P. Mintz, *The Liberty Lobby and the American Right: Race, Conspiracy, and Culture* (Westport, Conn.: Greenwood Press, 1985), 71–78; Turner, *Power on the Right*, 150–52, 162–63. For Carto's relationship with Yockey, see George and Wilcox, *Nazis, Communists, Klansmen*, 253–65. Yockey, a lawyer, anti-Semite, and National Socialist theoretician, received a psychological discharge from the U.S. Army during World War II. In 1947 he wrote a rambling, esoteric anti-Semitic philosophic tract, *Imperium*, under the pseudonym "Ulick Varange." Carto was so taken with *Imperium* that in 1963 he published a second edition through his Noontide Press, calling it the "Bible" of resurgent National Socialism. Yockey was arrested for passport violations in San Francisco in 1960 and committed suicide in his jail cell while awaiting arraignment. He killed himself with a cyanide capsule. Carto was his last visitor. In 1964, Rockwell denounced Yockey as a Soviet agent in the July and September issues of the *Rockwell Report*—a charge that may well have been true—causing the breach with Carto, who remained passionately committed to Yockey. Essential elements of the Rockwell-Carto-Yockey relationship verified by Kevin Coogan, interview by author, 29 September 1994. Coogan is a historian/researcher currently writing a biography of Yockey.

9. GLR to Willis Carto, 10 May 1960, and GLR to Willis Carto, 26 July 1960, private collection of James Mason.

10. Rockwell's speech at the University of Hawaii is the first verifiable occasion at which he made Holocaust denial a major component of his presentation. See GLR, audiotape, debate with Tony Todaro, director, NAACP Hawaii Chapter, n.d. [ca. 1964], KTRG-TV-Honolulu, Don Carter, moderator. After 1964 Holocaust denial was a frequent feature of Rockwell's presentations to college audiences and the regular subject of articles in his publications. See, for example, GLR, audiotape, address at the University of North Dakota, November 1965, and [GLR], "Big Lie of 6 Million!" *Stormtrooper*, (Spring 1966), 6–8.

11. Quoted in Lipstadt, *Denying the Holocaust*, 66.

12. Bruno Ludtke to GLR, 28 November 1961, private collection of James Mason; Lipstadt, *Denying the Holocaust*, 22, 40. Kenneth Stern categorizes Barnes's writings on the Holocaust as "anti-Semitism masquerading as objective scholarly inquiry." Stern, *Holocaust Denial*, 5.

13. "Luke" [Bruno Ludtke] to GLR, 28 September 1962, and Bruno Ludtke to GLR, 29 June 1963, private collection of James Mason; Lipstadt, *Denying the Holocaust*, 41.

14. Bruno Ludtke to GLR, 11 January 1963 and 26 January 1963, private collection of James Mason.

15. Bruno Ludtke to GLR, 28 September 1962 and 28 November 1964, ibid.

16. Bruno Ludtke to GLR, 28 November 1961, n.d. [ca. February 1962], 29 January 1962, and 10 May 1963, ibid.; Stern, *Holocaust Denial*, 5.

17. Bruno Ludtke to GLR, n.d. [ca. February 1962], private collection of James Mason; Lipstadt, *Denying the Holocaust,* 71–74; Mintz, *Liberty Lobby,* 71–78; Stern, *Holocaust Denial,* 7, 155; Dawidowicz, "Lies about the Holocaust," 155.

18. Bruno Ludtke to GLR, 18 August 1962, private collection of James Mason. Ludtke specifically identified German journalists Heinrich Hartle and Peter Kleist as among those "we ought to hang."

19. GLR to Conde McGinley, 29 June 1963, and GLR to Denis Pirie, 19 May 1963, ibid.

20. GLR to Bernard E. Horgan, 20 April 1966, ibid.

21. Bruno Ludtke to GLR, 8 January 1965, 27 March 1966, 17 April 1966, 31 July 1965, and 16 November 1965, ibid.

22. Bruno Ludtke to Matt Koehl, 18 November 1964; Bruno Ludtke to GLR, 17 April 1966; Bruno Ludtke to William L. Pierce, 11 December 1966, all in ibid.

23. Quoted in Bruno Ludtke to GLR, 31 July 1965, ibid.

24. Bruno Ludtke to Presiding Judge, Criminal Division of the District Court, Frankfurt, West Germany, copy to GLR translated by Bruno Ludtke, n.d. [ca. May 1965]; Bruno Ludtke to GLR, 9 September 1966, both in ibid.

25. Guide Heimann, "The Lie of the Six Millions," *Der Weg* 7 (1954), translated by Bruno Ludtke, and Bruno Ludtke to GLR, 17 April 1966, ibid.

26. GLR to Bruno Ludtke, 15 May 1966, ibid.

27. [George Lincoln Rockwell], *The Diary of Ann Fink* (pamphlet) (Arlington, Va.: Hoax-Busters Press [ANP], n.d. [1965]; William F. Buckley Jr. to Barry Goldwater, Roger Milliken, Bill Baroody, Lloyd Smith, Jerry Millbank, Brent Bozell, DeLoach [sic], memorandum, n.d. [1965], William F. Buckley Jr. Papers, Sterling Library, Yale University. Anne Frank's *Diary of a Young Girl* is commonly (albeit mistakenly) referred to as *The Diary of Anne Frank.*

28. Rockwell, "*Playboy* Interview," 71–82, 154–55. *Playboy* circulation figures for April 1966 are from the Audit Bureau Circulation report for the period ending 30 June 1966. Shanthi Srenivasan, interviewed by author, 7 August 1995. Srenivasan is manager of the Circulation Department, Playboy Enterprises, Inc. *Journal of Historical Review* circulation figures are from George and Wilcox, *Nazis, Communists, Klansmen,* 262.

29. Lew Cor [George Lincoln Rockwell], "When the Nazis Tried Human Vivisection," *Sir!* March 1958, 10–11, 36–37; George Lincoln Rockwell, "So-called 'War Crimes' . . . Exposed!" *Rockwell Report,* n.d. [1965]; Rockwell, "*Playboy* Interview," 78–79.

30. Leonard Weinberg, "Introduction," in *Encounters with the Contemporary Radical Right,* ed. Peter H. Merkl and Leonard Weinberg (Boulder, Colo.: Westview Press, 1993), 8. For a sense of Rockwell's role from the perspective of contemporary anti-Semitic leaders, see Mason, *Siege,* 92; Matt Koehl, "Holocaust or Hitler: Which Is It Going to Be?" *New Order,* 10 April 1993, n.p.

31. Robert Braun, "The Holocaust and Problems of Historical Representation," *History and Theory* 33.2 (1994): 176. See also Pierre Nora, "Between Memory and

History: Les Lieux de Memoire," *Representations* 26 (Spring 1989): 8–9. For problems in historical representation of the Holocaust, see Wulf Kansteiner, "From Exception to Exemplum: The New Approach to Nazism and the 'Final Solution'," *History and Theory* 33.2 (1994): 145–71; Hans Kellner, "'Never Again' Is Now," *History and Theory* 33.2 (1994): 127–44. Kellner warns: "Because we are a historical society, the Holocaust must become historical for its memory to survive" (128). He also argues that the normal process of historical revision threatens the validity of the historical memory, especially "as the survivors pass" and the "dangers of representation become more intense" (129). See also Berel Lang, "Is It Possible to Misrepresent the Holocaust?" *History and Theory* 34.1 (1995): 84–89; Young, *Writing and Rewriting the Holocaust.* Young argues that the "moral enormity" of the Holocaust makes it a "test case for historical representation" (88).

32. GLR to Bruno Ludtke, 15 May 1966, private collection of James Mason.

Chapter 11: Christian Identity

1. [R. E. Cooper], *NSV Report,* July/September 1991, 2.

2. The most comprehensive and reliable current study of Christian Identity is Michael Barkun's *Religion and the Racist Right: The Origins of the Christian Identity Movement* (Chapel Hill: University of North Carolina Press, 1994). See also James A. Aho, *The Politics of Righteousness: Idaho's Christian Patriotism* (Seattle: University of Washington Press, 1990); Leonard Zeskind, *The "Christian Identity" Movement: A Theological Justification for Racist and Anti-Semitic Violence* (Atlanta: Center for Democratic Renewal, 1986).

3. Barkun, *Religion and the Racist Right,* 3–22.

4. Zeskind, *"Christian Identity" Movement,* 9–10.

5. Quoted in Aho, *Politics of Righteousness,* 51–59.

6. James A. Aho, lecture at Pacific Coast Branch conference of the American Historical Association, Corvallis, Oregon, 14 August 1992, from author's notes.

7. Aho, *Politics of Righteousness,* 92–95, 103–11. Butler developed an Identity genealogy that "documented" the claim of Aryans to the status of true Israelites through Seth, the third son of Adam and Eve and the ancestor of Noah, and through Noah's son Shem to Abram (Abraham) and Jacob (Israel). Butler's major theological innovation, however, entailed the genealogical "documentation" of Jews as the literal offspring of Satan through Cain—who was, according to Butler, not Adam's son but the product of a sexual union between Eve and Satan. Butler taught that after Cain was driven from Adam's presence for murdering his half-brother Abel, Cain copulated with the "Witch Women of Nod" to create a race of humanoid devils, the Canaanites, who are the true ancestors of contemporary Jews.

8. Leonard Weinberg, "The American Radical Right: Exit, Voice, and Violence," in *Encounters with the Contemporary Radical Right,* ed. Peter H. Merkl and Leonard Weinberg (Boulder, Colo.: Westview Press, 1993), 188, 193–94. Weinberg includes William Potter Gale with Swift and Butler as adapting Identity theology "to American circumstances in the twentieth century."

9. Elden "Bud" Cutler to author, 23 June 1991. Cutler was an ANP stormtrooper and Christian Identity follower who knew both Rockwell and Butler.

10. Zeskind, *"Christian Identity" Movement,* 9–10; Turner, *Power on the Right,* 100–101; George and Wilcox, *Nazis, Communists, Klansmen,* 382–93; *Para-Military Organizations in California,* NSRP-10; AJC Trend Analysis Division, "Profile of an 'Acting Fuehrer': Matthias (Matt) Koehl, Jr.," 7 September 1967, box 138, AJC.

11. Turner, *Power on the Right,* 100. Some, like James K. Warner, actually functioned in both arenas, serving as ANP national secretary (1960–61), as "pastor" of the New Christian Crusade Church, a Christian Identity spin-off, and as publisher of the *Christian Vanguard,* a contemporary racist and anti-Semitic periodical in which tenets of Nazism and Christian Identity are indistinguishable. See *NSV Report,* October/December 1993, 4.

12. Emory Burke, Letter to the Editor, *NS* [National Socialist] *Bulletin* 328 (Second Quarter 1992): 5; Emory Burke, interviewed by author, 17 September 1995. When asked whether he believed that Rockwell actually implemented his plans later through Christian Identity churches, Burke emphatically answered "No." According to Burke, although many contemporary Nazis operate under the cover of Christian Identity churches, it is "immoral to hide politics in a church." When pressed whether this was his opinion or Rockwell's, Burke claimed Rockwell would have agreed with his position that "it is terribly dishonest to hide Nazism within Identity." Burke saw no incompatibility between his attribution of a morally based reluctance by Rockwell to exploit religion and Burke's later description of Rockwell as "an enormously pragmatic man" who believed in only "what will work" and that "if one way didn't work, he'd find another way that would." According to Burke, "Rockwell would do anything necessary to achieve power, for his ideas to gain power." All evidence regarding Rockwell's pragmatism, including Burke's own testimony and Rockwell's private correspondence on the strategic use of religion, suggests that it would have been enormously out of character for Rockwell to reject any promising strategy on moral grounds. The passage of time may have transferred Burke's own ethical standards to Rockwell, at least in Burke's mind. I believe Burke is mistaken about Rockwell's utilization of the Identity church structure for political purposes.

13. Bruno Ludtke to GLR, 30 May 1962, private collection of James Mason. Ludtke also sent Rockwell a ten-page letter detailing his own religious beliefs, including a proposed "Creed" in which Adolf Hitler is cast in the role of Jesus as son of God and redeemer of God's "Chosen People"—the German-Nordic Aryans. See Bruno Ludtke to GLR, 15 May 1962, ibid. Earlier, Ludtke wrote a long position paper for Rockwell on the organization and strategy of the Roman Catholic Church and suggested that the Church's history "should be one of the main courses in the training of our political officers." The Church's strength, wrote Ludtke, was in having "the most unchangeable dogmas, but [was] very flexible as to the methods." According to Ludtke, the Roman Catholic Church understood "that the greatest danger was not the power of the enemy" but "heresy." To combat "heresy" within the movement, according to Ludtke, Rockwell needed to speak with the political authority of the Führer and the moral authority of the Pope. See Bruno Ludtke to GLR, 5 March 1962, ibid.

14. GLR to Bruno Ludtke, 21 January 1963, and Bruno Ludtke to GLR, n.d. [ca. early February 1963], ibid.

15. Bruno Ludtke to GLR, 30 January 1963, ibid. When Ludtke and Rockwell suspected that their mail was being intercepted and read by government agents in West Germany and the United Sates, they adopted the code names "Paul" for Rockwell, "Luke" for Ludtke, and "Mark" for Colin Jordan, which reflected the extent to which evangelical imagery had permeated their thinking. See "Luke" to "Paul," 30 June 1962, ibid.

16. GLR to Bruno Ludtke, 11 February 1963, ibid.

17. Bruno Ludtke to GLR, 10 May 1963 and 29 June 1963, ibid.

18. Bruno Ludtke to GLR, 25 January 1964, ibid.

19. Bruno Ludtke to Colin Jordan, 22 June 1964, and GLR to Colin Jordan, 31 August 1963, ibid. Ludtke continued to try to appease Jordan by agreeing with his distaste for the Bible and Christianity while defending Rockwell's larger strategy. See Colin Jordan to Bruno Ludtke, 15 January 1966, and Bruno Ludtke to Colin Jordan, 18 January 1966, ibid. Both letters were in reaction to Rockwell's pressing Jordan to use Christian and biblical references to mobilize mass support for Nazis in Britain. See GLR to Colin Jordan, 1 January 1966, ibid.

20. Colin Jordan to GLR, 20 January 1966, ibid. See also Colin Jordan, *National Socialism: World Creed for the 1980s* (Harrogate, Eng.: Gothic Ripples, 1981), rpt. from *National Socialist* 3 (Winter 1981).

21. See GLR to Ron Gostick, 25 March 1964; GLR to Bernard E. Horgan, 20 April 1966; Bruno Ludtke to GLR, 8 January 1966 and 4 March 1966, private collection of James Mason.

22. Turner, *Power on the Right,* 102. GLR, audiotape, address to supporters, location unknown, 1965, in which Rockwell praises Swift and reports that he "just spent three days with him" on matters of mutual interest.

23. FBI File #9-39854, appendix 175-43-19, n.d. [2 August 1966], identifies Ralph Perry Forbes as captain and commander of the ANP's Western Division headquartered in El Monte, California. Forbes took command of that division on 1 May 1963. In an article on the Rockwell connection to Christian Identity, R. E. Cooper says that "Rockwell wanted Captain Forbes to head a Christian branch of the ANP" and elaborates on the implementation of that intention. Cooper writes that "Rockwell had the right idea about establishing a religious branch of the ANP." See *NSV Report,* January/March 1992, n.p. Forbes remains an active "minister" and publisher of anti-Semitic and racist tracts, with twelve full-time "helpers," through his Good News Ministries in London, Arkansas. His newsletter, *Straight Shoot'n: The Chaplain's Report to Christian Soldiers,* is one of the most influential Identity-type pseudo-Christian publications in current circulation. See, for example, "The Bible, Blacks, and Identity!" and "Cults, Identity and Kulture War," both in volume 1, published in 1994.

24. GLR to Ralph Forbes, 26 August 1965, private collection of James Mason. Excerpts from this letter also appear in *NSV Report,* January/March 1992, n.p. According to Michael Barkun, William V. Fowler, an eschatological prophet and militant survivalist, advocated arming white Christians in preparation for the Tribulation. See Barkun, *Religion and the Racist Right,* 111, 114, 213.

25. Barkun, *Religion and the Racist Right,* 111, 114, 213.

26. Quoted in *NSV Report,* January/March 1992, n.p. According to Michael Barkun and James Aho, the use of etymology to substantiate Identity claims is a common feature of British Israelism and Christian Identity. Barkun traces this practice to John Wilson in the mid-nineteenth century, who looked for "words in different languages that sounded the same, assuming, usually erroneously, that if the sounds were similar, then the languages and their speakers had to be connected" (*Religion and the Racist Right,* 7). Aho identifies the use of etymology as a "compelling literary tool to substantiate Identity claims." One frequent misuse, according to Aho, is the crossing of linguistic subfamilies to make a point. Hebrew, a derivative of the Afro-Asiatic Semitic root, and English, of the Germanic subfamily of the Indo-Aryan root, are carelessly interchanged by Identity propagandists to establish a desired point based on sounds and letter groupings. For example, Identity adherents connect the Hebrew *b'rith* (covenant) and *Ish* (man) and suggest that this amalgam is the root of the English word *British,* which, to them, translates as "covenant people" and which in turn "proves" that the Patriarch Abraham was British. Aho, *Politics of Righteousness,* 106–8.

27. Ralph Forbes to author, 25 August 1993.

28. [R. E. Cooper], *NSV Report,* January/March 1992, n.p. For an indication of Butler's revered position within the neo-Nazi movement, see *NSV Report,* January/March 1985, n.p. Butler's role as the prime transmitter of Nazi ideology through Identity theology is carried on through his own disciples, such as "Pastor" Thom Robb, who heads an Identity congregation in Harrison, Arkansas, and coordinates "Movement activities" throughout the state of Arkansas. See [R. E. Cooper], *NSV Report,* October/December 1987, n.p.; Zeskind, *"Christian Identity" Movement,* 6–8. Butler's influence in Christian Identity, neo-Nazi, white supremacist, and violent survivalist circles is pervasive. His disciples included the late Robert Jay Mathews and Gary Lee Yarbrough, the most notorious, violent white supremacists of the 1980s. Butler's followers have been implicated in virtually every major white supremacist and anti-Semitic act of violence since 1970, including the 1984 murder of Denver radio talk show host Alan Berg. According to a *Time* reporter who studied neo-Nazi activities in the 1980s, "a common thread in this network of bigotry is [Richard Butler's] . . . white supremacist organization in Hayden Lake, Idaho." See Robert T. Zinti, "Dreams of a Bigot's Revolution," *Time,* 18 February 1985, 42.

29. After Rockwell's death, Francis Joseph "Frank" Smith, Rockwell's personal bodyguard and one of his closest friends in the ANP, also became a Christian Identity minister with a congregation in rural Maine. Gordon Hall to author, 2 October 1995. Regarding the interconnectedness of Nazism and Christian Identity following Rockwell, see Southern Poverty Law Center, "Racist Identity Sect Fuels Nationwide Extremist Movement," *Klanwatch Intelligence Report* 79 (August 1995): 1, 3–5. In the same publication, Richard G. Butler is identified as a contemporary neo-Nazi Identity leader. See idem, "Aryan World Congress Focuses on Militias and an Expected Revolution," ibid., 1–2.

30. Matt Koehl, "Introduction" (published as an insert), in New Order, *The Religion of Lincoln Rockwell* (Milwaukee: New Order, n.d. [ca. 1972]).

31. The psychological attraction of Christian Identity to racists and neo-Nazis can be likened to that experienced by adherents to cults of many types. See R. Drew Smith, "Why Blacks Join Cults," *Emerge,* July/August 1993, 52–54.

32. [R. E. Cooper], *NSV Report,* July/September 1991.

Chapter 12: Settling for Notoriety

1. GLR to Bruno Ludtke, 18 July 1964 and 9 March 1964, private collection of James Mason.

2. The Commander [GLR] to Major [Matt] Koehl, 1 August 1966, memo, Criminal Archives, Office of the Clerk, Circuit Court of Arlington County, Commonwealth of Virginia, File C-5575, Defense Exhibit J.

3. FBI File #9-39854, "American Nazi Party." According to the FBI, Rockwell established the United White Christian Majority in July 1964. It operated through 1965 under the command of Rockwell's surrogate, Cecil Odom. The White Youth Corps was established in October 1961 and operated intermittently through 1965. Rockwell tried to energize the flagging group in 1964–65 under Marlin Wayne Thomas, a seventeen-year-old Queens College student. The ANP's Texas chapter, under the command of Robert A. Surrey and Jerald Thomas Walraven, was the most active ANP chapter during the period 1964–65. The southern California chapter, under the command of Ralph Perry Forbes, was also active and growing during this period.

4. The most accurate and comprehensive work to date on William Luther Pierce's career and beliefs is Brad Whitsel's essay "The Cosmotheist Community: Aryan Visions for the Future in the West Virginia Mountains." Whitsel generously made a prepublication copy available to me for this study. The essay is scheduled for publication in the *Journal of Terrorism and Political Violence.*

5. Under the pseudonym "Andrew Macdonald," Pierce wrote a futuristic novel, *The Turner Diaries,* which became a blueprint for white supremacist violence in the 1980s and 1990s. Pierce's protégé, Robert Jay Matthews, was a founder of The Order, a violent white supremacist revolutionary cadre that modeled itself on a fictional Pierce creation from *The Turner Diaries.* Matthews was implicated in several acts of criminal violence and was killed in a shoot-out with federal law enforcement authorities. See Eckard Toy, "Historical Sources of the Radical Right," paper read at the American Historical Association Pacific Coast Branch Conference, 14 August 1992, Oregon State University, from author's notes. For Pierce's political novels, see Andrew Macdonald [William L. Pierce], *The Turner Diaries,* 2d ed. (Washington, D.C.: National Alliance, 1980), and *Hunter* (Hillsboro, W.Va.: National Vanguard Books, 1989). For additional insight into Pierce's philosophy, particularly his racism and quasireligious millenarianism, see William L. Pierce, *Cosmotheism: Wave of the Future* (Hillsboro, W.Va.: National Vanguard Books, 1977), and *Human Dignity: A Racial Ethic* (Hillsboro, W.Va.: National Vanguard Books, 1978).

6. William L. Pierce to GLR, 1 November 1966, private collection of James Mason.

7. GLR to Colin Jordan, 19 January 1964, ibid. Rockwell's sense of personal loss regarding Thora and their children was a frequent topic in his voluminous correspon-

dence with Bruno Ludtke. Ludtke tried to instill in Rockwell the belief that "men like ourselves simply cannot be happy even with the best things that make normal men happy. Our kind of happiness would be an unbearable burden for normal beings." See Bruno Ludtke to Colin Jordan, 2 August 1965, ibid.

8. GLR to Claire Schade Rockwell, 4 August 1964, private collection of P. Claire Rockwell.

9. Jack Anderson, news release, 10 January 1966, private collection of R. E. Cooper.

10. See, for example, Barbara von Goetz to Claire Schade Rockwell, 6 July 1963, 5 February 1964, 11 July 1966, and 12 March [1967], private collection of P. Claire Rockwell.

11. Barbara von Goetz to Claire Schade Rockwell, 23 November 1964, ibid.

12. Ibid.

13. Barbara von Goetz to Claire Schade Rockwell, 11 July 1966, ibid.

14. GLR to Claire Schade Rockwell, 18 October 1966, ibid.

15. Stanley R. Tupper to author, 23 August 1995. Tupper was a close boyhood friend and classmate of Rockwell at Hebron Academy; during Rockwell's public career, Tupper represented Maine in the U.S. Congress. Doc Rockwell was Tupper's most prominent constituent and the two men, along with Doc's second wife, Madelyn, maintained a friendship.

16. Barbara von Goetz to Claire Schade Rockwell, n.d. [1966], private collection of P. Claire Rockwell. Rockwell's mother periodically sent him cash for food and other necessities. She also financed some dental work he urgently needed. See Barbara von Goetz to Claire Schade Rockwell, 6 July 1963, ibid.

17. Claire Schade Rockwell to GLR, 29 June 1966, and GLR to Claire Schade Rockwell, 18 October 1966, ibid.

18. GLR to [unnamed] IRS District Director, 18 February 1964; Chief, IRS Taxpayer Service Section, to GLR, form letter, 9 March 1964; H. N. Bono, Acting Chief, IRS Review Staff, to GLR, 23 December 1964; R. J. Stakem, Chief, IRS Exempt Organizations Branch, to GLR, 1 March 1965; GLR to R. J. Stakem, 27 March 1965; L. M. Chapper, Chief, IRS Review Staff, to GLR, 23 August 1965; GLR to L. M. Chapper, 28 August 1965; W. J. Powell Jr., Director, Division of Individual Taxes, Commonwealth of Virginia, to GLR, 30 December 1965; IRS Notice of Public Auction, 7 February 1966; GLR to Sam R. Edmundson, Collector of Internal Revenue, 19 February 1966; Lt. Col. [Alan] Welch to Commander Rockwell, ANP memorandum, 20 February 1966; GLR to W. J. Powell, 20 February 1966; GLR to [unnamed] IRS District Director, 20 February 1966; GLR to Mrs. Judith A. Rockwell, 20 February 1966; Judith A. Rockwell to "Gentlemen," 4 March 1966; GLR to W. J. Powell, 12 March 1966, 27 March 1966, and 21 May 1966; W. J. Powell to GLR, 22 March 1966 and 15 July 1966; James P. Boyle, IRS District Director, to GLR, 17 March 1966 and 23 June 1966; C. P. Smith, Acting Chief, IRS Conference Staff, to GLR, 30 June 1966; GLR to James P. Boyle, 26 June 1966; GLR to C. P. Smith, 2 July 1966; GLR to [unnamed] IRS District Director, 17 April 1967, all in the private collection of James Mason.

19. See, for example, *Sunbury* (Pa.) *Daily Item,* 10 January 1962, 17 January 1962, 22 January 1962, and 31 January 1962.

20. Fine and Himmelfarb, *American Jewish Year Book 1963,* 138–40.

21. According to the FBI, during this period Rockwell spoke at Carleton College (Minnesota), Western Washington State College, San Jose City College, San Francisco State College, Stanford University, Antioch College (Ohio), the University of Chicago, the University of Michigan, Colorado State College, and the University of Hawaii. See FBI File #9-39854, "American Nazi Party." This list, although accurate, is incomplete. Rockwell also spoke at San Jose State College, the Hilo and Honolulu campuses of the University of Hawaii, Hofstra University (New York), the University of New Hampshire, the University of Kansas, Rocky Mountain College (Montana), Colorado State College, Union Junior College (New Jersey), and the University of Washington. See Barbara von Goetz to Claire Schade Rockwell, 5 February [1964] and 23 November 1964, private collection of P. Claire Rockwell. See also GLR to Bruno Ludtke, 7 June 1964, and GLR to Euna Holmquist, 22 September 1964, private collection of James Mason.

22. "ADL Asks C.U. [Colorado University] to Explain Rockwell Appearance before 3000," *Intermountain Jewish News,* 17 May 1963, 1; Laird Wilcox, interviewed by author, 19 August 1991.

23. For a detailed description of the events at the University of Washington, see GLR to Bruno Ludtke, 7 June 1964, private collection of James Mason. The FBI reported that Rockwell surrogate Ralph P. Forbes drew a capacity crowd of 6,500 at the University of California at Berkeley on 22 May 1964. See FBI File #9-39854, "American Nazi Party," 26.

24. GLR to William L. Pierce, 19 December 1965, private collection of James Mason.

25. A partial list of Rockwell's bookings from mid-1965 through 1966, in addition to Harvard, Brown, and Columbia, include: the University of New Mexico, Ohio University, Northwestern University, Northern Illinois University, the University of North Dakota, New York University, Rice University, New Mexico Highlands University, State University of New York at Oneonta, State University of New York at Geneseo, and the University of Minnesota. See FBI File #9-39854, "American Nazi Party"; Morris Fine and Milton Himmelfarb, eds., *American Jewish Year Book 1966* vol. 67 (Philadelphia: Jewish Publication Society of America, 1966), 162; idem, *American Jewish Year Book 1967,* 70; GLR to Claire Schade Rockwell, 18 October 1966, private collection of P. Claire Rockwell; GLR, audiotape, lecture at the University of North Dakota, November 1965; GLR, audiotape, lecture at New York University, [1965]; Lee Larson to author, 30 November 1990.

26. GLR to Matt Koehl, 13 April 1967, Criminal Archives, Office of the Clerk, Circuit Court of Arlington County, Commonwealth of Virginia, File C-5575; GLR to Pedro del Valle, 18 April 1967, Pedro A. del Valle Papers, Special Collections, University of Oregon. See also Mason interview; Barbara von Goetz to Bruno Ludtke, 19 January 1967 and 10 February 1967, private collection of James Mason; Barbara von Goetz to

Claire Schade Rockwell, 12 March [1967], private collection of P. Claire Rockwell; contract between Don Awtrey and GLR, Wichita State University, 25 March 1967, Michigan Historical Collections, Bentley Historical Library, University of Michigan. Educational institutions at which Rockwell appeared in 1967 include: the University of Minnesota, Drake University (Iowa), Iowa State College, Phillipps Academy (Boston), the University of Utah, Wake Forest University, Idaho State University, the University of California at Santa Barbara, Ohio University, Bowling Green College (Ohio), Wichita State University, the University of South Carolina, Sonoma State College (California), and the University of California at Los Angeles. This partial list was assembled from fragmentary extant records and represents a small percentage of the campus appearances Rockwell made from January through August 1967.

27. Max Lerner, "A Sick Evening," *New York Post*, 28 September 1966, quoted in Fine and Himmelfarb, *American Jewish Year Book 1967*, 70.

Chapter 13: Betrayal and Death

1. Audiotaped conversation between Roy Frankhauser and Laird Wilcox, 21 August 1988, private collection of Laird Wilcox. Frankhauser was a ubiquitous presence within the anti-Semitic radical right. At one time or another he was a member of just about every radical right-wing group in the United States, including Rockwell's. Most often he operated as an informant for federal and/or local law enforcement agencies. Frankhauser claims that the ADL was "tied to Rockwell's killing" and used Patler to accomplish the deed. Frankhauser also claims that Patler tried to sell him the murder weapon a month before the assassination. A key element of Patler's defense is that the murder weapon had not been in his possession for several years prior to the murder.

2. Karl Allen to Pedro A. del Valle, 9 December 1967, Pedro A. del Valle Papers, Special Collections, University Library, University of Oregon.

3. John Patler to Judge Russell, n.d., Criminal Archives, Office of the Clerk, Circuit Court of Arlington County, Commonwealth of Virginia, File C-5575.

4. John N. Stanislaus, Acting Chief Probation Officer, Bronx (N.Y.) County Court, to J. J. Miller, M.D., Director, Morrisania Hospital Mental Hygiene Clinic, 5 September 1956, Re: John Patsalos [Patler], Case #22,798, Commonwealth Exhibit #1(a), ibid.

5. Pierre Rube, M.D., Report #16221, John Patsalos [Patler], Morrisania City Hospital Mental Hygiene Clinic, 26 October 1956 to 1 September 1960, ibid.

6. Edmundo de L. Yearwood, M.D., The City of New York, Department of Hospitals, History Continuation Sheet, Re: John Patsalos [Patler], Social Service Case No. 16221, 30 October 1957, ibid. See also Albert A. LaVerne, M.D., undated psychiatric examination notes, and Charles W. Gray, Deputy Chief Probation Officer, Bronx (N.Y.) County Court, to Bellevue Psychiatric Hospital, 30 January 1957, ibid.

7. John Patler to Judge Russell, June 1972. See also Edmundo de L. Yearwood, M.D., History Continuation Sheet, Re: John Patsalos [Patler], 26 October 1956.

8. John Patler to Judge Russell, June 1972. Ironically, it was Hooker who introduced Rockwell to Patler. Rockwell, like Patler, revered Hooker and regarded him as his men-

tor. In the dedication of *This Time the World*, Rockwell pays tribute to DeWest Hooker as the one "who first taught me to know the cunning and evil ways of the enemy" (v).

9. John Patler to Judge Russell, June 1972.

10. Rader, "Deadly Friendship," 14.

11. Gordon Hall, interviewed by author, 30 September 1995. See also David Bell, interviewed by author, 28 June 1991.

12. John Patler to Judge Russell, June 1972. For Patler's relationship with Dan Burros, an ANP officer who committed suicide when the *New York Times* revealed that he was a Jew and the son of Nazi death camp survivors, see A. M. Rosenthal and Arthur Gelb, *One More Victim* (New York: New American Library, 1967).

13. GLR to John Patler, [25?] June 1966, Criminal Archives, Office of the Clerk, Circuit Court of Arlington County, Commonwealth of Virginia, File C-5575, Commonwealth Exhibit #61; Captain [John] Patler to The Commander [GLR], 28 June 1966, Commonwealth Exhibit #60, ibid.

14. Captain [John] Patler to The Commander [GLR], 28 June 1966.

15. John Patler to GLR, n.d. [ca. summer 1967], Criminal Archives, Office of the Clerk, Circuit Court of Arlington County, Commonwealth of Virginia, File C-5575, Commonwealth Exhibit #5E.

16. Those closest to Patler and to the Rockwell murder case are fairly evenly split on the question of Patler's guilt. Helen Lane, Patler's defense attorney and a personal friend of Rockwell, remained "strongly convinced," years after the trial, that Patler was innocent. She based that opinion primarily on the belief that the physical circumstances of the murder proved Patler incapable of covering the distance from the place of the murder to the point of his arrest in the time allowed. Lane even engaged a high school track champion to attempt to duplicate the route the Arlington police claim Patler took following the murder. The young athlete, in much better condition than Patler, was unable to do so by a substantial margin. Lane's son, Bob, knew Patler prior to the murder, when Patler worked for Alice Ervin's father as a television repairman, and he believes John Patler was "incapable of the crime." Bob Lane, interviewed by author, 29 September 1995.

Gordon Hall, a journalist and writer who studied Rockwell and the ANP and knew both Rockwell and Patler well, is equally convinced that Patler is guilty. Hall interviewed Patler in his jail cell following his arrest and says he has "no doubt" that Patler killed Rockwell. Gordon Hall, interviewed by author, 30 September 1995. James Mason, a Rockwell loyalist with numerous contacts within the contemporary racist right, believes that Patler "probably was the triggerman" but that he was merely the pawn of a wider conspiracy to kill Rockwell. Mason interview; James Mason to John Jewell, 22 January 1982, private collection of James Mason. Mason's view is shared by former ANP officer Hal Kaiser (a.k.a. Joe Charles Carter). Hal Kaiser, interviewed by author, 17 July 1991. David Bell, the Arlington County clerk of courts, believes Patler, unassisted, was Rockwell's assassin. Bell interview. See also Thomas J. Harrigan, Counsel for John Patler, Petition for Writ of Error, 17 March 1976, Office of the Clerk, Supreme Court of Appeals, Commonwealth of Virginia, Record #7103. Harrigan cites multiple instances of evidentiary inconsistency in Patler's 1967 trial.

17. Rough draft of letter from "Major Koehl, by order of G. L. Rockwell, Commander," to John Patler, n.d. [ca. March 1967], Criminal Archives, Office of the Clerk, Circuit Court of Arlington County, Commonwealth of Virginia, File C-5575, Commonwealth Exhibit #58-A.

18. John Patler to "Brother Booker" [H. H. Booker II], 22 May 1967, Commonwealth Exhibit #72; John Patler to H. H. Booker II, 3 May 1967, Commonwealth Exhibit #73; and John Patler to H. H. Booker II, 19 April 1967, Commonwealth Exhibit #75, all in ibid.; John Patler to GLR, n.d. [ca. summer 1967]. If Rockwell ever specifically rejected Patler's plea for forgiveness, that rejection would bolster the prosecution's claim that the March 1967 break was absolute and would strengthen their case against Patler, but no Rockwell reply is extant. In the absence of documentary evidence to the contrary, it is reasonable to assume that the events of March to August 1967 would have followed the pattern long fixed in the Rockwell-Patler relationship: a breach instigated by Patler, followed by Patler's plea for forgiveness, followed by reconciliation. However, Patler's fragile mental state in mid-1967 must be kept in mind, which would preclude no act, no matter how irrational or how inconsistent with past behavior.

19. Hall interview.

20. Bell interview. Bell believes that "it was a love triangle, pure and simple." He identifies Bennie Taylor, the clerk at Patler's trial, as the source of this allegation.

21. John Patler to GLR, n.d. [ca. summer 1967].

22. Convicted of Rockwell's murder, John Patler was sentenced to twenty years in prison. He served less than eleven years and was paroled by the Commonwealth of Virginia on 6 October 1978. Upon completion of his parole, Patler changed his name and left Virginia. While in prison, he took college classes and graduated magna cum laude from New River Community College with an associate's degree in science; he also took courses in art education through Radford University, sought and received psychiatric counseling, and renounced his Nazi affiliations. Since his release, he has led a productive life and has not resumed his antisocial behavior. Judge Charles S. Russell, who presided at Patler's trial and went on to a distinguished career as a justice of the Supreme Court of Virginia, interceded on Patler's behalf with the parole board. Russell wrote to Patler in prison: "I wrote to the Parole Board in your behalf, recommending you for release as soon as you become eligible for consideration. Yours is the only case in which I have ever written such a letter, but all of the information which has come to me serves to confirm my belief that it was well deserved." See Julian Pugh to author, 5 December 1990; Charles S. Russell to John Patler, 7 October 1974, Criminal Archives, Office of the Clerk, Circuit Court of Arlington County, Commonwealth of Virginia, File C-5575; John Patler to Charles S. Russell, 14 September 1974, ibid.; John R. McGreeny, M.D., concluded that "there is no evidence to indicate any present psychopathology." See John R. McGreeny, handwritten notes from psychiatric evaluation of John Patler while in prison, n.d., ibid. John R. McGreeny, M.D., same file.

23. Max Amann [Robert Surrey] to "Admirers and Supporters of the late George Lincoln Rockwell," June 1968, private collection of James Mason. Surrey, Rockwell's "man in Dallas" and one of his closest and most trusted followers, openly accused Matt Koehl of plotting and directing Rockwell's assassination. Surrey identified Douglas Lindberg Niles, "the only man ever to receive a DISHONORABLE discharge from the party," as the assassin. R. E. Cooper, director of the National Socialist Vanguard and a former Koehl aide, shares Surrey's suspicion that former ANP stormtrooper Doug Niles "may have been Rockwell's assassin." Cooper does not go as far as Surrey in specifically naming Koehl as the mastermind of the assassination, but he does not discount that possibility. See R. E. Cooper to H. H. Booker II, 16 January 1982, and H. H. Booker II to R. E. Cooper, 22 January 1982, private collection of R. E. Cooper. Booker was not convinced of Koehl's complicity in Rockwell's death. See H. H. Booker II to R. E. Cooper, 7 January 1982, ibid.

24. Kaiser interviews, 17 July 1991 and 15 October 1991. Kaiser claims that Rockwell told him, weeks before the incident described, that he suspected Koehl, Pierce, and Lloyd were trying to take over the party. Koehl was not at ANP headquarters during the altercation but relayed the eyewitness account he received from the stormtrooper on duty to the author. Kaiser believes that Koehl, Pierce, and Lloyd manipulated Patler to kill Rockwell.

25. Burke interview; Mason interview.

26. Barbara von Goetz to Claire Schade Rockwell, 15 December 1967, 25 January 1968, and 25 March 1968, private collection of P. Claire Rockwell; Rockwell interview. Rockwell's sister confirms that Barbara von Goetz became increasingly uneasy with Koehl during the months following Rockwell's murder and didn't want him to know her whereabouts. While Arlington police and prosecutors were aware of a growing hostility between Rockwell and Koehl in the months before Rockwell's assassination, they inexplicably did not pursue that issue. In fairness, however, it must be kept in mind that the fractious radical right is fraught with feuds and vendettas, with the interactants alternating frequently between ally and enemy. The ANP was no exception. Ironically, von Goetz, the most credible proponent of the Koehl conspiracy theory, now lives with Matt Koehl in his fortified compound in New Berlin, Wisconsin. She serves as his secretary and chief aide under the pseudonym "William Wallace." Neither von Goetz nor Koehl would agree to be interviewed for this study. See The Commander [GLR] to Major [Matt] Koehl, ANP memo, 1 August 1966, Criminal Archives, Office of the Clerk, Circuit Court of Arlington County, Commonwealth of Virginia, File C-5575, Defense Exhibit K; and GLR to Matt Koehl, 13 April 1967, ibid., Defense Exhibit J.

27. Testimony of Francis Joseph Smith, 12 December 1967, trial transcript, p. 2292, ibid. Hal Kaiser reports that Rockwell expressed a similar sentiment shortly before his death. According to Kaiser, Rockwell told him in a private conversation, "There is a conspiracy to take my own party away from me." Kaiser interview, 17 July 1991.

28. Barbara von Goetz to Claire Schade Rockwell, 15 December 1967, 25 January 1968, and 25 March 1969, private collection of P. Claire Rockwell.

29. Stefani interview; Rockwell interview; *Concord* (N.H.) *Daily Monitor,* 31 August 1967, 20; *Manchester* (N.H.) *Union Leader,* 28 August 1967, 22.

30. "Der Tag," *Newsweek* 70 (4 September 1967): 30–31; "Ashes to Ashes," *Newsweek* 70 (11 September 1967): 23–24. Rockwell was cremated on 30 August 1967. The disposition of his ashes is unknown.

31. Rockwell interview; Jack Anderson, news release, 10 January 1966, private collection of R. E. Cooper. The child was born on 8 December 1961 at the District of Columbia General Hospital and died on 25 October 1962 of respiratory collapse in von Goetz's quarters at the ANP barracks at Hatemonger Hill. The baby was named Laurie Gissela Mapp, "Mapp" being the last name of von Goetz's former husband. For years, the death fueled a macabre rumor that a Rockwell-von Goetz infant was born horribly deformed and that Rockwell choked it to death. That story, although widely circulated among Rockwell's enemies on the racist right, is untrue.

32. Barbara von Goetz to Claire Schade Rockwell, 12 March 1967 and 28 June 1967; Barbara von Goetz and Ethel Harrison, letter of agreement for child care, 2 April 1967, all in the private collection of P. Claire Rockwell.

33. Barbara von Goetz to Claire Schade Rockwell, n.d. [ca. July 1967], ibid. In this letter, von Goetz says that Rockwell did not believe Gretchen suffered from Werdung-Hoffmann disease. Rather, he attributed her condition to abortifacient injections von Goetz apparently took on learning she was pregnant. The injections failed to abort the fetus, but Rockwell, who learned of von Goetz's abortion attempt after the baby was born, believed Gretchen was "poisoned" by the injections.

34. Barbara von Goetz to Claire Schade Rockwell, 8 August 1967, ibid.

35. Barbara von Goetz to Claire Schade Rockwell, 21 August 1967, ibid. After Rockwell's death, von Goetz wrote to Claire Rockwell and asked her to burn all letters and documents relating to Gretchen's paternity, birth, and death. "I have [burned] mine," she wrote, "and everything to do with the subject." Rockwell's mother did not comply with the request. Barbara von Goetz to Claire Schade Rockwell, 25 January 1968, ibid.

Conclusion

1. [Matt Koehl], "The Genius of Lincoln Rockwell," *NS* [National Socialist] *Bulletin* 329 (Third Quarter, 1992): 1, 3, 8. See also Matt Koehl, "Letter to Supporters," 10 April 1993, author's files, in which Koehl describes his organization's mission as carrying "the torch of Adolf Hitler and his National Socialist truth to the world." Koehl invokes Rockwell's spirit: "Just as Lincoln Rockwell once picked up that torch in the postwar years, so we must now hold it aloft and see that never does it fall."

2. William L. Pierce to author, 28 July 1995; Mason, *Siege,* 102, 119, xiii, 317.

3. Manfred Roeder to author, 29 July 1991; T. W. Adorno, "What Does Coming to Terms with the Past Mean?" in *Bitburg in Political and Moral Perspective,* ed. Geoffrey Hartmann (Cambridge, Mass.: Harvard University Press, 1988), 115. Roeder's current neo-Nazi platform is built upon anti-Semitism, Holocaust denial, racial cleansing, euthanasia for the weak, the feeble, and the infirm, and nationhood based on blood and culture—all in terms that mirror Rockwell's WUNS rhetoric from the 1960s—and proenvironmentalism, anticonsumerism, antifeminism, and antiabortion as added

planks for the 1990s. See Manfred Roeder, [open letter to readers], *Teutonic Unity* 4 (1991): n.p.

4. Colin Jordan to author, 7 September 1995.

5. Mason interview.

6. Richard Hofstadter, *The Paranoid Style in American Politics* (Chicago: University of Chicago Press, 1979).

7. H. Keith Thompson to author, 12 July 1993. Thompson met Rockwell in 1956 when Rockwell worked for Russell Maguire at the *American Mercury.* He remained a friend and supporter throughout Rockwell's career, although he was never a member of the ANP. Thompson had extensive connections with prewar Nazis, having been a member of Fritz Kuhn's German-American Bund in the 1930s and having served as a special agent of the Nazi government in the *Sicherheitsdienst* (SD), the Overseas Intelligence Service (his commission was signed by Adolf Hitler). In the 1970s and 1980s, Thompson became active in Holocaust denial circles. Background information on Thompson is from David McCalden, *Revisionist Newsletter* 21 (June 1983), private collection of H. Keith Thompson.

8. Stefani interview; Smyth interview; Wilcox interview; Stanley R. Tupper to author, 23 August 1995.

9. William F. Buckley Jr., handwritten notes from telephone conversations with Father Eugene V. Clark, 2 March 1964 to 4 May 1964, William F. Buckley Jr. Papers, Sterling Memorial Library, Yale University.

10. William F. Buckley Jr., *The Jeweler's Eye* (New York: G. P. Putnam's Sons, 1968), 327–29.

11. Benjamin Ginsberg, *The Fatal Embrace: Jews and the State* (Chicago: University of Chicago Press, 1993), 5.

12. Eugene D. Genovese, "When All Men Were Equal," *New Republic,* 4 September 1995, 36.

13. Rosenthal and Gelb, *One More Victim,* 88.

BIBLIOGRAPHY

A Note on Sources

Since there is no single repository of George Lincoln Rockwell's personal papers or official American Nazi party documents, this study relied heavily on previously unexamined personal collections, on interviews with Rockwell followers and family members, on several university collections, and on the holdings of organizations such as the American Jewish Committee and the Anti-Defamation League of B'nai B'rith. I now have in my possession a vast collection of primary Rockwell materials, including more than two thousand pages of photocopied documents and the sound and video recordings listed in the bibliography.

Two privately held collections were indispensable to my work. The James Mason Collection contains several thousand original letters, documents, and photographs from Rockwell's personal files, from 1958 to 1967. Mason, a former ANP member and one of the leading National Socialist theorists in contemporary America, rescued and preserved Rockwell's extensive correspondence, including the Rockwell-Ludtke correspondence. He made his collection available to me with no restrictions. The P. Claire Rockwell Collection contains extensive family correspondence, including a substantial number of letters between Claire Schade Rockwell and her son, as well as letters between Rockwell's mother and Barbara von Goetz. The P. Claire Rockwell Collection is also a rich source of rare family photographs and tape recordings of Rockwell speeches. I am indebted to James Mason, R. E. Cooper, and P. Claire Rockwell for their generous access to materials in their possession.

Interviews with Rockwell relatives, associates, followers, and foes, conducted over several years and preserved on tape in my files, provided critical insight into Rockwell's private and public life. Rockwell family members—including his sister P. Claire Rockwell and cousins Peter Smyth and Nancy Smyth Stefani—shared intimate, often painful, memories of a man they deeply loved; boyhood friends and classmates—Eben Lewis, Victor J. Hillery, and Stanley R. Tupper—shared their experiences with Rockwell in his pre-Nazi days; public officials, journalists, and scholars whose lives intersected Rockwell's, either in an official capacity or in opposition—notably, David Bell, Gordon Hall, Bob Lane, Al Lerner, Stuart McKeever, Herman J. Obermayer, Harvey M. Spear, Tony Ulasewicz, and Laird Wilcox—provided insightful accounts of their experiences with him; and former Rockwell followers and colleagues on the racist right—including Emory Burke, R. E. Cooper, Eldon "Bud" Cutler, Edward R. Fields, Colin Jordan, Hal Kaiser (a.k.a. Joe Charles Carter), Lee Larson, James Mason, William L. Pierce, Fred L. Surber, and H. Keith Thompson—shared Rockwell materials in their possession and, more important, allowed a nonmovement investigator into the private world of the postwar racist right. Finally, a number of former Rockwell followers and associates who demanded anonymity for personal and security reasons shared their experiences and verified the recollections of others. These sources illuminated Rockwell and his life's work far beyond the information available in the secondary literature.

The Laird Wilcox Collection at the Kenneth Spencer Research Library, University of Kansas; the Gerald L. K. Smith Papers at the Bentley Historical Library, University of Michigan, Ann Arbor; the William F. Buckley Jr. Papers at the Sterling Memorial Library, Yale University; and the Keith Stimely Papers and the Pedro del Valle Papers, both at the University Library, University of Oregon—all contain fragments of Rockwell's official correspondence that were important to my research. The Solomon Andhil Fineberg Papers in the Special Collections Department of the American Jewish Committee's Blaustein Library is the repository for a number of indispensable documents about Rockwell, the ANP, and the American Jewish community's response to him, and the Publications Archives of the Anti-Defamation League of B'Nai B'Rith houses a fairly complete collection of ADL publications and membership memoranda from the Rockwell era.

Archives and Collections

American Jewish Committee, New York
    Blaustein Library, Special Collections
Anti-Defamation League of B'nai B'rith, New York
    Publications Archives
Bentley Historical Library, University of Michigan, Ann Arbor
    The Gerald L. K. Smith Papers
    Michigan Historical Collections
    Special Collections
Kenneth Spencer Research Library, University of Kansas, Lawrence
    The Wilcox Collection
Sterling Memorial Library, Yale University
    The William F. Buckley Jr. Papers
University Library, Special Collections, University of Oregon, Eugene
    The Keith Stimely Papers
    The Pedro A. del Valle Papers

Government Documents and Records

California Department of Justice, Office of Attorney General Thomas J. Lynch. *Para-Military Organizations in California: A Report to the California State Senate Judiciary Committee.* 12 April 1965.

Commonwealth of Virginia, Circuit Court of Arlington County, Office of the Clerk, Criminal Archives, *Commonwealth vs. John Patler.* File C-5575.

Commonwealth of Virginia, Supreme Court of Appeals, Office of the Clerk. *John Patler, Plaintiff in error vs. Commonwealth of Virginia, Defendant in error.* Record No. 7103.

U.S. Department of Justice, Federal Bureau of Investigation. FBI File #9-39854: George Lincoln Rockwell.

Interviews

David Bell, 28 June 1991

Emory Burke, 17 September 1995

R. E. Cooper, 24 April 1991, 13 August 1991

Edward R. Fields, 7 August 1991

Gordon Hall, 30 September 1995, 1 October 1995

Hal Kaiser, 17 July 1991, 15 October 1991

Bob Lane, 29 September 1995

Eben Lewis, 7 August 1995

James Mason, 22 August 1991

Stuart McKeever, 16 June 1991

Herman J. Obermayer, 15 August 1995

P. Clair Rockwell, 17 August 1991

Peter Smyth, 24 July 1991

Harvey M. Spear, 18 and 21 August 1995

Shanthi Srenivasan, 7 August 1995

Nancy Smyth Stefani, 6 June 1991

Fred L. Surber, 21 July 1995

Stanley R. Tupper, 23 August 1995

Tony Ulasewicz, 20 July 1991

Emile Walter, 17 August 1991

Laird Wilcox, 19 August 1991

Sound and Video Recordings

American Nazi Party. Promotional videotape, n.d. [ca. 1965].

Rockwell, George Lincoln. Audiotape of address at the University of North Dakota, November 1965.

———. Audiotape of address to supporters, Dallas, Texas, 1964.

———. Audiotape of address to supporters, Dallas, Texas, 1965.

———. Audiotape of address to supporters, location unknown, 1965.

———. Audiotape of appearance on "The Michael Jackson Show," 9 May 1965, KNX-LA Radio.

————. Audiotape of debate with Tony Todaro, director, NAACP Hawaii Chapter, n.d. [ca. 1964], KTRG-TV-Honolulu, Don Cater, moderator.

————. Audiotape of lecture at Brown University, n.d. [Fall 1966].

————. Audiotape of lecture at New York University, n.d. [1965].

————. Audiotape of speech at Lynchburg, Va., City Armory, 30 August 1963.

————. Sound recording, "Commander George Lincoln Rockwell Speech at Brown University, 1966." Arlington, Va.: G. L. Rockwell Party, n.d.

Articles in Journals and Periodicals

Abcarian, Gilbert, and Sherman M. Stanage. "Alienation and the Radical Right." *Journal of Politics* 27 (November 1965): 776–96.

"*The American Mercury* and Russell Maguire." *Facts,* October/November 1959, 1.

"Anti-Semitism in the South." *Facts,* October/November 1958, 127–34.

"Are Europe's Jews in Danger?" *ADL Bulletin* 22 (September 1965): 1–2, 6.

Bagdikian, Ben H. "The Gentle Suppression." *Columbia Journalism Review* 4 (Spring 1965): 16–19.

Bancroft, Nancy. "American Fascism: Analysis and Call for Research." *Phylon: The Atlanta University Review of Race and Culture* 43 (1982): 155–66.

Barker, Edwin N. "Authoritarianism of the Political Right, Center and Left." *Journal of Social Issues* 19 (April 1963): 63–74.

Barth, Alan. "Report on the Rampageous Right." *New York Times Magazine,* 26 November 1961, 25, 130–32.

Berger, Alan L. "The Holocaust, Second-Generation Witness, and the Voluntary Covenant in American Judaism." *Religion and American Culture* 5 (Winter 1995): 23–47.

Berman, Paul. "Gas Chamber Games." *Village Voice* 26 (10 June 1981): 1, 37.

Bettelheim, Bruno. "Why Does a Man Become a Hater?" *Life,* 7 February 1964, 78–80.

Braun, Robert. "The Holocaust and Problems of Historical Representation." *History and Theory* 33.2 (1994): 172–97.

Clark, Susan Canedy. "America's Nazis." *American History Illustrated,* April 1986, 40–49.

Cook, Fred J. "The Ultras: Aims, Affiliations and Finances of the Radical Right." *The Nation,* 30 June 1962, 565–606.

Cooper, Mary. "The Growing Danger of Hate Groups." *Editorial Research Reports,* 12 May 1989, 262–75.

Cor, Lew [George Lincoln Rockwell]. "When the Nazis Tried Human Vivisection." *Sir!* March 1958, 10–11, 36–37.

Daly, Charles U. "The Man Who Would Bring Back Hitler." *Cavalier,* June 1961, 56.

Dawidowicz, Lucy. "Lies about the Holocaust." *Commentary,* December 1980, 31–40.

Eco, Umberto. "Ur-Fascism." *New York Review of Books,* 22 June 1995, 12–15.

Eisen, Arnold M. "The Rhetoric of Chosenness." *Society* 28 (November/December 1990): 26–33.

Eisenstadt, Shmuel A. "The Jewish Experience with Pluralism." *Society* 28 (November/December 1990): 21–25.

Ellerin, Milton. "To Take Credit or Not." *ADL Bulletin,* April 1960, 6–7.

Elrod, Rod. "The Wizard of Awes." *Gallery,* November 1990, 62–66, 72, 76, 96–97.

"Extremists: Ashes to Ashes." *Newsweek,* 11 September 1967, 23–24.

"Fascists: Booby Prize." *Time,* 17 August 1962, 19.

Ferkiss, Victor C. "Political and Intellectual Origins of the American Radical Right and Left." *The Annals* 344 (November 1962).

"The 54th Annual Meeting." *ADL Bulletin,* February 1967, 1–2, 4–6.

Fineberg, Solomon Andhil. "Checkmate for Rabble-Rousers: What to Do When the Demagogue Comes." *Commentary,* September 1946, 220–26.

———. "How Fight Rabble Rousers?: Fight on the Real Battle Line." *Commentary,* November 1946, 465–66.

———. "Rockwell and the Abuse of Freedom." *AJC Reporter,* Summer 1962, 1–3.

Finger, Justin J. "The Exploiters." *ADL Bulletin,* November 1966, 3–4.

Forster, Arnold. "Violence on the Fanatical Left and Right." *The Annals* 364 (March 1966).

Foxman, Abraham H. "Holocaust Denial: The Growing Danger." *Dimensions* 8.1 (1994): 13–16.

Franklin, Raymond S. "The Political Economy of Black Power." *Social Problems* 16 (Winter 1969): 286–301.

Genovese, Eugene D. "When All Men Were Equal." *New Republic,* 4 September 1995, 36.

"George L. Rockwell, U.S. Nazi." *Facts,* October 1963, 271–80.

Glatstein, Irwin Lee. "How Fight Rabble Rousers?: Against 'Silent Treatment.'" *Commentary,* November 1946, 460–62.

Glazer, Nathan. "American Jewry or American Judaism." *Society* 28 (November/December 1990): 14–20.

Green, Barbara B., Kathryn Turner, and Dante Germino. "Responsible and Irresponsible Right-Wing Groups: A Problem in Analysis." *Journal of Social Issues* 19 (April 1963): 3–17.

Hertzberg, Arthur. "Is Anti-Semitism Dying Out?" *New York Review of Books,* 24 June 1993, 51–57.

Hofstadter, Richard. "The Pseudo-Conservative Revolt." *American Scholar* 24 (Winter 1954–55): 9–27.

Howe, Irving. "How Fight Rabble Rousers?: The Value of Mass Action." *Commentary,* November 1946, 462–65.

"How to Handle Rockwell." *ADL Bulletin,* April 1967, 6.

Ianniello, Lynne. "Rockwell on the Campus." *ADL Bulletin,* April 1963, 6–7.

Jenkins, Philip. "Home-Grown Terror." *American Heritage* 46 (September 1995): 38–46.

"The Jewish Nazi." *Newsweek,* 15 November 1965, 110–12.

Kansteiner, Wulf. "From Exception to Exemplum: The New Approach to Nazism and the 'Final Solution.'" *History and Theory* 33.2 (1994): 145–71.

Kellner, Hans. "'Never Again' Is Now." *History and Theory* 33.2 (1994): 127–44.

Koehl, Matt. "Holocaust or Hitler: Which Is It Going to Be?" *New Order,* 10 April 1993, n.p.

Krause, Charles. "George Lincoln Rockwell: A Myth or Real Threat to America's Peace?" *Private Affairs,* June 1962, 52.

Ladd, Everett C., Jr. "The Radical Right: White Collar Extremists." *South Atlantic Quarterly* 65.3 (Summer 1966): 314–24.

Lang, Berel. "Is It Possible to Misrepresent the Holocaust?" *History and Theory* 34.1 (1995): 84–89.

Langer, Elinor. "The American Neo-Nazi Movement Today." *The Nation,* 16/23 July 1990, 82–107.

Lind, Michael. "Power to the People," *New Republic* 185 (4 September 1995): 37–41.

Lipset, Seymour Martin. "The Radical Right: A Problem for American Democracy." *British Journal of Sociology* 6 (June 1955): 176–209.

———. "A Unique People in an Exceptional Country." *Society* 28 (November/December 1990): 4–13.

Lipstadt, Deborah E. "Deniers, Relativists, and Pseudo-Scholarship." *Dimensions* 6 (1991): 6.

———. "Holocaust Denial: An Overview." *Dimensions* 8.1 (1994): 3–7.

Lourie, Richard. "To Combat Denial." *Dimensions* 8.1 (1994): 9–12.

Marable, Manning. "Martin Luther King's Ambiguous Legacy." *WIN Magazine* 19 (15 April 1982): 15–19.

McGovern, Michael. "The Problems of a 'Fuehrer.'" *ADL Bulletin,* November 1966, 4–5.

Meier, August. "The Dilemmas of Negro Protest Strategy," *New South* 21 (Spring 1966): 1–18.

———. "On the Role of Martin Luther King." *New Politics* 4 (Winter 1965): 52–59.

"Murders: Der Tag." *Newsweek,* 4 September 1967, 30–31.

"The Nazi Mind." *America* 110 (14 March 1964): 329.

Nora, Pierre. "Between Memory and History: Les Lieux de Memoire." *Representations* 26 (Spring 1989): 8–9.

"Notes and Asides." *National Review,* 18 November 1961, 331.

Orgell, Mrs. Richard. "George Lincoln Rockwell: American Nazi." *Spot News,* December 1960, 1, 5.

Patler, John. "That Liberal Rockwell." *KILL! Magazine,* September 1962, 1, 9.

Prager, Arthur. "Here Come the Hate Groups." *Nation's Cities,* November 1964, 22–24.

Proshansky, Harold M., and William Evans. "The 'Radical Right': A Threat to the Behavioral Sciences." *Journal of Social Issues* 19 (April 1963): 86–106.

Rader, Dotson. "The Deadly Friendship: George Lincoln Rockwell and John Patler." *New Republic* 157 (23 September 1967): 13–15.

Roberts, Gene. "The Story of Snick: From 'Freedom Rides' to 'Black Power.'" *New York Times Magazine,* 25 September 1966, 27–29.

Rockwell, George Lincoln. "An Analysis of Four Years of Nazi Success." *Rockwell Report* (Special Anniversary Issue), Winter 1962, 1–10.

———. "From the Commander." *The Stormtrooper,* February 1962, 1–23.

———. "Jew Ostriches Beating Nazis to Death with Fat Bottoms!" *Rockwell Report,* 1 July 1962, 2–4.

———. "Jews Expose Themselves as Terrorists at Colorado University." *Rockwell Report,* 1 June 1963, 1–5.

———. "Nazism: The White Man's Ultimate Weapon." *RIGHT,* May 1960, 6.

———. "No Wonder Iceland Hates Us!" *American Mercury,* January 1957, 7–13.

———. "Office of the Commander." *National Socialist Bulletin,* September 1961, 3.

———. "*Playboy* Interview: George Lincoln Rockwell." By Alex Haley. *Playboy,* April 1966, 71–72, 74, 76–82, 154, 156.

———. "So-called 'War Crimes' . . . Exposed!" *Rockwell Report,* n.d. [1965].

———. "Who Wants Panty-Waist Marines?" *American Mercury,* April 1957, 117–22.

[Rockwell, George Lincoln]. "The American Nazi Party Is Not Subversive!" *National Socialist Bulletin,* September 1961, 2, 10.

[———]. "Big Lie of 6 Million!" *Stormtrooper,* Spring 1966, 6–8.

[———]. "Tax Problems Now Solved!" *National Socialist Bulletin,* September 1961, 10, 16.

"Rockwell." *Facts,* September 1960, 161–66.

"Rockwell: The Road to Nowhere?" *ADL Bulletin,* April 1961, 6–7.

Roeder, Manfred, [open letter to readers], *Teutonic Unity* 4 (1991).

Rosenthal, A. M., and Arthur Gelb. "The Life and Death of a Nazi." *ADL Bulletin,* November 1967, 4–5.

Rothman, Stanley. "American Catholics and the Radical Right." *Social Order,* April 1963, 5–8, 37.

Rush, G. B. "Toward a Definition of the Extreme Right." *Pacific Sociological Review* 6 (Fall 1963): 64–73.

Rustin, Bayard. "'Black Power' and Coalition Politics." *Commentary* 42 (September 1966): 35–40.

"Savitri Devi: A Souvenir." *NS* [National Socialist] *Bulletin* 330 (Fourth Quarter 1992): 7.

Schlesinger, Arthur M., Jr. "The Threat of the Radical Right." *New York Times Magazine,* 17 June 1962, 10, 55, 58.

Schmuck, Richard, and Mark Chesler. "On Super-Patriotism: A Definition and Analysis." *Journal of Social Issues* 19 (April 1963): 31–50.

Shapiro, Fred C. "The Last Word (We Hope) on George Lincoln Rockwell." *Esquire,* February 1967, 101–5, 137–43.

Shapiro, Richard M. "Atlanta: The Deep South Says 'Yes.'" *ADL Bulletin,* October 1961, 1–2, 6.

Simonelli, Frederick J. "The American Nazi Party, 1958–1967." *The Historian* 57 (Spring 1995): 553–67.

———. "Preaching Hate with the Voice of God: American Neo-Nazis and Christian Identity." *Patterns of Prejudice* 30.2 (1996): 43–54.

Smith, R. Drew. "Why Blacks Join Cults." *Emerge,* July/August 1993, 52–54.

Southern Poverty Law Center. "Aryan World Congress Focuses on Militias and an Expected Revolution." *Klanwatch Intelligence Report* 79 (August 1995): 1–2.

———. "Racist Identity Sect Fuels Nationwide Extremist Movement," *Klanwatch Intelligence Report* 79 (August 1995): 1, 3–5.

Starr, Mark, et al., "Violence on the Right." *Newsweek,* 4 March 1985, 23–26.

Stewart, D. K., and T. C. Smith. "Celebrity Structure of the Far Right." *Western Political Quarterly* 17 (June 1964): 349–55.

Stewart, Dan. "About National Socialism (Nazism)." *NSV [National Socialist Vanguard] Report,* October/December 1989, 1–2.

"This Month: Notes." *ADL Bulletin,* December 1967, 6.

Walton, Hanes, Jr. "The Political Leadership of Martin Luther King, Jr.," *Quarterly Review of Higher Education among Negroes* 36 (July 1968): 163–71.

Waxman, Chaim I. "Whither American Jewry?" *Society* 28 (November/December 1990): 34–41.

Whitsel, Brad. "The Cosmotheist Community: Aryan Visions for the Future in the West Virginia Mountains." *Ms.* 1995.

Wilcox, Laird. "What Is 'Political Extremism'?" *Free Inquiry,* Fall 1990, 13–16.

Wilkins, Roy. "Whither 'Black Power'?" *Crisis,* August/September 1966, 354.

"WUNS Reorganized." *NS* [National Socialist] *Bulletin* 330 (Fourth Quarter 1992): 1–3.

Zangrando, Robert L. "From Civil Rights to Black Liberation: The Unsettled 1960s." *Current History* 62 (November 1969): 281–86, 299.

Zia, Helen. "Women in Hate Groups." *Ms.* March/April 1991, 20–27.

Zinti, Robert T. "Dreams of a Bigot's Revolution," *Time,* 18 February 1985, 42.

Books and Chapters in Books

Abernathy, Ralph David. *And the Walls Came Tumbling Down: An Autobiography.* New York: Harper Perennial, 1990.

Abraham, Gary A. *Max Weber and the Jewish Question: A Study of the Social Outlook of His Sociology.* Urbana: University of Illinois Press, 1992.

Adams, Brooks. *The Law of Civilization and Decay: An Essay on History.* New York: Alfred A. Knopf, 1951.

Adorno, T. W., Else Frankel-Brunswick, D. J. Levinson, and R. N. Sanford. *The Authoritarian Personality.* New York: Harper, 1950.

Adorno, T. W. "What Does Coming to Terms with the Past Mean?" In *Bitburg in Political and Moral Perspective.* Ed. Geoffrey Hartman. Cambridge, Mass.: Harvard University Press, 1988.

Aho, James A. *The Politics of Righteousness: Idaho's Christian Patriotism.* Seattle: University of Washington Press, 1990.

Allport, Gordon W. *The Nature of Prejudice.* 1954. Rpt., New York: Anchor Books, 1958.

Almog, Shmuel, ed. *Antisemitism through the Ages.* Trans. Nathan H. Reisner. New York: Pergamon Press, 1988.

Anti-Defamation League of B'nai B'rith. *Hate Groups in America: A Record of Bigotry and Violence.* New York: Anti-Defamation League, 1982.

Apter, David, ed. *Ideology and Discontent.* New York: Free Press, 1964.

Barkun, Michael. *Religion and the Racist Right: The Origins of the Christian Identity Movement.* Chapel Hill: University of North Carolina Press, 1994.

Beaty, John. *The Iron Curtain over America.* Dallas: Wilkinson Publishing Co., 1951.

Bell, Daniel, ed. *The New American Right.* New York: Criterion Books, 1955.

———. *The Radical Right.* New York: Doubleday-Anchor, 1963.

Bell, Leland V. *In Hitler's Shadow: The Anatomy of American Nazism.* Port Washington, N.Y.: Kennikat Press, 1973.

Bennett, David H. *The Party of Fear: From Nativist Movements to the New Right in American History.* Chapel Hill: University of North Carolina Press, 1988.

Bollinger, Lee C. *The Tolerant Society.* New York: Oxford University Press, 1986.

Branch, Taylor. *Parting the Waters: America in the King Years, 1954–1963.* New York: Simon & Schuster, 1988.

Brown, J. F. *Psychodynamic of Abnormal Behavior.* New York: McGraw-Hill, 1940.

Buckley, William F., Jr. *In Search of Anti-Semitism.* New York: Continuum, 1992.

———, *The Jeweler's Eye.* 8th ed. New York: G. P. Putnam's Sons, 1968.

Canedy, Susan. *America's Nazis—A Democratic Dilemma: A History of the German-American Bund.* Menlo Park, Calif.: Markgraf Publications Group, 1990.

Carlson, John Roy [Avedis Derounian]. *Under Cover: My Four Years with the Nazi Underground of America.* Philadelphia: Blakiston Co., 1943; rpt., New York: American Books–Stratford Press, 1943.

Carmichael, Joel. *The Satanizing of the Jews: Origin and Development of Mystical Anti-Semitism.* New York: Fromm International Publishing Corp., 1992.

Carson, Clayborne. *In Struggle: SNCC and the Black Awakening of the 1960s.* Cambridge, Mass.: Harvard University Press, 1981.

Cohen, Naomi W. *Not Free to Desist: The American Jewish Committee, 1906–1966.* Philadelphia: Jewish Publication Society of America, 1972.

Caplovitz, David, and Candace Rogers. *Swastika 1960: The Epidemic of Anti-Semitic Vandalism in America.* New York: Anti-Defamation League of B'nai B'rith, 1961.

Dinnerstein, Leonard. *Antisemitism in America.* New York: Oxford University Press, 1994.

Duckitt, John. *The Social Psychology of Prejudice.* New York: Praeger, 1992.

Finch, Phillip. *God, Guts, and Guns: A Close Look at the Radical Right.* New York: Seaview/Putnam, 1983.

Fine, Morris, and Milton Himmelfarb, eds. *American Jewish Year Book.* Philadelphia: Jewish Publication Society of America, 1960–67.

Fineberg, Solomon Andhil. *Appraising the Quarantine Treatment.* New York: [American Jewish Committee,] Community Relations Service, 1949.

————. *Deflating the Professional Bigot.* New York: American Jewish Committee, 1960, 9.

————. *Punishment without Crime: What You Can Do about Prejudice.* New York: Doubleday & Co., 1949.

————. *Overcoming Anti-Semitism.* New York: Harper & Bros., 1943.

Ford, Henry, Sr. *The International Jew: The World's Foremost Problem.* Ed. G. F. Green. London: Privately printed, 1948.

Forster, Arnold, and Benjamin R. Epstein. *Danger on the Right: The Attitudes, Personnel and Influence of the Radical Right and Extreme Conservatives.* New York: Random House, 1964.

————. *The New Anti-Semitism.* New York: McGraw-Hill, 1974.

George, John, and Laird Wilcox. *Nazis, Communists, Klansmen, and Others on the Fringe: Political Extremism in America.* Buffalo, N.Y.: Prometheus Books, 1992.

Gerber, David A., ed. *Anti-Semitism in American History.* Urbana, IL: University of Illinois Press, 1986.

Ginsberg, Benjamin. *The Fatal Embrace: Jews and the State.* Chicago: University of Chicago Press, 1993.

Glock, Charles Y., and Ellen Siegelman, eds. *Prejudice U.S.A.* New York: Frederick A. Praeger, 1969.

Golden, Harry. *Only in America.* New York: Permabooks, 1959.

Greene, Melissa Fay. *The Temple Bombing.* New York: Fawcett Columbine, 1996.

Haines, Herbert H. *Black Radicals and the Civil Rights Mainstream, 1954–1970.* Knoxville: University of Tennessee Press, 1988.

Hampton, Henry, and Steve Fayer, *Voices of Freedom: An Oral History of the Civil Rights Movement from the 1950s through the 1980s.* New York: Bantam Books, 1990.

Hentoff, Nat. *Free Speech for Me—but Not for Thee.* New York: Harper Collins, 1992.

Higham, Charles. *American Swastika.* Garden City, N.Y.: Doubleday & Co., 1985.

Hoffer, Eric. *The True Believer.* New York: Harper & Bros., 1951.

Hofstadter, Richard. *The Paranoid Style in American Politics.* Chicago: University of Chicago Press, 1979.

Jaher, Frederic Cople. *A Scapegoat in the New Wilderness: The Origins and Rise of Anti-Semitism in America.* Cambridge, Mass.: Harvard University Press, 1994.

Janson, Donald, and Bernard Eismann. *The Far Right.* New York: McGraw-Hill, 1963.

Jeansonne, Glen. "Combating Anti-Semitism: The Case of Gerald L. K. Smith." In *Anti-Semitism in American History.* Ed. David A. Gerber. Urbana: University of Illinois Press, 1986. 152–66.

————. *Gerald L. K. Smith: Minister of Hate.* New Haven, Conn.: Yale University Press, 1988.

Judis, John B. *William F. Buckley, Jr.: Patron Saint of the Conservatives.* New York: Touchstone, 1990.

Klarsfeld, Serge. *The Holocaust and the Neo-Nazi Mythomania.* New York: Beate Klarsfeld Foundation, 1978.

Kurland, Philip B., ed. *Free Speech and Association: The Supreme Court and the First Amendment.* 8th ed. Chicago: University of Chicago Press, 1975.

Kuzmack, Linda Gordon. *The Hate Business: Anti-Semitism in America.* New York: Franklin Watts, 1993.

Langmuir, Gavin I. *Toward a Definition of Anti-Semitism.* Berkeley: University of California Press, 1990.

Le Bon, Gustave. *The Crowd: A Study of the Popular Mind.* 5th ed. New York: Viking Press, 1966.

Lederer, Laura, and Richard Delgado, eds. *The Price We Pay: The Case against Racist Speech, Hate Propaganda, and Pornography.* New York: Hill & Wang, 1995.

Lewis, Bernard. *Semites and Anti-Semites: An Inquiry into Conflict and Prejudice.* New York: W. W. Norton & Co., 1986.

Lipset, Seymour Martin. "Prejudice and Politics in the American Past and Present." In *Prejudice U.S.A.* Ed. Charles Y. Glock and Ellen Siegelman. New York: Frederick A. Praeger, 1969.

Lipset, Seymour Martin, and Earl Raab. *The Politics of Unreason: Right-Wing Extremism in America, 1790–1970.* New York: Harper & Row, 1970.

Lipstadt, Deborah. *Denying the Holocaust: The Growing Assault on Truth and Memory.* New York: Plume/Penguin, 1993.

Macdonald, Andrew [William L. Pierce]. *Hunter.* Hillsboro, W.Va.: National Vanguard Books, 1989.

———. *The Turner Diaries,* 2d ed. Washington, D.C.: National Alliance, 1980.

Mason, James. *Siege: The Collected Writings of James Mason.* Ed. Michael M. Jenkins. Denver: Storm Books, 1992.

Merkl, Peter H. "A New Lease on Life for the Racist Right?" In *Encounters with the Contemporary Radical Right.* Ed. Peter H. Merkle and Leonard Weinberg. Boulder, Colo.: Westview Press, 1993. 204–27.

Mintz, Frank P. *The Liberty Lobby and the American Right: Race, Conspiracy, and Culture.* Westport, Conn.: Greenwood Press, 1985.

Myers, Gustavus. *History of Bigotry in the United States.* 1943. Rpt., New York: Capricorn Books, 1960.

Nicholls, William. *Christian Antisemitism: A History of Hate.* Northvale, N.J.: Jason Aronson, 1993.

Oates, Stephen. *Let the Trumpet Sound: The Life of Martin Luther King, Jr.* (New York: NAL, 1982).

Overstreet, Harry, and Bonaro Overstreet. *The Strange Tactics of Extremism.* New York: Norton, 1964.

Parkes, James. *Antisemitism.* London: Vallentine, Mitchell & Co., 1963.

Pierce, William L. *Cosmotheism: Wave of the Future.* Hillsboro, W.Va.: National Vanguard Books, 1977.

———. *Human Dignity: A Racial Ethic.* Hillsboro, W.Va.: National Vanguard Books, 1978.

Quinley, Harold E., and Charles Y. Glock. *Anti-Semitism in America.* New York: Free Press, 1979.

Rabinowitz, Dorothy. *About the Holocaust: What We Know and How We Know It.* New York: American Jewish Committee, 1980.

Ridgeway, James. *Blood in the Face: The Ku Klux Klan, Aryan Nations, Nazi Skinheads, and the Rise of a New White Culture.* New York: Thunder's Mouth Press, 1991.

Roberts, Frank C. "George Lincoln Rockwell," in *Obituaries from the "Times," 1961–1970.* Reading, Eng.: Newspaper Archive Developments, 1975, 681.

Rockwell, George Lincoln. *This Time the World.* 3d ed. Liverpool, W.Va.: White Power Publications, 1979.

———. *White Power.* 3d ed. Reedy, W.Va.: Liberty Bell Publications, 1983.

Rosenstone, Robert A. *Protest from the Right.* Beverly Hills, Calif.: Glencoe Press, 1968.

Rosenthal, A. M., and Arthur Gelb. *One More Victim.* New York: New American Library, 1967.

Salomon, George, ed. *Jews in the Mind of America.* New York: Basic Books, 1966.

Schultz, Donald O. *The Subversive.* Springfield, Ill.: Charles C. Thomas & Stanley K. Scott, 1973.

Schwartz, Alan M., ed. *Hate Groups in America: A Record of Bigotry and Violence.* New York: Anti-Defamation League of B'nai B'rith, 1988.

Seidel, Gill. *The Holocaust Denial: Antisemitism, Racism and the New Right.* Leeds, Eng.: Beyond the Pale Collective, 1986.

Selznick, Gertrude J., and Stephen Steinberg. *The Tenacity of Prejudice: Anti-Semitism in Contemporary America.* New York: Harper & Row, 1969.

Shapiro, Shelly, et al., eds. *Truth Prevails: Demolishing Holocaust Denial—The End of "The Leuchter Report."* New York: Beate Klarsfeld Foundation, 1991.

Sherwin, Mark. *The Extremists.* New York: St. Martin's Press, 1963.

Simonelli, Frederick J. "The World Union of National Socialists and Postwar Transatlantic Nazi Revival." In *Nation and Race: The Developing Euro-American Racist Subculture.* Ed. Jeffrey Kaplan and Tore Bjorgo. Boston: Northeastern University Press, 1998. 34–57.

Stern, Kenneth S. *Holocaust Denial.* New York: American Jewish Committee, 1993.

Summers, Anthony. *Official and Confidential: The Secret Life of J. Edgar Hoover.* New York: Pocket Books, 1993.

Thayer, George. *The Farther Shores of Politics: The American Political Fringe Today.* 2d ed. New York: Simon & Schuster, 1968.

Turner, William W. *Power on the Right.* Berkeley, Calif.: Ramparts Press, 1971.

Ulasewicz, Tony. *The President's Private Eye.* Westport, Conn.: MACSAM Publishing Co., 1990.

Varange, Ulick [Francis Parker Yockey]. *Imperium.* 2d ed. Sausalito, Calif.: Noontide Press, 1963.

Vidal-Naquet, Pierre. *Assassins of Memory: Essays on the Denial of the Holocaust.* Trans. Jeffrey Mehlman. New York: Columbia University Press, 1992.

Volkman, Ernest. *A Legacy of Hate: Anti-Semitism in America.* New York: Franklin Watts, 1982.

Weinberg, Leonard. "The American Radical Right: Exit, Voice, and Violence." In *Encounters with the Contemporary Radical Right* Ed. Peter H. Merkl and Leonard Weinberg. Boulder, Colo.: Westview Press, 1993. 185–203.

———. "Introduction." In *Encounters with the Contemporary Radical Right.* Ed. Peter H. Merkl and Leonard Weinberg. Boulder, Colo.: Westview Press, 1993. 1–15.

Walker, Samuel. *Hate Speech: The History of an American Controversy.* Lincoln: University of Nebraska Press, 1994.

Wilcox, Laird. *Guide to the American Right: Directory and Bibliography.* Olathe, Kans.: Laird Wilcox Editorial Research Service, 1991.

Wistrich, Robert S. *Anti-Semitism: The Longest Hatred.* New York: Pantheon Books, 1991.

Young, James E. *Writing and Rewriting the Holocaust: Narrative and the Consequences of Interpretation.* Bloomington: Indiana University Press, 1988.

Zatarain, Michael. *David Duke: Evolution of a Klansman.* Gretna, La.: Pelican Publishing Co., 1990.

Zeskind, Leonard. *The "Christian Identity" Movement: A Theological Justification for Racist and Anti-Semitic Violence.* Atlanta: Center for Democratic Renewal, 1986.

Pamphlets and Flyers

American Jewish Committee. *Bigot Seeking Buildup: The 'News' Techniques of George Lincoln Rockwell.* New York: American Jewish Committee, May 1962.

———. *Extremism in America Today.* New York: American Jewish Committee, 1966.

———. *"News" That Isn't News: Fact Sheet on George Lincoln Rockwell and His American Nazi Party.* New York: American Jewish Committee, February 1962.

[American Jewish Committee.] Community Relations Service. *What to Do When the Rabble-Rouser Comes to Town.* New York: Community Relations Service, n.d.

Burros, Dan. *American Nazi Party Official Stormtrooper's Manual.* Arlington, Va.: American Nazi Party, 1961.

Fineberg, Solomon Andhil. *Appraising the Quarantine Treatment.* New York: Community Relations Service [AJC], 1949.

———. *Deflating the Professional Bigot.* New York: American Jewish Committee, March 1960.

———. *"Quarantine Treatment."* New York: American Jewish Committee, 15 August 1947.

Gillespie, William. *Dietrich Eckart: An Introduction for the English-Speaking Student.* 2d rev. ed. Milwaukee: NS Publications, 1976.

Jordan, Colin. *National Socialism: World Creed for the 1980s.* Harrogate, Eng.: Gothic Ripples, 1981.

Koehl, Matt. *Adolf Hitler: German Nationalist or Aryan Racialist.* Arlington, Va.: NS Publications, 1974.

———. *America: A Racial Mission.* 2d ed. Arlington, Va.: NS Publications, 1977.

———. *Faith of the Future.* N.p. Reprinted from *National Socialist,* Spring 1982, n.p.

———. *The Future Calls.* Arlington, Va.: World Union of National Socialists, 1972.

———. *Official Program: National Socialist White People's Party.* Cicero, Ill.: NS Publications, 1980.

———. *The Revolutionary Nature of National Socialism.* 2d ed. Milwaukee: NS Publications, 1987.

————. *Some Guidelines for the Development of the National Socialist Movement.* Arlington, Va.: NS Publications, n.d.

Mason, James. *George Lincoln Rockwell: A Sketch of His Life and Career.* Chillicothe, Ohio: Universal Order, n.d.

New Order. *The Religion of Lincoln Rockwell.* Arlington, Va.: New Order, n.d. [post-1967]; rpt., Milwaukee: New Order, n.d. [ca 1972].

N.S. Kindred. *The Wisdom of Adolf Hitler.* 3d ed. Nevada City, Calif.: N.S. Kindred, 1990.

Peabody, John N. *Cathedral of the Incarnation: A History.* Baltimore, 1976.

Pierce, William L. *Lincoln Rockwell: A National Socialist Life.* Arlington, Va.: NS Publications, 1969.

Rockwell, George Lincoln. *Fable of the Ducks and the Hens.* Chillicothe, Ohio: Universal Order, n.d. [1958].

————. *In Hoc Signo Vinces.* 3d ed. Arlington, Va.: World Union of National Socialists, 1971.

————. *Legal, Psychological and Political Warfare.* 1965. Rpt., Reedy, W.Va.: White Power Publications, 1977.

————. *Proof That Goldwater Is a Plant!* Arlington, Va.: American Nazi Party, n.d. [1964].

————. *Who's a "Hate-Monger"?* Arlington, Va.: World Union of Free Enterprise National Socialists, 1958.

[Rockwell, George Lincoln]. *The Diary of Ann Fink.* Arlington, Va.: Hoax-Busters Press [ANP], n.d. [1965].

————. "Proof of the Pudding—from the Jews!" Arlington, Va.: [American Nazi Party], n.d. [1961].

————. "White Man on the March!" Arlington, Va.: American Nazi Party, n.d. [1960].

Warner, James K. *Swastika Smearbund.* Wilkes-Barre, Pa.: American Nationalist Book Store, 1961.

INDEX

Abernathy, Ralph, 76
Adams, Brooks, 17
ADL. *See* Anti-Defamation League of B'nai
  B'rith
Adorno, T. W., 142
African Americans. *See* racism
agnosticism, 16, 115
AJC. *See* American Jewish Committee
Alabama, 75–76
alcohol problems, 23, 31
Allen, Karl, 76, 131
Amaudruz, G. A., 166n36
American Jewish Committee (AJC): ANP
  surveillance, 35–36, 37–38; and quaran-
  tine strategy, 52–71
American Mercury, 25
American Nazi party (ANP): formation of,
  31; funding of, 37–43, 56, 128, 129–30,
  163n4; homosexuality in, 77–79; member-
  ship numbers, 33–37, 123–24; merger
  with Christian Identity, 120–22; name
  change, 104; platform, 33; racial tension
  in, 101–2, 136; role in Rockwell's death
  and burial, 136–39. *See also* National Socialist White People's party
Anglo-American Israelism, 116
Anglo-Israelism, 115–16
ANP. *See* American Nazi party
Anti-Defamation League of B'nai B'rith
  (ADL): accused of orchestrating

Rockwell's death, 131, 180n1; ANP surveillance by, 35–36, 37, 38, 42; and quar-
  antine strategy, 65
anti-Semitism: Butler's genealogical docu-
  mentation of Jews, 173n7; in Christian
  Identity movement, 115–22; of Rockwell,
  2, 22–23, 33, 72–73, 74–75, 97; in
  Rockwell family, 11–13, 29; Rockwell
  legacy of, 141–45; Temple bombing, 28–
  29, 151n23; in U.S. before WWII, 107.
  See also Holocaust denial
Argentina, 90
Arrowsmith, Harold Noel, Jr., 26, 27–28, 40
Aryan Unity faction, 102
Atlantic City High School (N.J.), 14–15
Aufbau, 62–63
Aultman, Judith. *See* Rockwell, Judith
  Aultman
Aultman, Merwyn L., 19
Australia, 90

Back Door to War (Tansill), 109
Bagdikian, Ben H., 69–70
Barnes, Harry Elmer, 109
Beattie, John, 91, 165n35
Belgium, 93–94
Bellfeuille, Andre, 90–91
Black Power/White Power slogans, 99–100
blood contamination issue, 72–73
Booker, Herbert Hillary, 79, 162n30

Frederick J. Simonelli received a Ph.D. degree from the University of Nevada at Reno. He is an assistant professor of history at Mount St. Mary's College in Los Angeles.

Typeset in 10/13 New Caledonia
with Helvetica Neue Extended display
Designed by Paula Newcomb
Composed by Jim Proefrock
at the University of Illinois Press
Manufactured by Thomson-Shore, Inc.